27-50

Collected Poems

Humphrey Moore
wearing a Canadian train driver's hat.
Photographed by John Simpson in 1954.

Collected Poems

Humphrey Moore

with a Memoir
by John Bridgen

The Lutterworth Press
Cambridge

To All the Teachers, Staff and Boys and Girls
of Clayesmore School,
Past, Present and To Come

First published in 1997 by
The Lutterworth Press
P O Box 60
Cambridge
CB1 2NT
England

British Library Cataloguing in Publication Data:
A catalogue record is available from the British Library.

ISBN 0 7188 2959 X

Printed in Great Britain by
St Edmundsbury Press Limited, Bury St Edmunds, Suffolk

Contents

Illustrations

Preface

Humphrey Moore had a special gift for friendship. It has not been possible to name all of his many friends. I hope that any friends who have not been mentioned in the Memoir will understand.

I should like to express my warmest gratitude and my indebtedness to all of the following: my wife, Ruth, for her typing of the memoir and the indexes and for her constant encouragement and help; Adrian Brink of The Lutterworth Press for his editing of the memoir and for his continuous help, his encouragement and his patience – and to all at The Lutterworth Press who have helped in so many ways; Cdr. Oliver Moore for making sure that I received all of Humphrey's, papers, for much information about Humphrey's life and for help in contacting several of Humphrey's friends and for all his encouragement; Francis King for his very much appreciated help in selecting the best of the poems and for all his encouragement; Dr. John Auden for some information relating to W. H. Auden; Beryl Platts for first suggesting to me the appropriateness of writing a memoir to accompany Humphrey's collected poems; P. S. Morrish and C. Sheppard of the Brotherton Library at the University of Leeds for all their help and access over many years to Humphrey's books and papers which now form the main part of the 'The Bridgen, McEachran, Moore Collection of W. H. Auden and Thirties Poets' at the Library, for permission to quote from this material and to reproduce two photographs; the Rt. Rev. Michael Fisher, SSF, and the Rt. Rev. Peter Walker who both made several very helpful suggestions; Dr. George Rylands for some very helpful suggestions regarding the poems; F. E. Templer for information relating to Bradfield; Michael Charlesworth for information relating to Shrewsbury; Lt. Col. P. F. Steer for information from the archives of the British Schools Exploring Society; B. W. H. Coulson for lending me his letters from Humphrey and 'Mediterranean Travellers'; Gavin Ewart for his encouragement; Katherine Middleton Murry for some helpful suggestions; Anthony Dickins and Laurence Clark for their enthusiastically shared memories of their time at Cambridge with Humphrey; Lord Annan and T.E.B. Howarth for quotations about Stowe and Cambridge; Tony Chew for information from the Clayesmore archives; Dr. John Simpson for lending me back copies of *The Clayesmorian*; and of course all of the many friends of Humphrey who responded unfailingly to my requests for information and wrote to me with an enthusiasm like that of the subject about whom they were writing.

Twenty four of the poems in this book were first published in a privately circulated booklet entitled *Poems* which was printed at The Hillingdon Press and was edited by John Bridgen in 1974. Forty one of the poems were published, eighteen of them for the first time, in 'Collected Poems', a booklet which was produced with financial assistance from Miss Anne Winslow and was edited by Howard Sergeant for Outposts Publications in 1975.

John Bridgen
Cambridge

Foreword

I was rather surprised when John Bridgen asked me to write a foreword to his book on Humphrey Moore and his poetry for, although an Old Clayesmorian and Chairman of the Governing body for over twelve years, I never had the pleasure of knowing, in contradistinction to being acquainted with, Moore.

My first inclination was to profess how truly flattered I was to be asked, but politely to refuse. However, on reflection, it occurred to me that an entirely objective and disinterested approach might be desirable, so I agreed.

I have heard much of Moore from those who knew him, but it did not bring the man to life as does Bridgen's splendid biography. To me he emerges as one of a breed of Public School masters who existed before the war and who had certain characteristics, most of which were excellent. In the main they were as devoted to their profession as priests are to theirs; they were products of Public Schools and Oxbridge and were gentlemen in the best or Newman's sense of the word; they were individualists with many extra-mural skills and interests in which they sought to involve their pupils; they were usually firm but fair disciplinarians, and the school and their pupils were their life not only in term time but often in the school holidays.

Another characteristic was that they were usually bachelors but were they therefore homosexual? I suppose that the answer is that often their sexual orientation was in that direction, but it was inevitably suppressed, for any overt demonstration would have led to instant disgrace and dismissal.

In Moore's poetry can be found a sort of cryptic autobiography, the cypher for which can be found in Bridgen's biographical introduction. When I have the leisure, I shall much enjoy trying to equate biography and autobiography and I recommend this exercise to the reader. Fortunately, Moore's poetry has a quality of immediacy, is unmannered, pleasingly fresh and honest and, as it scans and rhymes, is very readable and often profound and lyrical.

If what I have written suggests that Moore was simply a typical school-master of his generation, I have been misunderstood: the greatest characteristic of his 'type' was individuality.

Moore deserved a biography and his poetry needed to be immortalised; nobody could have accomplished this tribute of affection and admiration better than John Bridgen, his former pupil and friend.

J.P. Brooke-Little, CVO, MA, FSA
Clarenceaux King of Arms

MEMOIR: Early Life

Oh you rocking atoms and you tireless spheres. . . .
When I am gone, when all of me is dust, let this my gift be given
unto some little child, who'll bear it purely till it flower; for flower it
must.
Lead on, lead on, you processes of life. I'll hold aloft the torch.
Humphrey Moore, Cambridge 1932

Humphrey was born on 21 November 1913 at 70 Bracondale, a suburb of
Norwich. His father, Montague, always known as Monty, was then an H.M.
Inspector of Schools in Norfolk. Humphrey was the second son of Monty and
Amy (née Peacock) who had met at a dance not long after the turn of the
century and were quite swept away by one another at first sight. Monty came
from the lower echelons of the middle classes. He had a very good brain, a
classical education, great charm, and a gentle manner. His father, Arthur Lewis
Moore, had been a highly skilled craftsman of low-church background who
made stained-glass windows, many of which are still to be seen in churches
around Britain. Amy, tall, comely and vivacious, and decidedly the dominant
partner in the marriage, had been brought up in a lifestyle nearer to what used
to be called the haute bourgeoisie. Her sister Gladys, Humphrey's godmother,
emigrated to America in the 1920s. Their father had been a well-to-do food
importer in London.

In the early years of their marriage the Moores moved house several times
because of Monty's work. After periods in Essex and Cornwall, they eventu-
ally settled in Somerset. Monty's work increasingly centred on the West Country
and in 1926, after he had been appointed Chief Inspector of Schools for Som-
erset, the Moore family found the home where they were to stay. This was
'Byams', a beautiful Elizabethan house, a little outside the tiny village of
Fitzhead, near Taunton. From the lovely garden with its white dovecot one can
see the classic line of the Quantock hills. It was this home with its idyllic
setting that the whole Moore family were very soon to come to adore. Every
Sunday morning they would decorously travel the few miles to Parish Com-
munion at the little village church at Bagborough on the edge of the Quantocks
in one of the earliest family Austins. The Moores by now had three sons: Peter
the eldest, later a Brigadier; Humphrey, the middle son, who became a public
school master; and Oliver, the youngest, who became a naval Commander.

The Moores settled in quickly to their newly rooted life of the country. The
countryside around 'Byams' was wonderful territory for the boys to grow up
in. Humphrey in particular very quickly began to discover the natural wonders
round his lovely Somerset home; he began to jot down in notebooks all the
birds and animals, trees and flowers that he saw – describing them in detail
and getting to know them intimately. 'Byams' itself was charmingly secluded.

It had the feeling of a haven of beauty and quiet. Most of Humphrey's friends were to be taken there and were to know this: the feeling of a real old-world country family home, where in surroundings of ordered calm and beauty, they would be welcomed (very often from the far less settled and less beautiful world outside) and met with warmth and kindness. It became for most of Humphrey's friends in the fullest sense one of life's 'good' places.

In 1924 shortly before the family settled in Somerset, Humphrey was sent to Durlstone Court Prep School in Swanage, Dorset. He enjoyed his three years there. Above all, he was delighted to be near the sea, for which his love and fascination grew. However, I should point out that his first impressions of the sea had both been Cornish, formed during the family's earlier year at Carbis Bay and during the family's frequent holidays at their favourite seaside place, Treyarnon Bay. In Cornwall Humphrey would spend his days, frequently in solitude, exploring the shores and rocks for their wildlife, completely absorbed, delighting in all that he found, and sowing there the first seeds of what became his lifelong passion for natural history.

It was at Treyarnon Bay that Humphrey underwent his initiation into the world of poetry. Among Monty's books he discovered Matthew Arnold's poems. He read 'The Forsaken Merman', and was completely captivated. Later on Humphrey would always introduce the young to this poem. Second only to 'The Forsaken Merman' stood 'The Scholar Gypsy' in his boyhood love and affection. Of the peculiar haunting sadness of Arnold's poetry Humphrey later tellingly commented: 'He was a man of regret seeking affirmation. He would have been better as a revolutionary or a vagabond. Instead of which he was a Civil Servant conscious of a strange aching in his heart'. I wonder if Monty (an H.M.I. like Arnold) sometimes knew a similar aching in his heart.

One night lying awake in his bed while still quite a small child Humphrey had his first intimation of what music would mean to him as he heard the clearly audible strains of a classical concert coming from his parents' radio in the room below. He lay listening all at once mysteriously rapt into a new dimension of experience. The music, he felt, was addressing him and claiming him with an all important message of an ineffable sweetness and sadness that he must heed. He would listen more intently after this whenever his mother played the piano, as she frequently did when he lay awake at night. He seemed to have a foresight of that journey towards beauty that he would travel all his life.

While the children were all growing up at 'Byams' Monty and Amy found a Danish governess for them. Gudrun Hammershaimb was a Faroe Dane whose grandfather had translated the ancient Danish sagas into Faroese and thereby rescued the Faroese language for posterity. She was married to Gusti Hofmann, a ski instructor in the Swiss Army. The family's friendship with Gudrun and Gusti was to be deep and lifelong.

Humphrey's childhood was very happy. He knew well, however, the pressures involved in growing up as the middle, and the most sensitive, one of three brothers in a close-knit family at a time when there were far fewer diversions than are found today. He experienced how the young can often be as he later put it, 'hemmed in by the weights of childhood'. Monty and Amy had an excellent marriage, but Amy could not help chafing Monty on occasions, sometimes calling him an old stick-in-the-mud and getting into fits of laughter over some of his antics, much to his annoyance. Humphrey thus experienced how sometimes the intensity of feeling in a family of strongly contrasting personalities can suddenly turn into love-hate and back to love again. Moreover his parents old-world values were sometimes too oppressive for the young rebel in him. On several occasions he protested by running away from home. Despite a certain emotional ambivalence, however, towards their old world conventions he loved his parents and nobody was to be more devoted to them in later life.

Humphrey knew also how much unhappiness there can sometimes be in a nursery fracas among three brothers; how three boys can contend for first place in their parents' love, especially their mothers; and how warring loves and woes from this very early period can sometimes seem at the time to place emotional obstacles like boulders in the way of the child; but amidst the conflicts and pains of growing up in a quite large household still mainly Edwardian in its basic atmosphere of rectitude and propriety, there was always the refuge of what Humphrey called 'the Spring of Helicon', where the muses dwell – that most precious gift that the child first discovers, in fact he who does not discover it as a child probably never will discover it – the gift of the pure creative freedom of the spirit in books and music and art, an ever accessible 'wings away' and a refuge to which the imaginative child can always withdraw whenever he needs to. Humphrey was to idealise childhood all his life. He had already made up his mind at prep school that he wanted 'to remain a boy always', and to go on experiencing the world just as a boy does. Indeed, in a sense he was to remain an eternal child. He would have been pleased to have been so called. For he believed that most of the creative spirits of mankind have been found in people who have in some sense retained the child's sensitive quality of wonder as well as the child's essential sincerity.

In later life Humphrey became conscious of the world into which he had been born as representing a kind of dying fall of the Victorian era. The First World War began only nine months after he was born. This was more of a profoundly traumatic experience for those who had lived in the Victorian and Edwardian aura of imperialist Britain, as had Humphrey's parents, than those of later generations can possibly conceive. It caused a fault in the massive rock face which grew and brought about eventually a shattering of the calm British assumption of rule and precedence. Monty and Amy were all their lives stalwarts of what they saw as the paternalistic British Empire; but already, when Humphrey was born, the British bourgeoisie was experiencing the early onset of that feeling of being 'doomed' which was to characterise the whole era to come. A fall down the slope on the other side of the Victorian high civilisation had begun for them. And the First World War of course was to precipitate the decadence of the British Empire and the changes which were to cause that privileged world to disintegrate and all its settled assumptions to be thrown to the winds.

In the Moores' cultured home education in general was looked upon as the potential leaven for the future salvation of British society. As a genteel middle class H.M.I. Monty followed in the tradition of the Arnolds and the enlightened Victorians in wanting the benefits of culture and education to be spread throughout society to all classes with the least possible lowering of standards. Though very conservative by nature, the Moores were inheritors of the faith of many of the leading Victorians in education as the way forward into a vital and enlightened democracy.

At the same time, the British educational system they believed would also be one of the leading means by which Britain would maintain a pre-eminent place in the world. This, however, would only be so if the British educational system, and especially the public school sector, which had fallen into such laxity in the earlier part of the nineteenth century, could be reformed and revitalised. Monty was one of those administering the Public Schools Act of 1868 whose aim was to raise educational and intellectual standards. Then after 1902 he was one of those who put into effect Morant's Education Bill, one of whose aims was, while enabling the public schools to retain their position as both the leaders and the prototypes of secondary education, to extend its development in England and Wales. So from his earliest childhood Humphrey lived in a public school centred milieu and he imbibed, though often of course unconsciously, very many of his educational assumptions and ideals.

After the First World War Europe failed to regenerate a newly reconstructed order which would make the world safe for democracy. The First World War instead was to be followed by a time of crisis and violence and anxiety, a time over which the threat of war continuously loomed. Culturally this was to be reflected in the iconoclastic emergence of modernism. Owing to the particular nature of his early experience Humphrey had his first and instinctive roots in the earlier British and European traditional order, but owing to the cataclysmic events that were occurring at the time when he was born, he grew up in a world of breakneck transition and change. Most significantly for us he was to live and record his experience of this travailing time of transition in the heart of the traditionalist English public school world.

All his life Humphrey was to experience a close connection between his wondering childlike delight in beauty, natural and artistic, a capacity for what he frequently terms in his earliest diaries 'ecstasy', and a kind of nagging psychological unease. This was not just the effect of his consciousness of his homosexuality as he grew up, though that was doubtless a connected factor. An insistent regret frequently haunted him – memories of magical moments, echoes of childhood, painfully at variance with the more ordinary habitual world. The bright strands in his imagination were in a sense always to be shot through with the dark. He had tasted the savour of a privileged family life in a more rooted and a more gracious age and these idyllic memories he carried with him all his life. He was indeed to be very excited by all the cultural changes taking place during his lifetime but he had been exquisitely sensitive to his childhood. As a result in the ensuing gradual disintegration of that world as he grew up he felt something like a sense of a kind of spiritual loss – though at the same time in his public school environment he still kept more in touch with aspects of the earlier order than he would have done in most other walks of life. Still, however, the ecstasy and the angst were in a sense always to coexist within him.

Humphrey's early childhood, it is important to stress, was mostly blissfully happy. He looked back on it as a golden idyllic age. Though the seeds of emotional and class ambivalence were already within that blissful period, yet Humphrey did not feel to the same extent as Auden, who was from the same contemporary class background, though predominantly urban rather than rural, 'isolated' from his family or 'haunted' by its ancestral ghosts. He would have understood Auden's reaction perfectly, but his relation to his own childhood was more positive and romantic. He had in fact very much the innate capacity always to welcome the vitally new with open arms but, in some ways, it was the archaically tinged past that he loved most. This set up a lasting dialect within him, for his memories lived on ineradicably. He remembered especially, and with the purity of devotion that only a child can know, his earliest years by the legend-haunted seas of Cornwall and his prep school years overlooking the sea on the cliffs above Swanage in Dorset, and no less indelibly all those boyhood years passed with the family at 'Byams' within sight of the Quantock Hills in Somerset – the life in its essential character of a still largely Edwardian country gentry family. He looked back always with love and nostalgia on the settled peace, the spacious beauty and the natural graciousness of that way of life, so soon to pass. It was a way of life that the shockwaves of iconoclastic change going on in the world at large were only then, when he was a boy, beginning to filter through to very gradually. It was a way of life still almost entirely untouched by the precipitous growth of industrial ugliness in a great deal of Britain – something which was all but hidden from him throughout his childhood. It was a golden age for him indeed. It was a golden age that as it happened Humphrey was in a sense to have a unique opportunity to prolong. He was not to be so suddenly or traumatically uprooted and cast out from it as were so many in his time.

BRADFIELD

At Michaelmas 1927 it was time for Humphrey to transfer from Durlstone Court to a public school. His parents, under the influence of Dr (later Sir) A.W. Pickard-Cambridge, the great Oxford educationalist, who was a family friend, decided on Bradfield College in Berkshire, a momentous decision that was to affect Humphrey's whole life profoundly. He had shown academic aptitude at Durlstone Court. Monty had heard, from Pickard-Cambridge, that Bradfield was on the academic ascendancy under the exceptional Headmastership of the Rev R.D. Beloe.

Bradfield (founded in the 1850s like Lancing and Radley) was an offshoot of the Oxford Movement. Its Church connection pleased Monty and Amy. Besides, the school's record in the First World War, which was second to none, was widely recognised and admired throughout the country, not least by a couple like the Moores who were to dedicate two of their sons to the armed services – Peter was now training for the Army at Woolwich and Oliver for the Navy at Dartmouth.

Moreover Bradfield possessed a wonderful Greek Theatre, the idea of which had been conceived and realized by the Rev H.B. Gray, Beloe's most distinguished predecessor at Bradfield. This innovation was to give Bradfield a unique and special place in the annals of the Public Schools. Indeed it has been said that the Greek Theatre at Bradfield ranks equal to 'Tom Brown's Schooldays' as one of the most effective advertisements ever exhibited, without meaning to advertise at all, for Public Schools. As a classicist himself, Monty warmly applauded Beloe's courageous decision to revive the Greek plays at Bradfield after the First World War.

Beloe wanted Bradfield to take its place among the 'great' Public Schools in the old sense. He was no egalitarian: he wanted Bradfield to be for 'the sons of gentlemen'. The most heinous sin, he convinced all Bradfield boys, was that of 'letting the place down', of falling below the standard that membership of Bradfield required of them. He found his own way to meet the bitter postwar disillusionment that swept over so many of the public schools. He kept much of the prewar public school idealism alive and responded vigorously to the challenge of the First World War itself. Beloe had enabled the boys at his school to participate in the war effort by making munitions in the school engineering workshops. He kept the heroism and sacrifice of the war generation ever before the eyes of Bradfield boys.

Beloe wanted to uphold and carry forward the old public school idealism while reorganizing it along modern lines. In many ways he was the last of the great nineteenth century public school headmasters. He stood for the greatness of a great tradition, but he was also forward thinking. While in response to the war he fostered 'hardiness' in the boys, setting an outstanding example of it himself in his whole manner of living, at the same time he also considerably demonasticised Bradfield, in particular by introducing more married teachers and more feminine influence. He wanted to achieve good friendly relations between masters and boys and a 'family' atmosphere in the school at large, even though he himself was something of an olympian presence. Above all he saw to it that the things of the mind were held in the highest regard. The arts were to be cultivated. And, somewhat unusually for a leading public school at that time, science too stood in high esteem. Academic achievement was sought after and the sixth form had the primary prestige in the boys' hierarchy. Games were to be enjoyed but not worshipped. The sway of the 'bloods', that bane of the older public schools, which had affected Bradfield in the early days, had all but disappeared by the time Humphrey reached the school. Public opinion centred around the enlightened although somewhat daunting figure of Beloe himself.

Beloe was determined that Bradfield should be no conventional public school. He created a unique and inspiring public school republic at Bradfield. The school really did revolve around the axis of christian humanist ideals and, as a Greek play programme of the time expressed it, 'the kinship between the Greek BODY and certain aspects of our Public Schools'. The Bradfield boy

The Rev. R.D. Beloe in his study at Bradfield in about 1927.
Beloe of Bradfield was one of the heroes of Hunphrey's youth and his
constant ideal of the public school headmaster.

was taught to love his school as the Greek citizen loved Athens. Both the chapel and the Greek Theatre were to be inspiringly central to his life.

Beloe loved and encouraged above all originality, individuality and creative achievement. He made it clear to all that he disliked ordinariness. To this end he composed his staff of original and striking personalities. He saw to it that the Bradfield boy loved his school and was loyal to it with heartfelt affection. This special public school mystique inspired Humphrey with an unswerving lifelong devotion. The legendary Beloe was one of the chief role models for his whole life, as well as one of the main heroes of his youth and his constant ideal of what a public school Headmaster should be.

Humphrey was put in 'Army' House. In fact many boys in those days actually used to go from 'Army' House directly into Woolwich and the services; but this was never Humphrey's aim. It was obvious from very early on that Humphrey was the least military of people. In 'Army' House he came under the influence of his Housemaster, Cecil Bellamy, who was also Beloe's first special 'Greek Play' appointment at Bradfield. Bellamy, of whom I shall say more later, befriended Humphrey and was a decisive influence in bringing out his latent enthusiasms for literature and the arts.

The head of Biology was Alan Poole Gardiner – another of Beloe's many inspired appointments – a delightful and slightly eccentric teacher who rather lent himself to schoolboy teasing. Being a brilliant all-round field naturalist years ahead of his time, it was he who laid the foundation for one of Bradfield's abiding parts of work and achievement. He was above all a marine biologist and a leading British conchologist, i.e. an expert on shells. The boys always knew him as 'Sniffers' – probably from his habit of sniffing between sentences. Humphrey and Gardiner quickly became friends. They had a great respect for one another which did not prevent Humphrey from delighting in Sniffers' eccentricities. Many were the tales of Sniffers he told in later life. Sniffers used to whistle his 'esses' and an oft-repeated threat to any miscreant in class was 'Look here you sssilly little ssssnipe, I'll dust the ssseat of your trouserssss if you don't behave'. Sniffers' favourite hobby was collecting 'molluscsss' from the seashore, and this was how he liked to spend most of his holidays, usually with a group of Bradfield boys. Sniffers was very fond of Humphrey whom he used to refer to as 'the young snipe Meohr'. I suppose that Sniffers would today certainly be classed as something of an eccentric, but Humphrey always had a particular love for the colourfully individual and the eccentric.

Humphrey had come to his Biology very much through his childhood love of natural history; and Alan Poole Gardiner was the chief agent responsible for fostering this into the lifelong pursuit and devotion that it became. Under Gardiner's influence Humphrey was to become a leading member of Bradfield's 'Scientific Society'. The annual natural history prize, the Hollowell (later renamed the Hollowell-Gardiner) was won by Humphrey many times. *The Chronicle* (Bradfield's school magazine), especially between 1930 and 1932, is full of entries regarding Humphrey's achievements in natural history and biology. It was Gardiner who inspired

Humphrey into what became his chosen career.

It certainly wasn't science alone, however, that claimed Humphrey's enthusiasm at Bradfield. In what is often regarded as a very philistine period in the independent schools, the artistically and musically inclined boys very much enjoyed 'a place in the sun' at the school. Meanwhile Humphrey was being just as inspired in the two other spheres which would be equally central to his life: poetry and music. He was especially fortunate at this seminal stage of his life to come under the influence of the classicist, Cecil Bellamy, and the musician, Douglas Fox. Humphrey loved and admired both men and they became his lifelong friends. Bellamy, who had come to Bradfield from Oxford, initiated Humphrey's generation at Bradfield, and several subsequent generations, into a dynamic knowledge of what Greek theatre is really about. He made Greek drama live for them as a vital experience in the modern world. This influenced Humphrey profoundly and it is no exaggeration to say that it played an essential part in forming his whole outlook on life.

Douglas Fox, the director of music, Humphrey would always refer to as one of the 'sacred' names of his youth. Like Bellamy, Fox came to Bradfield from Oxford. At Oxford he had been a pupil of Sir Hugh Allen. He was a most distinguished musician and one of the many 'originals' appointed by Beloe. He had lost his right arm in the First World War, but this terrible tragedy did not prevent him from being a brilliant organist and pianist. Fox was held in very high regard and affection in the musical world at large; and very many leading musicians of the day visited Bradfield at his invitation. Humphrey first took up the piano, which was to be an abiding love of his life, under Fox's direction. Fox was a deeply religious man with a strong sense of interconnection between religion and music. He was completely devoted to teaching and to youth. Music was for him a bond of love between people. As a teacher Fox deepened the musical love and understanding of his pupils into a reverence for the great classics. His whole life can be seen as being given to the service of youth and the great composers. Under his guidance his pupils learnt to love the greatest best. He was one of those rare teachers who can give to their pupils a vision of greatness.

Monty's high expectations of Bradfield were certainly being fulfilled. Beloe headed a team of teachers of outstanding calibre, and he himself, Humphrey always said, had the stamp of greatness. It was a greatness that yet encompassed within its high idealism a genuine humility. The person whom he reminds one of in many ways is Dr Arnold of Rugby – the patriarch inspirer of the young, strict but kind, binding his republic together with religious fervour. Humphrey would tell countless sagas in later life about Beloe. He would tell, for example, of how Beloe used to read poems to the whole school in assembly simply because he liked them. He would tell of how Beloe would sometimes interrupt classes in great excitement to tell the young of an important discovery he had made, or something he had experienced, in order to share it with them: it might be perhaps a new author or some new insight into science. With him the young realised that education is an exciting adventure that they and their teachers are embarked on together.

In the chapel Beloe made all the varied experience and activity of the school cohere in Christ, who alone, he taught, really enables one to make sense of human life and provides an anchor for the whole of the rest of a boy's life. A few years after he left Bradfield Humphrey summarised Beloe's achievements when he wrote in his diary: 'religion must be the centre of a school and the Headmaster must be the leader of the religion'. This was certainly the old public school ideal and it lived on in Beloe in a revitalized way. For the humanist Christianity at Bradfield, centred as it was in the ritual of the chapel was also in vital connection with the ritual of the Greek Theatre. So Bradfield religion actively involved the majority of the boys and appealed in a unique way to their imagination as well as to their faith. It awakened in them a sense of reverence and wonder and beauty and it bound them together with respect for individuals as well as community. Beloe was a most gifted and sincere educator and he stood for true and inspiring values. His way of prefixing his statements to outsiders with 'I'm Beloe of Bradfield' became legendary. Some of the stories about him may be apocryphal. For instance, did he really go into a garage one day, as Humphrey used to later tell, and grunt in his inimitable style 'I'm Beloe of Bradfield and *I want oil*'? It was certainly not possible for any other Headmaster to replace Beloe in Humphrey's esteem and affection, and when he retired his successor E.A. Whitworth could not compete for Humphrey's affection or indeed for that of his generation at Bradfield.

It was in the spring of 1928 that Beloe's health gave out. He was only fifty nine. He had constantly overworked and he had worn himself out in devotion to Bradfield. He lived only two more years. So great was the love and loyalty that Humphrey's generation felt to Beloe that E.A. Whitworth in his first two terms was actively mobbed by the boys. There could hardly have been a greater contrast of personalities. Beloe had in fact only been Humphrey's headmaster for one year; but Humphrey kept a framed photograph of Beloe in his study for the rest of his life.

Woven into the very texture of Bradfield's deeply patriarchal republic were Humphrey's friendships among his contemporaries. These friendships were the emotional substratum of his ensuing life. In the Bradfield of the 1920s much of the old public school propriety still held sway in personal relationships, though eased somewhat by the more than usually familial kind of ethos. Older boys were discouraged from befriending younger boys. Friendships moreover were usually between boys in the same House. *Esprit de corps* and good form had to be upheld at all costs. Boys were supposed to call one another only by surnames. Breaches of the customary code were usually frowned upon. Humphrey, nevertheless, entered upon several romantic friendships at Bradfield, and none of them in fact were with boys in his own House. One can't help wondering whether his special friendships were not at least in part an expression of his need for privacy in the enforced group life of the school, the chance for someone who was in many ways a natural loner to share something more personal and inward amid the encroaching and fairly regimented communal life. Though in general Humphrey probably required somewhat more privacy than the school setting actually allowed, until he became a prefect at any rate, it would be wrong to see his romantic friendships as a kind of short cut to community. Eric (later Sir Eric) Faulkner, a contemporary, though not a close friend at Bradfield, recalled Humphrey there as 'very companionable and happy'. Humphrey found the overall ethos at Bradfield far too congenial, and he had far too strong a sense of belonging and of feeling at one with his environment, to be seeking any kind of personalised escape. In a way it was Bradfield itself that was always in danger of being for him, both then and in later life, his ideal 'island'. His friendships there were in many respects a kind of crowning affirmation of his love for the school and all that it stood for.

Of the many friends that he made in his six years at Bradfield probably emotionally the most important, and certainly the most lasting, for Humphrey was John Paine. John was the eldest of a Kent farming family of six children, five brothers and a sister. Two of John's brothers followed him to Bradfield: Michael, who became almost as great a friend of Humphrey as John, and Toby, whom he knew slightly less, who later was to become Britain's Registrar General and to receive a knighthood. John arrived at Bradfield in 1928, a year after Humphrey. Neither he nor Michael after him were in 'Army' House, but in 'The Close'; so John and Humphrey didn't really get to know one another until well on into their time at Bradfield when they met together in the Biology Sixth. What started off then as an adolescent romantic friendship developed, perhaps somewhat rarely for such cases, into a permanent friendship. Humphrey became a lifelong visitor to 'Morry House' near Maidstone where the Paine family farmed. It was there that he first struck up friendship with John's younger brother Michael. He also got to know well another of John's younger brothers, Peter, and he became a lifelong friend of John's wife and all their children. Humphrey loved and cultivated his visits to the Paines and valued the warmth of their family life.

John Paine recalled Humphrey at Bradfield as above all 'a leader, a practical joker and a breaker of rules'. He already exhibited the qualities of the 'natural anarchist', which was how he was later to describe himself throughout his early life. But as many of his contemporaries have told me, he was a popular figure with both staff and boys alike. Another contemporary, F.E. Templer, has told me 'he was unmistakable, being fair and tall, and even then he had his curious way of holding his head to one side'. He was clearly a leader among his peers and occasionally led himself and them into trouble but none of them exceeded him in their devotion to Bradfield.

Humphrey was actually 'in love' with John. It was to him that very many of Humphrey's earliest poems were addressed, but two further main friendships also blossomed for Humphrey while he was at Bradfield. The first was with Oliver Garrod ('Og' inevitably after the King of Bashan) who was for two years a fellow prefect with him. He was a highly intelligent scientist who later became a famous doctor at St Bartholomew's Hospital in London. As well as being very accomplished on the piano and a poet, he was also very athletic. Oliver's uncle, an Air Chief Marshal, was Warden of Bradfield. Sir Eric Faulkner told me of Oliver 'he was an amusing and likeable boy who attempted to write poetry most of which was a pale copy of Rupert Brooke (who was Laureate to all my generation).'

Humphrey's other main friend at Bradfield – and intellectually by far the most important for him – was Martin Wight. Martin was a highly intelligent boy in E House. They were exact contemporaries and they also became prefects of their respective Houses at the same time; but, being in different Houses, their friendship did not begin until near the end of their time at Bradfield. Martin was the middle of three sons of a distinguished Brighton doctor. The family background was conservative, religious and intellectual. Dr Wight stood for the old-fashioned virtues, the good and gracious things of life. A particular advocate of Hilaire Belloc, he was the founder and president of a poetry society in Brighton to which he gave frequent talks.

Humphrey's great friendship with Martin Wight blossomed in 1931 and 1932. He talked to me later in his life about the vital importance of this friendship to him. In fact it was very important to them both. The friendship centred on their shared passion for Rupert Brooke and T.E. Lawrence, whose *Seven Pillars of Wisdom* had recently been published, and their sense of an associated national glamour and nobility of purpose living on in Beloe's Bradfield.

Humphrey first got to know Martin at the Public Schools Camp at Tidworth in the Summer of 1931. At this time boys from several public school OTCs (Officers' Training Corps) used to join together with army volunteers at their regimental volunteers camp for a week of very spartan living in country (usually Home Counties) surroundings. It appears that the informal closeness and simplicity of the Camp life quickly kindled the warm new friendship between Humphrey and Martin. It developed all the more rapidly since Humphrey was in a highly emotional state as he neared the end of his time at Bradfield. He confided his feelings in Martin as this, for him, elysian and emotionally fermenting period of his adolescence drew towards its close. Humphrey was very apprehensive at the prospect of leaving Bradfield. He pleaded for Martin's understanding and sympathy; and he found that Martin was in exactly the same boat. Their intimate avowals rose to romantic commitment when they discovered that they both loved poetry and especially the poetry of Rupert Brooke.

Early in 1932 Martin bought Humphrey his first Collected edition of Brooke's poems (with the Memoir by Edward Marsh). Later Martin inscribed it to him 'in memoriam 1931-32'. During 1932, Humphrey's last year at Bradfield, in their free time they cycled all around Berkshire together, exploring the countryside and reading Brooke's poetry. Humphrey marked in this book the exact date and place where they read together every poem. This was the time when Humphrey first got to know intimately all of Rupert Brooke's poetry, and his love of Brooke was to be especially deep, abiding and unique, as we shall see.

Like all boys at Bradfield, Humphrey and Martin were involved in the school OTC. It absorbed a considerable part of their young lives. It is perhaps rather surprising for those who knew Humphrey later to learn that he was at this time a Senior Under Officer. In fact while at Bradfield both Humphrey and Martin were devoted to the school OTC. The irony is that both of them within quite a short time of leaving the school would become ardent pacifists. The seed of their pacifism was already there, for while being lovers of the British Empire at the same time they were both greatly disillusioned by the contemporary clash of imperialisms. They were both deeply religious and it was with great difficulty that they could relate their Christian values to contemporary power politics. However while at Bradfield both Humphrey and Martin believed that in their overriding religion of youthful love, their reverence for all of life and for beauty, lay the answer to all wars.

Humphrey was somewhat wilder by nature than Martin, who already had a fundamental commitment to Anglicanism and something of the biblically based realism that was to become increasingly the hallmark of his thinking. Humphrey was inclined at Bradfield to be 'agin all governments'. In his notebook of this time he records that he worshipped Beethoven as 'a defyer of convention and a force of nature'. He felt that it is the power nexus, the power relationships themselves, which are wrong – a belief he held until after the Second World War. Significantly, he was with Martin, one of the few in a very conservative contemporary establishment, who expressed a lot of sympathy for 'the other half of the two nations'.

Martin was a complex and brilliant intellectual. Sir Eric Faulkner recalled spending a somewhat 'uneasy year' as a fellow prefect sharing the same study with him. Sir Eric told me: 'Wight was always an intellectual though also a brilliant swimmer, but introspective, moody and given to deep and long depressions. He was also a rebel and scorned Whitworth, the Head Usher when Beloe retired'. Later in his life Martin wrote a letter to his mother describing his generation at Bradfield as follows: 'Headmasters in the long run impose their personality upon a school. The Bradfield of 1930 reflected Beloe, the enterprising and rebellious generation of John Peters, Eric Faulkner and Humphrey Moore. None of Basil's (Martin's brother who preceded him to Bradfield) contemporaries or mine were lacking in personality. That was the hangover of Beloe which Whitworth had to deal with. In the succeeding ten years he managed to reduce everything to a dead and uniform level of respectability which reflected himself. Now Hills comes and has to deal with this hangover of Whitworth'.

Some idea of the quality and intensity of his platonic friendship with Martin emerges from notebooks and letters and from remarks that Humphrey made to me in later life. He saw his love of Martin as a meeting on equal terms with a special being for whom he believed his destiny had prepared him. Their friendship established an essential 'soul contact' in each of them. They could in their love for one another learn to be themselves completely. The essential emergent person in each of them was triumphant during the two years of their joint spiritual awakening. What they castigated as the mask of mere social convention was thrown down, before it ever really needed to be lifted up by them, and the gold of their youthful being was shared fearlessly and honestly. They felt as if a godhead lived within them as they wondered wholeheartedly at the vision that they shared and at the spontaneous life power within them, as yet unchanneled, uncharted, and open to high and courageous adventure.

They knew that they must in their ongoing lives maintain the essential courage of youth which embraces all of life in wonder – a courage which, it seemed to them, many lose in what they then saw as the unnatural process of 'growing up' into socialisation. Humphrey wrote in his diary during 1931: 'To establish contact with life one must have ones sensibility open and naked – in growing up into socialisation one finds that one can no longer stand so much beauty, so much wonder, surrounded as one is by so much hypocrisy and evil: and so one looks to ones own protection, self consciousness is developed and a protective intention of will which protects the soul from the evil in the world – So one closes the senses doors. Then no longer does one wholeheartedly wonder at a single human being. Such things come no more, or but rarely, when we become worldly-wise and get beyond our adolescence.'

Inexperienced as he still was, Humphrey felt that in his friendship with Martin he had been enabled to lift the veil from conventional life. They had experienced together while still at school that timeless world in which the living beauty of all things is known and they believed that they had been granted a glimpse in their own lives of the destiny of which that knowledge of beauty is a sign. So they felt that in their youth they had been given a kind of high spiritual trust to fulfil – a flame to guard and to hand on to those who could receive it. In a sense for those who have early known such experience their lives henceforth must be in one essential aspect attempts to clarify and elucidate their vision in relation to the practical everyday world of society and its demands; from Humphrey's point of view the attempt would be far from easy. Looking back in later life Humphrey said of his love for Martin: 'Such loves are rare in life. If they were common then life and poetry would be inseparable.'

Martin won an Open Scholarship to Hertford College, Oxford. He then went on to become one of the most distinguished historians of his generation, a leading authority on international relations, and on the academic planning boards which brought about the founding of the Universities of Sussex and Kent. He married fairly late in life, but very happily.

Given the intensity of his friendships and of his response to Bradfield, it is not surprising that Humphrey was beginning to write poetry. His first poems were written under the influence of Rupert Brooke, A.E. Housman, Matthew Arnold and classical legend. Many of his earliest poems are about Bradfield and his romantic attachments to John and his other friends. He was bewitched by the beauty of Bradfield itself, its rich landscape of a chalk river valley near the first rise of the Berkshire Downs, its wonderful beech and elm trees, and the peacefulness and seclusion of its setting. Within this idyllic setting in several poems he attempts to distil into verse something of his early experience of music. Humphrey's deepest experiences of poetry and music were very closely interconnected. Indeed his passionate love of music in a sense came first. All his earliest spiritual experience was in a way woven around the ineffable experience of music. Humphrey wrote in his Bradfield diary of his 'emotional religion' which took precedence for him over 'reasoned life'. He was trying, he said, in his earliest poems to do homage to an 'emotional religion of divine melancholy' which is yet 'all joyful'. Music often opened up in him the sense of a great sadness which was mingled with joy because he felt in it the existence of a pure beauty which the world denied.

Humphrey and his friends at Bradfield were very conscious of the marvellous heritage that they so richly enjoyed. Another enthusiasm which further sealed them together in a kind of spiritual bond was an impassioned interest in natural history (and especially botany), which they pursued in inextricable relation to their love of the English countryside. John still has the Bentham and Hooker *Illustrated Flora* (then 'the' edition) which Humphrey gave him. It is inscribed 'In mem. 3. Oliver Garrod h.m. and John Paine. Bradfield 1932'.

By the time he left Bradfield at the end of the summer term of 1932 Humphrey was undoubtedly one of her stars. He had won most of the prizes available to him and he was probably more active in a wider variety of spheres of school life than most of his peers. In one of his poems of 1932 Humphrey even avowed in Brookean vein that Bradfield was where he would finally like to be laid to rest. During his last year a large part of the school, and Army House especially, were under the sway of his personality.

We can be sure that there were tears in Humphrey's eyes when on the last Sunday evening of his final term Dr Gray's hymn 'Praise to our God who with love never swerving' ('Swervers') was sung in the school chapel, and especially when he reached the words:

Though never more in one place all may gather,
Though in life's battle we struggle apart,
One be our Saviour and one be our Father,
Bind us together in faith and in heart.

Bradfield had given Humphrey a vision of what human greatness is; together with a sense of magnificent tradition, an indelible feeling for the beauty and greatness of England, her history, her countryside and her poetry; and a quality of reverence for life. Perhaps it had not prepared him all that specifically for the actual world of the 1930s that he was to go out and encounter. For it had implanted in him what by this time was an increasingly rare kind of prewar heroic idealism which, despite the drift of the times, he would endeavour to emulate throughout his life. Humphrey left Bradfield with a springlike sense of beauty and promise welling up everywhere around him and within. The actual sadness and wrench of leaving was overwhelming. He felt an almost painful happiness, the spiritual state of one with all of a boy's hopes of the high heroic adventure of life stretching before him and all the wild light of a passionate sincerity and an untarnished wonder undimmed in his heart.

Cambridge and Teaching

Looking back over his schooldays in later life, Humphrey was to realise that in a sense his love of Bradfield had in some ways been almost too intense for his own good. It was as if he had found his goal at the start of his life – and in a sense he had; but how was subsequent experience to live up to such a dawning? And how was he to avoid resting complacently on his Bradfield laurels? There are probably only two places in Britain that could match up to such a seedtime youth, bringing it to a maturer flowering and ushering it gradually into a larger knowledge of the world without brushing the bloom from off the flower, and fortunately Humphrey was soon to take up residence at one of them. In October 1932 he took up the place that he had been awarded at Corpus Christi College, Cambridge. Inspired by Sniffers and all the opportunities for natural history at Bradfield, as well as at home in Somerset, he had made biology his chosen subject; although music and poetry would in fact be equally absorbing pursuits for him in the next three years.

When Humphrey arrived in Cambridge he knew no one. All of his Bradfield friends were going to either Oxford or London. He missed them terribly of course. In his initial loneliness he suffered greatly from self consciousness and shyness so that it was not easy at first to make new friends. Quite a lot of personal readjustment would clearly be needed before he could relax into Cambridge and appropriate the riches and the opportunities that it offered, but he appreciated quickly the beauty of his new environment.

One of the earliest entries in his first Cambridge diary captures a vivid first impression: 'Bells in Cambridge. The stars in their courses as seen from Old Court. The waiter Fritz, walking towards hall. His moustache "Ohay". The joy of bright colours; black enamel of bed; cream bell push and sea-green walls. Books, new and still in their covers. The excitement that one day one will meet someone interesting. The untold Windes that is locked up in Cambridge.

David the bookseller –

And of course –

The rose of dawn on King's Chapel – at 7.0 a.m.'

He was given a room over the Westminster Bank in King's Parade. So that from the geographical point of view he was certainly made to feel right at the centre of things from the start; but he would suffer agonies of shyness and apprehension in his new environment.

At this stage of his life he was still suspicious of 'society' at large from which he had been until this time mostly sheltered and the spiritual benefits of whose influence, as we have seen, he doubted. He felt, wrongly as it happened, in his Cambridge environment, that 'society' would not understand or value the sensitive idealist and the poet. He brought his Bradfield enthusiasms to Cambridge and he feared greatly lest they be slighted or met with incomprehension. Cambridge seemed to him at first very far removed from his

Bradfield world. University is of course much more than an extension of school and Humphrey had far too vital and curious an intelligence not to respond to its newness, and the particular accent of the enthusiasms that he brought with him to Cambridge in themselves prove that he had indeed come to the right place. In his first year his diary is full of three names in particular: Brooke, Beethoven and Beloe of Bradfield. Now, here he was in the city of Rupert Brooke where many who had known Brooke were living; at a University with innumerable strong links with the world of the public school (Corpus Christi had incidentally been Beloe's College); and in a city that could still justify the claim to be what the poet W.J. Turner had called it in the 1920s, 'the most musical town in England'.

On his arrival at Cambridge Humphrey recorded in his diary 'music was my religion'. He soon joined the Corpus Christi choir as a volunteer member. He also hired a piano (always a necessity for him), and he joined the CUMS choir which was under the direction of Cyril Rootham. It was Rootham who had conducted the notable performance of 'The Magic Flute' in Cambridge in 1910, an acknowledged Mozart landmark in Britain. In this production Rupert Brooke had walked on as one of the Nubian Slaves in the first Act.

At first Humphrey felt disappointed with university life and very much on the outside of it. He was to say later how many of his memories of his lonely first year were of rushing from one part of Cambridge to another along its grey stone pavements. He did, however, apply himself very hard to the Biology Tripos. He wrote long letters to John and Martin and other Bradfield friends, and he joined the Old Bradfieldian Society. He kept hoping that he would soon meet some kindred spirits, though still not too confident that he would; but he gradually began to feel more settled and at home. For one thing he started to appreciate how unique the College was which he had joined; and Corpus Christi was indeed at a most interesting stage of its development.

The College had been at something of a low ebb just before 1914. It had then undergone a transformation under the outstanding Mastership of Sir Will Spens, a man of whom all Humphrey's generation always spoke with the greatest affection and respect. During Humphrey's time at Cambridge Spens was to begin work on the Report which brought about the reorganisation of secondary education in England – one effect of which was that the author of this Memoir was able to enjoy public school education and thereby meet Humphrey. One of the Fellows of the College at this time was R.A. Butler (who in 1944 was to put the recommendations of the Spens Report into effect). How curious it is that two of the men who were eventually to enormously alter secondary education and the position of the public schools within it were Master and Fellow of Humphrey's College! Several of the other Fellows either had been or were to become Public School Headmasters. Humphrey's favourite don however was the lovable and unworldly 'Archie' Clarke-Kennedy, whom he didn't in fact get to know until his final year. Spens pursued a policy of entertaining the famous and influential in the College which was greatly appreciated, not least by Humphrey who was especially pleased as many of the famous visitors were musicians. A contemporary recalled: 'We often had musical evenings, concerts or Bene't meetings in the Master's Lodge as well as in the Dean of Chapel's rooms'.

In *Cambridge Between Two Wars*, T.E.B. Howarth evokes much of the intellectual climate of Corpus Christi at this time when he says that members of the College were 'expected to be very good academically and also adjudged likely to "fit in",' for which the main criteria were 'sincere churchmanship; intelligent conservative politics . . . and preferably a tacitly understood agreement not to marry under the age of thirty'. Humphrey may be said in the main to have met these criteria later in his life; but the first two read somewhat ironically in view of his outlook at this time. At this stage he was very inwardly divided about the church. He had imbibed from home and Bradfield an instinctive respect for Christianity, but of course public school religion in the enclosed community is in many ways very different from religion in society at large; and Bradfield's religion had been unique. Another part of himself, pulled strongly by his feelings, rebelled and saw religion, as did Rupert Brooke, as an important part of the middle-class philistinism that the young above all should be devoted to unmasking. Humphrey had been surrounded by the church all his young life; and, as with Brooke's 'neo-paganism', Humphrey's young rebellion expressed the need of the young poet to break the mould and find his own way. Because of his background the seeds of the churchman had been implanted deep; but the rebel in him at this time was stronger. The second criterion, 'intelligent conservative politics', is perhaps the one that reads most ironically in the light of his actual three years at Cambridge.

The university ethos in the early 1930s was registering very markedly the changes in the ethos of the nation at large. The exclusivity of the 1920s was breaking down and a new militancy for social justice was abroad in society as a whole. A Labour government had been elected in 1929. By the time Humphrey arrived at Cambridge overall the lower middle-classes were beginning to get more into the driving seat among the undergraduates, although the privileged bourgeoisie still held the social scene. Moreover the great economic Depression of the 1930s had gained hold upon the nation. Fascist dictators were rising up in many parts of the world, and the more fully aware among the privileged in Britain could see that there was a milder and more muted fascism at large in the British nation. Within this complex situation the influence of Karl Marx was in the ascendant – much more so among the university undergraduates and the intelligentsia than among the working classes in the nation at large. It was the privileged classes who, as they held on somewhat guiltily to their rosy inheritance, were increasingly assailed by the sense of being doomed by the movement of history. Many intellectuals felt a strong appeal in the austerity of communism. All of this greatly affected Humphrey and for a good many years he shared the prevailing sense of the onset of the dialectic. Like most Cambridge intellectuals of this time he went through a kind of communist phase.

While at Cambridge, however, Humphrey was an interested sympathiser with the left-wing cult rather than in any way actively involved. He was not primarily a political person. His was a Socialism of the heart; he believed that

Socialism and the teaching of Christ were connected; but, no matter how much he was to be swept along by the new socialist sympathies he still remained conscious that 'I am a bourgeois'. The new International Socialism may have affected his conscience, but more important for him was the fact that Socialism had been the faith of Rupert and the faith of Oscar Wilde, and it was the faith too of certain new voices on his poetical horizon.

When John Paine came to Cambridge to visit Humphrey they had long discussions about all these things. Humphrey told John of the growing attraction for him of leftwing politics. He told John how since he had arrived in Cambridge he had been swept off his feet by the new 1930s poets – Auden, Spender and Day Lewis – whom he used to refer to at that time as 'the red triangle'. They were the emergent young poets of his own generation and their leftwing sympathies were very influential on his own politics. In one of his wartime diaries Humphrey wrote: 'the dawn of communism was brought to me by Auden and Harry Kemp of Stowe'. The latter was an influential Cambridge contemporary.

Humphrey knew that this political reorientation would almost certainly cause quarrels and misunderstanding at home. He was right. His home was ultra-conservative. His parents and his elder military brother, Peter, could not sympathise with his changing views; but, he later said, his mother did try to. However Humphrey did have one convert in the household, his younger brother, Oliver. Humphrey in fact was beginning to be like a mentor to Oliver in intellectual and artistic matters. He took Oliver's literary and musical education in hand. He wrote a vivid *History of English Poetry* in typescript for Oliver and inspired him with all his literary and musical enthusiasms. In their youth and beyond they shared many devotions, including one to A.A. Milne. Of Humphrey's new identification with the 1930s poets and his left-wing sympathies, Oliver has told me: 'I think the real trouble was that my parents did not approve of the Thirties writers. They had misconceptions about their way of life and so would not try to understand the poetry. Humphrey's influence on me was total. Our elder brother, Peter, was a good deal older and was often held up as a paragon of virtue. This threw Humphrey and me very much together, and Humphrey's enthusiasms were very infectious. I was a very willing pupil. I bought it all although I often did not understand what he was trying to tell me at all. And Humphrey was a great relief from and antidote to the very regimental society into which I had been sent at an early age, viz. Royal Naval College, where to be interested in anything smacking of the aesthetic at that time was scorned and discouraged.'

Devoted son though he was, Humphrey's feelings about his class background were always to be somewhat ambivalent. I believe that he saw much of the haute bourgeoisie life style of his background as in some ways the contemporary inheritance of the late Victorian morality in the propriety and rectitude of which, as he later expressed it, 'all the virtues had their prescription written on the bottle'. This could do little for the increasing sense he had in early life of complex inner psychological struggle and the concomitant need for spiritual healing and renewal which was closely connected with his growing sense of contemporary middle class British life. His parents, though they were cultured in their old fashioned way, were not really fully aware of the iconoclastic changes that were taking place in the world at large. Nor was it at all easy for them to follow the range and novelty of Humphrey's interests. Humphrey knew that they were holding on to the past. His mother's irrepressible sense of humour, however, as well as his father's ingenuous charm in the main prevented what he saw as atavistic class failings from actually dominating his own particular household; and it made things a bit easier having Oliver as an ally.

Humphrey's relationship with his mother was especially close, but it was not an easy relationship. Amy, who was very strong willed, wrestled emotionally to dominate the household. For all his deep love for her, Amy's effect on Humphrey over long periods was frequently to make him feel emotionally stifled. He couldn't help feeling angry sometimes at the emotional power she exercised over him. She was possessive; and she worked on his feelings. He sometimes felt that she actually resented his life away from home. As a result he felt a very great need for independence. As for many middle class intellectuals in his time school was for Humphrey in some ways his liberation from an overdominant home background. At the same time he was from early manhood onwards at least partly conscious of the fact that his relationship with her was the source in him of what Auden called 'the wound' – that psycho-sexual core of identity which he both suffered from and yet cherished.

For all of his first year at Cambridge Humphrey lived in something of an ivory tower. In a sense he cultivated what he called 'a kind of defensive egotism' as he felt out and found his feet in his new environment. Contemporaries have told me that he would sometimes play the piano all day long. In a diary he describes the state of being that he practised most in his first year as a kind of 'refined' or 'archaic melancholy'. Music would sometimes lift the melancholy for a while and give periods of ecstatic happiness. Chopin above all became the bosom companion of his loneliness; the composer, he would often later say, from whom the adolescent is most likely to begin a musical pilgrimage. He wrote of Chopin at this time: 'once addicted to Chopin who can ever again claim to be entirely sober'. He was under the spell of what he described as Chopin's 'lingering sort of beauty, tinged with some distant melancholy for past ages and past events – and a yearning, for what?' Of the pianist, Cortot, he noted at this time: 'a life devoted to Chopin is a pure aim'.

During his first term at Cambridge Humphrey made a pilgrimage to Grantchester on his own. He had longed for this moment. For him Grantchester was Rupert Brooke, and all the places there most directly associated with Rupert were shrines to his memory. Arrived in Grantchester, he went first to the Old Vicarage and introduced himself to the people living there. Unfortunately he didn't record in his notebook whom he spoke to, (it is likely to have been Rupert's close friend, Dudley Ward, or a member of his family) but he had begun now to enquire of all living sources about Rupert – which he was to do later throughout Cambridge. He found out some unique information too about Samuel Widnall, who had previously lived at the Old Vicarage. He was also to make his own discoveries about Rupert, some of which were otherwise

Humphrey as a young man.
During his time at Cambridge Humphrey's poetry developed under
the influence of Brooke and Auden.

unknown. He visited the church and walked along by the river. He lay in the long grass and dreamed. Then he had tea in the Orchard tearooms and stayed to savour the dusk and walk again by the river. There he jotted a few ideas for a poem about Rupert which would germinate later on holiday abroad. He recorded in his diary: 'first really sacred day at Cambridge'.

Humphrey was of course actually in love with Rupert Brooke or rather he was in love with the idealised memory of Rupert Brooke; but he did have a real understanding of the human being behind the legend. He deeply regretted that fortune had as it were separated him personally from Rupert. For he felt that had they been able to know one another they would certainly have been intimates. Indeed Humphrey felt as if by a cruelty of fate, Rupert and he were meant for one another – and yet at the same time he knew this could never be. There were some important differences between them as people, but they were from the same kind of roots. Their family backgrounds, their school experiences and also their temperaments had so much in common. Rupert in some ways lived on in Humphrey. He lived on in a certain shared sense in Humphrey of being an inheritor of a uniquely glorious tradition and growing into his heritage. Rupert and Humphrey shared too a similar kind of exuberant idealism, shot through with puritanism; they both mingled aestheticism with humour; and they both wrote poetry that attempts magnanimously to win over and to share: that displays in fact pre-eminently the gifts of the teacher. Humphrey however did not share Rupert's difficult bisexuality. He was of course aware of Rupert's love of women, but he transposed all the heterosexual love poetry into a homosexual key.

Because of Rupert's tragically young death in the First World War, Humphrey saw him as a kind of sacrificial torch bearer for the youth of his own generation – dying for his idealised vision of England and her heritage, such a vision as Humphrey and all his friends at Bradfield had shared. In Rupert's death he saw a kind of destiny. He wasn't primarily concerned with Rupert as a 'war poet' – though he was aware of course that the war sonnets had been the basis of Rupert's original reputation. He believed, however, that by a kind of tragic necessity Rupert had to die when he did – laying down his life for his country at the age of twenty eight with all his promise unfolding and with all his awareness of beauty still 'pristine, absolute and incandescent'. For Humphrey Rupert was above all the public school and University poet of youth and love – always linked to Rugby School even after he had left. He believed that Rupert was divinely chosen for his looks and charisma as well as for his poetic gifts to enshrine as it were sacrificially one of the final flowerings of the 'golden ages of poetry' – ages in which poetry reflected the beauty and romance and wholeness in people's lives, qualities such as Humphrey and all his generation had experienced at Beloe's Bradfield.

Humphrey sometimes fantasised that Rupert was still alive and that they went about together. He cherished his dreams of close friendship with this most handsome of poets; but, while he knew of Rupert's bisexuality, it is doubtful whether he knew of Rupert's repudiation of homosexuality in his later years. Even if he had known, I doubt whether this or anything else could have diminished his love. A friend gave him what I think is an unique photo of Rupert, which he treasured. He bought one of the Rupert Brooke wall plaques which were then on sale. This period was in fact the height of Rupert's idolisation in Cambridge, although Humphrey frequently wished that more of the undergraduates really appreciated Rupert's poetry. This was the time when Rupert's statue was raised on Skyros and his plaque placed beside Arnold's and Clough's in Rugby chapel. Humphrey found out strange little known facts about Rupert, such as that he was once charged with trespassing and causing damage when he went out to catch moths while at Cambridge and for this he was charged ¼d. Interestingly enough, Humphrey himself was to become during his lifetime one of the best known moth collectors in the South West of England.

During all his first year Humphrey's intellectual interests were fermenting and expanding in many directions. He started exploring many of the great philosophers and filling notebooks with quotes and comments on them. He was especially concerned to explore the relation between the everyday world and the world of dreams and fancies. He noted: 'The impression of apparently solid matter in a settled state on my mind hurts. I am becoming convinced that the everyday solid and brittle life is an illusion, by reason of its false appearance of stillness and its abstracted nature: the world of dreams and fancies and the imagination is nearer for me to reality.' Elsewhere he noted: 'Rupert Brooke exhorted his friends to live poetry i.e. to cast off from the shore and swim in the so called 'illusions' of their dreams and fancies. When an artist successfully does this, the 'illusions' lead to vision'. He read a lot of 'Uncle' Aldous Huxley whom he found to be a very sympathetic guide and point of reference for all this richness of new discovery, but despite his intellectual ferment he lived all his first year in a kind of assiduous vagueness of as yet unpinpointed potential waiting and hoping for the friendship that he knew he needed in order to be able to realise and manifest his gifts.

ANTHONY DICKINS AND LAURENCE CLARK

Friendship suddenly flowered for Humphrey at the beginning of his second year at Corpus. Anthony Dickins arrived as the assistant Organ Scholar of the College. He came to Cambridge from Stowe where he had been a pupil of Roxburgh. He was the son of a Brigadier General in the Indian Army and he was reading Modern Languages. They had seen one another frequently at Choir practices and at the glee singing after dinner. Then one evening in early 1934 Anthony has written to tell me: 'Humphrey came to my rooms after Choir practice to ask to talk to me. He told me the tale of how he had been let down by a friend, Eric Faulkner. They had been great friends and then came this rift. This is how our friendship started, for I had no real friend then but only a myriad of 'social acquaintance', and both Humphrey and I needed a real friend. We soon found common ground, especially in music and poetry and in our mutual orientation towards young men.'

Eric Faulkner had come up to Corpus one year after Humphrey from Bradfield where, though they had not been close, they had known one another quite well as fellow Prefects. As his only fellow Bradfieldian in Corpus Humphrey now looked to him hopefully for a more permanent and ongoing friendship. They were even given adjacent rooms in College. It looked as if a friendship was on the cards, but this was not to be. (Sir Eric Faulkner later became an Honorary Fellow of Corpus, Warden of Bradfield from 1965-1984, and the Chairman of Lloyds Bank). Sir Eric told me that his friendship cooled mainly because Humphrey attempted to take charge of his intellectual and artistic development and also because Humphrey would habitually play the piano in the early hours of the morning.

This is how Anthony tells the ongoing story in his contemporary Cambridge diary: 'John told me that Faulkner on whose friendship he had counted had turned out differently from what he had expected. John says he feels very alone – he feels the need of a friend. . . . When we finished talking it was 3.45 a.m. It was a very fine morning so we climbed out through the area (where one of the balustrades in the staircase could be removed to give access to the street – known only to initiates). Glorious feeling of freedom as we ran down Silver Street escaping into the grass and trees and birds. We went very fast along the river until we came to the swimming-shed where we climbed in and swam naked in the river for a while – the water was very warm and the birds came flying down low to inspect the intruders. We ran up and down the grass afterwards to get dry and warm, dressed, climbed out and walked on to Grantchester, and beyond to Canteloupe Farm. Here we lay down in the long grass under a hedge to get half-an-hours sleep from 5.45-6.15. The colours of the dawn were sombre, evanescent purples and blues, and a slow drizzle soon began. At half past six we went to the Red Lion and fortunately found the good lady of the house just getting up and looking very tired. After a long wait we were brought a grand breakfast set out in a very fine way on the best crockery and best furniture in the place. An enormous quantity of scrambled eggs on toast, plenty of bread and butter and marmalade and very good coffee. Never have I so relished a breakfast. After this Rabelaisian meal we commandeered the local taxi to bear us in triumph back to Corpus – and it was sobering to re-enter the portals, but a necessary purge to our exalted emotions, and I was only just in time for my tutorial.'

Life now began to blossom for Humphrey though he was still wrestling with introversion and an inner lack of ease in society. This was largely due to his growing realisation that he was homosexual and all that this implied. He certainly at this stage had not properly come to terms with his homosexuality. He kept it secret from the world at large. Few can fully realise now the dilemma for the young man who at that time was discovering that he was homosexual. It meant growing into the awareness that he was going to be at odds with normal society all his life – an awareness that was aggravated for Humphrey by the prevailing cult of manliness among the undergraduates. One must remember too that for a long time yet any homosexual practice was to be against the law. From a note in a Cambridge diary we can see that up until this time Humphrey had always regarded his 'homosexuality as the natural prelude to heterosexuality'. However intense and special his Bradfield loves were he never thought at the time that he was developing irrevocably in such a way as to preclude normal sexuality in later life, but he was now beginning to clearly see that this was not to be so. His suffering was tempered by a mixture of puritanism and defiance. He notes how very angry he felt when he read of the treatment that Oscar Wilde had received. He then goes on to contrast his mainly chaste delight in the company of males with the talk of many contemporary undergraduates who 'talk about their women as I do about my stamps and birds eggs . . . and imagine that because they have labelled some of the sex factors, they have solved the mystery of love'. It is clear that he rarely sought sexuality as such – what he really sought was love, and this he needed for his happiness and in order to be creative. In contrast to today's more sexual homosexual love one could say that his homosexual love, and that of most of his generation, had a quality of innocence about it. Nevertheless because of his homosexuality he felt that things were stacked against him, and this feeling was frequently apparent to others. Some who knew him well as a young man at Cambridge described him as often 'anguished' in his demeanour. By contrast, Anthony was more sanguine. He settled down to accept his homosexuality and he was certainly more socially at ease.

Together Humphrey and Anthony launched more fully into Cambridge life. They joined a poetry group just forming called 'The Merry Meeting'. It was named after the café in Silver Street, which no longer exists, in a room above which they used to meet. The prime mover of the group was Stanley Richardson. He was later tragically killed in the bombing of the Café de Paris in the West End. Tom McKitterick was the second most prominent convenor. But the group in a sense revolved around Stanley Richardson's Patroness, Alicia Cameron-Taylor, a lady who queened it among the undergraduate men in the group and sometimes caused them enormous amusement. However, they were all more than a little in awe of her. She was in fact related to the Stephen family. She was an extraordinary lady, a figure of the demimonde, and a well known Cambridge institution of the period. She lived by the Arts Theatre. Everybody who met her would be regaled with tales of Oscar Wilde whom she had known. She invariably had two comments to make about him which seemed to alternate with fairly consistent regularity. Either she would say: 'I didn't like him' or 'I liked him'. When 'The Merry Meeting' produced in the Spring of 1935 their beautifully printed Quarto, on its very high quality paper in a luxuriant buff-grey cover, of the 'Poems read aloud at the Merry Meeting', of which George Rylands has recently told me he still possesses a copy, it was largely she who had financed it. The Quarto was dedicated to Alicia. Several of the contributors, of whom Humphrey was one (he contributed three poems), did try to recoup as much of the outlay as they could by attempting to hawk copies in Huntingdon market. They are now collectors' items. Tambimuttu later implored me for a copy.

Humphrey and Anthony were among the earliest founder members of 'The Merry Meeting'. They brought along their mutual friend from Peterhouse, Laurence Clark. He in turn introduced his friend, Tony Conybeare. The other members were: Olive Fraser, Geoffrey Hann, David Lea, Patrick Dudgeon,

R.J. Rees, David Edwardes, David Alexander, and W.K. Gibson. 'The Merry Meeting' was to be a prime factor in sealing the trio of friendship between Humphrey, Anthony and Laurence.

Anthony sent me the following which he said is a fairly typical entry about 'The Merry Meeting' from his 1934 Cambridge diary: 'Laurence Clark's supper party. Then off to 'The Merry Meeting'. Good meeting. Commanded in rather official manner by Laurence with occasional fruitless remarks by Quicktrick (McKitterick). Afterwards tremendous send off to Miss Cameron-Taylor as she mounts her four-wheeled chariot. Door is slammed and Miss C.T., firmly confined yet still smiling, is whisked away'.

'The Merry Meeting' has not been mentioned in any of the accounts that I have read of Cambridge in the Thirties. It had, however, a profound influence on those who belonged to it. All its members had a passionate commitment to poetry. Rupert Brooke was the presiding spirit. 'Poems read at the Merry Meeting' show how all pervasive his influence was on the group. They all remembered its meetings with joy. Humphrey would recount in later years how much sheer fun and laughter inspired its activities, but it was also a serious enterprise and an early valuable experience for three people at least whose lives would in many respects be largely devoted to poetry. After leaving Cambridge Anthony at first thought that his career might be in music and for a time he studied conducting under Sir Henry Wood. This, however, was not to be. In 1938, having walked out for good from his military father's household, and living at the time in bohemian poverty in Fitzrovia he founded with Tambimuttu, Dylan Thomas, and Keidrych Rhys, what became the leading poetry magazine of the Forties, *Poetry London*. Laurence was to be a frequent contributor to *Poetry London* and he also published several impressive volumes of his own poetry. Humphrey and Laurence and to some extent Anthony all continued to write poetry throughout their lives.

The stimulus of 'The Merry Meeting' was undoubtedly a foremost factor in Humphrey's development as a poet. His membership of a group both enthusiastic and discerning led him to take more care over his poems. He began for the first time to work on his poems and to produce some really completed ones. His first published poems appeared at Cambridge in 'Poems read at the Merry Meeting' and in another Cambridge literary magazine, 'Contemporaries and Makers'.

Laurence Clark was to become second only to Anthony among Humphrey's Cambridge friends. Both these friendships were to last. In the case of Laurence their common bond was poetry, not music. Laurence was in many ways the perfect whimsical English eccentric individualist. He had a most active enquiring mind and he had an enormous zest for living. He was somewhat unique among Humphrey's friends in that he was rich. His wealth came from the family food firm of Foster-Clark. Some of his friends questioned whether his wealth really did him much good. He certainly enjoyed it, however, while he was young. He was the only person whom Humphrey knew who enjoyed such amenities as a Bauhaus home in Moor Park, a comfortable flat in Bermuda, his own private aeroplane, and a yacht. But apart from keeping an eye on stocks and shares, Laurence took comparatively little interest in the family firm. Poetry was his passion.

Laurence had gone to Rugby and it was there that he began writing poems inspired by Rupert Brooke. He still remembers a small picture of Rupert Brooke in the Rugby chapel on an aisle pillar that he used to gaze on, admiring his beauty, his long hair and the unconventional clasp he used to wear instead of a necktie. He was Laurence's ideal of what a poet should be. At Rugby Laurence started a school paper inspired by Brooke. It was called 'Sparrow Pie' and it lasted two issues.

When Humphrey and Laurence met there was an immediate rapport between them. For it was surely inevitable and right that these two passionate devotees of Rupert Brooke should meet together at Cambridge. Their other main shared literary enthusiasms were for A.E. Housman and E.M. Forster – both of whom were in fact in Cambridge at that time.

One day Humphrey and Laurence were highly thrilled to see A.E. Housman himself in a Cambridge street. Humphrey wrote in his 1934 Cambridge notebook: 'We actually saw A.E. Housman this morning. We followed him down the street. He looked in a shop window. On his nose was a dewdrop. He had difficulty in blowing his nose. He wore an umbrella and a green cloth cap: at a jaunty angle. He looked somewhat decrepit.' Humphrey loved to recall this sighting of the great man in later years and relished the somehow so appropriate details of the dewdrop and the green cap at a jaunty angle.

It was with Anthony and Laurence that Humphrey now shared in all 'the severe contentions of Friendship' his enthusiasms and discoveries. In these crucial years they developed and grew in relation to one another. Though they had much in common they were also in many ways very different and complementary. Humphrey could enthuse over their virtues and also be very critical of them at other times. He noted in his 1934 diary: 'Most of Tony's utterances are worth looking at again. They are by no means valueless sparks thrown out by the groaning, developing being. He put me on to Nietzsche'; and 'Today because of Laurence Clark I have got through to the real nature of things'. Of the rapport between himself and Humphrey and Laurence Anthony told me: 'H.J.M. and L.W.C. gave me the hard, strong, stark intellects that I could appreciate, though they were very different from each other'. Both Anthony and Laurence of course were very soon invited to 'Byams', and they both took to his family as they had to Humphrey. Anthony noted: 'It was a great thrill to be invited to 'Byams' and to meet the unforgettable Amy Moore, who became almost as much a friend as Humphrey himself, for she and I got on like wildfire.'

With Anthony and Laurence, Humphrey established his new poetic bearings. They discovered Eliot and Pound with something of a shock; but it was an invigorating shock. Eliot was always to be of the greatest importance for Humphrey. Soon he and his undergraduate friends would be chanting the new music of Eliot as their forerunners had chanted the music of Swinburne. Humphrey in fact still often chanted the music of both. As they extended their horizons they discovered also Hopkins and Yeats. Above all, with a shock of thrilling recognition, they discovered Auden, Spender and Day Lewis. Here they realised was the voice of their own generation, speaking most directly to them and mainly originating from the same public school milieu and ethos.

And, something we don't always realise now, speaking of a new hope of spiritual renaissance for England, a revolutionary conception of a 'love' that would revitalise both the individual and society, a kind of courageous taking of a regenerative step forward in a confused and debilitated era.

Humphrey, as we have seen, was deeply emotionally rooted in the Georgian world of his childhood. He had imbibed to a rare extent the now vanishing pre-war liberal idealism. He had identified with that world first, but he discovered at Cambridge as great a commitment to Auden and his circle as in childhood he had discovered to the Georgians and the romantics. He was to see the Thirties poets as bringing a kind of new poetic age in a manner in some ways akin to the Georgians' earlier attempt at an English poetic renaissance among the middle class public. It was the strong impact of Auden and the Thirties poets on a sensibility moulded first in the Georgian world that I believe made Humphrey the original voice that he increasingly became. It was the creative dialectic between these two worlds of influence, plus his hellenism, that formed him as a poet. Auden above all challenged him to relate his religion of beauty to the actual complexities of the contemporary world and to actively engage with it. 'Today', Humphrey wrote in his Cambridge journal, 'we have an Auden for a Brooke.'

Laurence was more bowled over by Spender than by Auden; Anthony was most bowled over by Eliot and Pound; but everybody who knew Humphrey would realise the extraordinary closeness of his self-identification with Auden's life and work from this point onwards. As a poet who was also from an upper middle class professional background, a homosexual and a schoolteacher, in Auden Humphrey recognised an articulation of his own situation – or, in the case of the school teaching, what would soon become his own situation. Here is Humphrey writing soon after his discovery of Auden: 'Everything that Auden writes haunts me and runs on the tip of my tongue all day. He controls my behaviour more than I am aware. I find myself arguing with his effect, like a conscience. He represents my social conscience.' 'The one responsible poet' – he wrote on the title page of his copy of 'Poems' 1930. In Auden he perceived the stature of an emergent leader – an emergent intellectual leader from the milieu of the Independent schools. The young Auden, the privileged liberal individualist/socialist, with all his inner divisions, guilts and ambivalencies, at first lamented the loss of the heroic dimension in the modern world. In 'The Orators' 1932, a study of hero worship against a private school background, he analysed the flaws in the romantic conception of personality, while showing considerable sympathy for what he was analysing. By the time he wrote 'The Ascent of F6' in 1936 Auden had laid to rest any fantasies he had of being an heroic redeemer figure for his age. For many of his generation, nevertheless, including Humphrey, this kind of romantic and heroic aura of the early English Auden stayed with him for the whole of his life. As the Marxist dialectic gained its hold on peoples consciences in the Thirties Auden found himself drawn in two directions. He felt its strong appeal but he was all the time conscious of his own bourgeois roots. For a time he sought meaningfully to place his somewhat isolated life within the context of an evolving life force, a kind of Idealist version of the dialectic, which he called 'History'. He believed that the natural beneficence of this life force, if unimpeded, would move society towards 'the reign of love'. It is however thwarted by the impositions of state politics. But he soon came to see that this belief is utopian. Auden realised that in the Thirties history was no longer steadily evolving in such a way that the individual could pursue his private life largely oblivious of politics. Liberal values were everywhere under threat. History was becoming the reflection of the public realm in an increasingly collectivised and polarised world. In the contemporary public chaos, while seeking the regenerative political path, Auden sought in his poetry to preserve a vital sense of the individual's private sphere of life, and an awareness of the sense in which the individual could still take ethical responsibility as an agent of his own history. All of this helped Humphrey to elucidate his own situation; while giving him important bearings in his early life.

Auden moreover Humphrey saw as a phenomenon quite new in the modern world: a poet who knew about science and had taken stock of it; and a poet who showed that the successfully mature modern poet's mind could be 'objective and ordered in some ways like that of a scientist' while still writing whenever he wished with the quality of poetic song. Above all Humphrey perceived Auden to be a spiritual 'healer' – partly in the heroic redemptive sense, but also in a more generalised sense. Humphrey saw him as a poet who was as it were working with nature to diagnose the real ailments of the age. For Auden, whose father was a doctor specialising in Psychology, had begun his studies in Oxford in Biology – a significant fact for one with his early evolutionary view of history – and he was developing his own interest in Psychology. These influences, together with the liberal philosophy of his upbringing which, despite his temporary utopian realignment with the Left, still exercised a strong hold on him, and his basically Christian monist understanding of life, all appealed to conceptions of an underlying vital natural order. They gave the young Auden the perfect training to be as it were the spiritual doctor of the Thirties, both the warning and the healing voice of his times.

Humphrey's response to the discovery of Spender was also intense. 'Spender', he wrote in his Cambridge diary, 'is a descendent of the poet Shelley. He has something akin to Rupert Brooke in his style and his way of investing words with a shining value. His rightness, like Rupert's, lies in his accepting his own rightness without any doubt. He is not complicated like Day Lewis. And it is this one sided element that makes him attractive. He is worth a thousand people today because he is not against life; because he stands like a sword.' And after first reading Day Lewis Humphrey recorded: 'In Day Lewis' mind the bond between religion and poetry is strong. They both start from love, but he sees that religion has gone out of the land. The people are sinking with their cares. The heart is buried. So any action with religion as a basis is destined to be lost as a ripple on the lake. . . . The stream may not mingle in the waters of the people, and so carves its separate course. It can only affect the spirit when the spirit is open i.e. in youth. It must teach; and not books but wonder and fire and beauty.'

Looking back a few years later, Humphrey reveals that Anthony was in fact a main influence in leading him to his greatest love in music, Mozart: 'I discovered some Mozart at Bradfield', he noted in 1936, 'but it was a door through which I did not go immediately; of which I am grateful. At Cambridge I met Anthony Dickins who had been to Stowe and spent some time in Salzburg. He spent his first year considerably engrossed with Mozart, and it was this which led me to investigate the Piano Sonatas.' This investigation led to one of the most profound and central loves of his life.

In *Roxburgh of Stowe* Lord Annan tells of how Anthony first came through Roxburgh's influence to visit Salzburg: 'knowing that his parents were in India. J.F. (Roxburgh) asked a boy (Anthony) how he proposed to spend his summer holidays. Bicycling across Holland to Germany to improve his German. Did he know Dutch? No. That was unfortunate – he had far better to accept a return ticket to Salzburg and Vienna where he could listen to music.' 'This' said Anthony 'was the most wonderful, the most educative and the most formative holiday in my life. It was to that journey that I owed my music Scholarship to Cambridge.' This holiday and its consequences was also a fertilising seed of experience that was to extend its strong active influence into Humphrey's life, as we shall see.

Mozart now had prime place in Humphrey's musical pantheon, even ahead of Beethoven. 'Mozart' he noted a little later, 'was probably the purest genius that has ever lived. He is the man who I admire through his works above all others. The tradition of the pure-in-heart lies in him as in Blake. Chopin's request 'play Mozart in memory of me', knowing the music of both, is as germinal a saying as has ever been uttered.' Humphrey said that he was glad to come to Mozart a little later lest at school he had got the idea of him as 'a simple being, composing merely elegant music for the drawing room and the court'. Humphrey tried many time to define something of the inexhaustible profundity within Mozart's seemingly innocent simplicity. It was a quality that he associated with European family and court life before the French Revolution. He used to say that we are coming into a new era of the understanding of Mozart: and that our age really understands Mozart while the 19th century did not. Among his many formulations about Mozart I especially like the following:

Hungry music is Mozart's.
Unsatisfied with a salt taste on the tip of the tongue as acid leaves –
Think of the longing, the desire for completion, that is put with such
    light swift, complete certainty –
Encompassing the paradoxical doubt in reasoned thought.

Humphrey now started his Mozart library. It expanded alongside his collection of the Thirties poets. From now onwards he had a standing order at Bumpus' bookshop in London for every new book by Auden, Spender, Day Lewis and Macneice (who had been added to the original three), and also for every new book on Mozart. In due course his collection of the Thirties poets and his Mozart library were to be extraordinarily complete. They became a marvellous source of knowledge and a fount of inspiration for generations of boys later.

All his life Humphrey was in love with the music of the piano; and he pursued great pianists hungrily. In his last year at Cambridge he recorded in his journal that he heard a pianist the experience of whose playing, like that of hearing Rachmaninov and Paderewski in his childhood, stood out amid all his experiences in pursuit of the great virtuosi. For this pianist his enthusiasm knew no bounds. Humphrey was electrified through his consummate virtuosity, as of the Paganini of the piano. This was the legendary Vladimir Horowitz. Humphrey first heard him play at the Guildhall in Cambridge sometime early in 1935. He reproduced the programme of the recital entire in his journal and he also drew an extremely good and dramatic pencil drawing of Horowitz in action to accompany the eulogy in his journal. This is what Humphrey wrote after the concert:

> Tonight I heard him play. 3½ feet away on the platform. He has got me. I am tied to him. I will live when I hear him again. Small, impudent diabolo. No one will ever play Schumann like you, nor Brahms, nor anyone. He plays with his backbone – sitting on the edge of the chair, the right foot lightly on the pedal, the left foot probably back under the chair on tip toe. Balanced on the edge of the chair, he plays with his shoulders, arms, crouching over the keys. He has black powder in his fingers and a devil in his heart. One couldn't listen to the music in ones usual way. He had Power – held you in his hand. What use, words. He is the greatest pianist alive. Surely the years will be altered – A.V.H. anno Vlad. Horowitzo!

In the May of 1935 Humphrey noted in his diary: 'bought a car'. It was his first car – a bullnosed Morris. He was branching out and manifestly becoming less introverted than he had been. Anthony had probably whetted his appetite to run his own car when, during Humphrey's second year, he bought his own 'snub-nosed' Morris Oxford two seater which he called 'Towser'. Humphrey used to have the use of 'Towser' provided he paid for the petrol. These were still fairly early and very exciting days for motoring and the sheer adventure of driving is reflected in many of Humphrey's poems. It was the unfettered freedom of the open road that he always loved. The sense of exhilaration in driving his own car, frequently at speed, somehow never seems to have left him. His car was always to remain for him a great symbol of his freedom.

During 1935, Humphrey's last year at Cambridge, Anthony introduced him to several of his other friends. Some of these friends, like Steven Runciman the historian for example, were 'Apostles' and moved in Cambridge's most elite society. These friends were often invited to Anthony's rooms at Corpus, the rooms that the poet Marlowe had once occupied which Humphrey once referred to as 'Anthony's queer little episcopal rooms', in which fairly small space Anthony had nevertheless managed to squeeze a grand piano. It was here that Humphrey met many of the leading and most colourful figures of the time, for example Burgess and Philby who were quite frequent visitors – that is, until Anthony made it clear to them that he was not going to be converted. It would be interesting to know more about Humphrey's meeting with Maclean, who also came to Anthony's rooms and whom Humphrey refers to in a Cambridge diary.

The most interesting of these meetings for Humphrey was one with an undergraduate from Trinity College, who was a poet and who had been at Stowe with Anthony. His name was John Cornford, and he was a strikingly good looking young man and one of the most glamorous of his generation. He was the son of the Lawrence Professor of Ancient Philosophy at Cambridge and his poetess wife, Frances Darwin, and he was a fiercely committed and intensely idealistic Communist with a great admiration for Auden and the Thirties poets. This meeting had a special meaning for Humphrey. For both of Cornford's parents had been among Rupert Brooke's closest friends at Cambridge. Indeed it was Rupert Brooke who in a sense had first brought them together. John was even named Rupert John after Brooke. Humphrey saw Cornford as a kind of link between Brooke and Auden. Although they only met once, Humphrey never forgot him. And, when Cornford was killed in the Spanish Civil War in the following year, the day after his 21st birthday, the memory of this heroic Cambridge contemporary sunk especially deeply into Humphrey's mind.

Humphrey made a new friend at Corpus in his last year. Basil Gough was reading for the Theological Tripos; and like himself was a volunteer member of the Corpus Christi choir. Humphrey found in Basil Gough straightaway a challenging antithesis to himself. He wrote: 'He often destroys or paralyses my thoughts and feelings. He is anti romantic: but his influence on me is enormous. I love him.' I think that in this friendship there was an element of undergraduate adventure, and an attempt to live out something of his sexual nature. Several poems of Humphrey's later period at Cambridge were addressed to Basil Gough. They also went on a hiking holiday to the North West of Scotland in the Summer of 1937. Humphrey wrote a poem about the holiday which ends with the lines: 'Before Summer is over and the days are grown short/Like horsefly, like mayfly we'll frolic till caught'.

By the time Humphrey had reached his last year at Cambridge the horizon was clouded by the Fascist threat. Everyone had been vaguely conscious of it steadily growing for many years. All knew that Germany was rearming and that there was the probability of another war. It is very hard for people of later generations, and especially for those born after the Second World War, to imagine the mood and temper of this time and the tragic feeling of helplessness and doom as people waited for a war that they knew would come. Men of Humphrey's generation very often held a tragic view of life. In many, including Humphrey, a kind of desperate pacifism grew which was determined to try and ensure that there would not be another war, though in most cases hardly as yet remotely realising the full extent of the wickedness into which the world was to be plunged.

Meanwhile life was to be enjoyed as much as possible. While one had the precarious privilege it was to be all the more prized. Every one of Humphrey's holidays from Cambridge up until the outbreak of the Second World War was to be packed with experience and enjoyment; and he made sure that he revisited as many of his most loved places as possible in case he never saw them again.

In October 1935 he received a surprise letter from Laurence written from the Greek island of Skyros and informing him that Laurence was there with Stanley Richardson (main convenor of 'The Merry Meeting') and Bobby Alan (a rich ship owner who later got a life peerage). Humphrey was understandably jealous. Laurence has handed on to me the letter which Humphrey then wrote to him, which, as it is vintage Humphrey, I will quote in its entirety:

Byams 10th October '35

Dear Clark,

Thank you for your communiqué. I was not in Kent save for a day, to see a man who wanted me to canoe down the Zambesi with him for a year. However as he required £500 he didn't find me.

No I am not at Bradfield. Nor likely to be yet. There are no jobs as yet. You are a Devildevildevil, the lucky sort, being in Skyros. In fact its rather a nerve that you should go there before me. Is it a possible place? Is it very dry? Are there hundreds of Hamadryads knocking around? (David Lea?)

In return for this bald script write me a hundred page document giving your whyfore, and wherewhither, with a sketch map of everything. Incidentally come here when you can, but let me know, as there is a likelihood that I may be away learning teaching during school term time. You're the sort of person who must write and say 'I will be coming on. . . .' Your post card excited me for a whole day. It had a lovely creep of possibilities, and nearly stirred me up to the wildest schemes. It seems so stupid to be muddling about here to get a job I didn't want, when one might be wandering about. It's so like you, and so absolutely right. I having dreamed of just slipping off to Skyros, etc. and meeting people at the Taj Mahal, receive a pc from Clark installed in the Peloponnese (?). Were you hailed as Byron? Did the workmen lay down their tools, while you adjusted your spectacles, and fiddled with your pipe? Did you look like a tourist, or were you clad only in decent straightforward National Government tax collecting heathermixture?

I see you went with Richardson. How could you? Mrs Moore sends wishes, and re-emphasises that you must come here whenever possible.

Did you take notes on the temperature? Was it a comfortable island? (I received a long and stupid letter from John Moore yesterday).

H.J. Moore

[Below in pencil] Thank you for the Greek stamp.

Laurence, Stanley and Alan needless to say had visited Rupert Brooke's grave. It was to be many years before Humphrey himself was able to visit Skyros to pay homage. Despite the tone of his letter, to say that he was not a little put out and sore that Laurence had got there before him is to indulge in understatement.

As his three years at Cambridge came to an end Humphrey had to face the very serious question of finding his first job. The good Second that he got in the Finals of the Tripos would stand him in good stead. There was never any real doubt but that he would teach; he had a vocation. Besides which what else could a 'gentleman' of his idealistic persuasion do? He had no desire to go into the Services; on the contrary, he dreaded such a thought. The Church he had decided was out of the question for him. His upbringing had blocked a good many other ways of life. He had been brought up from his earliest days in the now completely anachronistic belief that any kind of trade or money-making career is dishonourable. Moreover he had an innate distaste for the mercenary motive. His gifts and everything seemed to be pointing him logically towards public school teaching. At first he wanted to return to Bradfield to teach. Then he saw that, much as he would love to do so, it would not be a wise step at this juncture. He decided to seek for a post at another public school.

What had Cambridge done for Humphrey? It had introduced him to a wider world while still enabling him to naturally maintain his public school links. While bringing his conception of society to greater maturity it had confirmed and even increased in him the love of personal freedom. As it gave him a growing sense of his own innate powers, at the same time it had made him begin to strive towards realising his values and his place in society. Honours had come his way more easily at Bradfield. Cambridge had tested his mettle and he said: 'taught me to avoid easy satisfactions'. It had taught him a greater intellectual discipline. In another place he says: 'It taught me a kind of puritanism of thought'. He would go on striving to find a more active realisation of that elusive spiritual freedom which would be like a graceful adult expression of the child's vision. He saw more clearly now that he wished to attempt to realise this vision in a life of service where his ideals could be put into practice.

DAUNTSEY'S

After a magical Christmas holiday in Switzerland with Gudrun and Gusti, in January 1936 Humphrey began his public school teaching. January, named after the god who faces in two directions, may well have been an appropriate month for him to start. He felt that all logical arguments pointed towards him teaching, and yet he was inwardly divided in his feelings about the public schools and about teaching as a profession. Cambridge had given him the sense of a newly blossoming personal freedom. Was that now to be regimented away into obtuseness? He was fearful that this was what his chosen way of life might mean. However Dauntsey's School in Wiltshire was probably in many ways a good place for him to learn to teach. It happens to be situated on the western edge of the Salisbury Plain quite near to the part of the West Country where he would eventually settle for most of his teaching life. The countryside around the school is beautiful and very good indeed for natural history. Dauntsey's, moreover, had a very good reputation as a school of a progressive kind.

When Humphrey joined the staff Dauntsey's was in the midst of a major expansion under the adventurous headmastership of G.W. Olive – himself a biologist. It is a fairly small public school but it had been recently elevated to membership of the Headmasters' Conference. It had started life as an Agricultural College. Olive, a pupil and devotee of Sanderson of Oundle, had since the 1920s presided over its development into a public school in which the farming nucleus was transmuted into a more science-oriented emphasis. Though having no Officer Training Corps at that time its board of governors showed a strong representation from the Forces. As with so many public schools there was also a strong leaning towards the British Empire discernible in its history. Most appropriately for its new trainee teacher the current expansion was especially taking the direction towards biology and natural history interests.

In many ways outwardly according to his colleagues Humphrey appeared to be quite happy during his two terms at Dauntsey's. He was clearly a born teacher. Capturing the attention of a class of boys came as second nature to him. The senior biology master, I.T. Hamilton, to whom he was assigned as an assistant, claimed that he had discipline trouble, and certainly Humphrey was no stickler for discipline at this time. He relied mainly on the co-operation which the boys gave him because they liked him, and so he settled into his teaching. He got on well with the other staff. He began to enjoy his natural history pursuits, and he founded a bird club called the 'Bird Trust' while he was at the school. This fired the enthusiasm of many boys and led to Humphrey's friendship with the second of his biologist colleagues at Dauntsey's, B.W.H. Coulson. Coulson became very involved in the 'Bird Trust'. When Humphrey left, Coulson took over the running of the club until he moved to Oundle in 1948. Humphrey and he kept in contact throughout the years leading up to the war and they corresponded after that. In the migration period in 1938 they took Dauntsey's boys to the Bird Observatory on the Isle of May off the coast of Fife. They also went on two natural history expeditions, both of them at Easter time, during school holidays. In 1937 they went to the Camargue and in 1939 to Greece. On both expeditions they were accompanied by the ornithologist, R.B. Sibson. As well as a shared enthusiasm for natural history, B.W.H. Coulson has told me that he owes his interest in W.H. Auden to Humphrey. Despite his friendship with B.W.H. Coulson and his flourishing natural history pursuits, however, Humphrey's journal shows that he was not happy at Dauntsey's. In fact he was going through a kind of emotional crisis which had little if anything to do with whether or not he was experiencing any difficulties with class discipline.

For a start he could not help comparing Dauntsey's with Bradfield, and inevitably for him Dauntsey's fell far short. And now that he was in the public school world he had to completely face up to and wrestle with his ambivalent feelings towards his own class and towards 'the profession' of education that he had chosen. He feared that in going into public school teaching he may have committed himself to 'a buried backwater of belief: a cove of retreat with linnet songs and no thunder'. He went on, however, 'the adventure of being part of a tradition and yet standing outside it, and if needs be criticising it, has its value' and it is in any case what he feels fate has in store for him.

Thus at a slight distance as it were from his routine work, he hopes to be able to get on with his reading and his writing. Soon after beginning work at Dauntsey's he noted in his journal: 'I am alarmed at the stolid and contented way in which I do my work. It is like one of those cross-country grinds when one thinks of nothing, but goes on acting! My life-plan of late was to find an occupation which would earn me sufficient bread, which should depend in no way on the bought labour of others, but should be mulcted from those meet to be mulcted, the stupid and snobbish bourgeoisie! All this was to enable me to go on reading and writing.'

There were also times at first when he felt the urge to break out and escape from the 'hothouse' of institutional education in which he now found himself. His urge was to run free from the enclosed communal regime and to find the hidden depths of the natural world where he could fling loose the inhibitions and proprieties imposed on him. He frequently wondered how he was going to be able to bear such constriction. However he found his inner solace as always in literature and music.

Nobody at Dauntsey's was to have any real conception of his private life. The school was dedicated first and foremost to the concept of service to the community. Humphrey was given very little opportunity or occasion for privacy, so he felt a painful kind of public/private dichotomy in his life. He liked the boys at the school very much; there was also much about the school itself that he enjoyed. He became friendly with several of the masters and joined in their staffroom banter, but, with the exception of B.W.H. Coulson, he made no close friends while he was at the school. He found the overall ethos of the regime rather too unrelaxed in its efficient conscientious striving to allow him real contentment. He often felt that the public life he was leading was like a kind of acting to meet the requirements of society. His private life was his real life and that nobody saw. Doubtless because of his hidden homosexuality, too, within what he soon found to be a very proper establishment he began to feel even more enforced into an internal privacy. Although very adequately performing the public part that was expected of him, he began to feel almost stigmatised in his inner isolation.

He had a little room in a house in the village adjoining the school. In what spare time he had he read a great deal, and he also found the refuge he needed in music. There was no space in his room for a piano though he could sometimes play one of the pianos up at the school. He relied mainly on his radio for music. In his Dauntsey's diary he noted: 'Great music speaks to suffering, striving man in the sense of healing, consoling and lifting him. Anyone who has really lived in music knows the value of suffering. He knows how suffering is inseparable from the furthest joy. I believe that those who have not understood this have stepped round life. I have known this since I was fifteen. But it is none the less true now.'

His reading during his first term shows a temporary self-identification with a more decadent conception of the poet. He read a lot of Oscar Wilde, Baudelaire and Rimbaud and, no doubt as a necessary counterbalance to the propriety of the school environment, felt for a while a curious appeal in the idea of redemption through aestheticism. His contemporary notes on Nietzsche reveal a progress towards self mastery. Nietzsche was a pointer he needed at this time on the path towards complete self acceptance, mastery of his own fate and the joyful affirmation of his unique life – with the attainment thereby of a higher than the conventional morality. For after all the homosexual both is and has to prove himself to be the exceptional man.

Through his reading of Nietzsche he discovered the philosophy of Heraclitus: the ancient Greek whom Nietzsche above all admired. It is Heraclitus who gave Humphrey what was to be a central symbol for his poetry. 'The primary element from which all things take their rise' he noted in his diary 'is not water or air but something finer, more subtle and mysterious – Fire.' It is at once the symbol and the essence of life: 'the restless, all consuming, all transforming and vivifying activity, now vibrating as a flame, now sinking to an ember, now soaring up and vanishing as smoke – at every moment it seems to pass away. The contents change but its substance is the same.' And Humphrey adds: 'The poet sees the fire behind every voice. He automatically arranges nature and life as a dramatic setting to his song, his song of fire and joy. He is all fire; and when he goes he leaves you his poems as ashes. But even the ashes are eloquent of flame.'

While he was at Dauntsey's Humphrey delved deeper into the Thirties poets. They were his lifeline with what really mattered to him most; moreover they were producing some of their finest work at this time. Reading Day Lewis's 'A Hope for Poetry', he was moved to write to Stephen Spender on the subject of Auden. After quoting Day Lewis on page 46 in his notebook: 'Auden is an expert at diagnosis . . .' he writes 'that is my own complaint of Auden as I wrote to Spender – Auden is not positive enough: or only in bursts, as in "John, son of Warner".' Tantalisingly, this is all that Humphrey wrote at this point of his notebook, but from a remark that he made to me in later life and from the nature of his admiration for Stephen Spender, I think that I know what the essential gist of his letter was. He regarded Auden as the greatest poetic genius since Eliot, but at times he regretted that Auden, with whom he felt so great an affinity, keeps himself so much in the background of his poems. Auden is so often, as Humphrey once said, like 'the white-coated dentist, self-effacing and dextrous, somewhat impersonally dealing with the patient'. He is nearly always objective. Humphrey sometimes wished that he would write more often from his own resonant heart; he wanted Auden to write more often in an affirmative, and even romantic, vein; and he wanted Auden to more often take up the mantle that he felt was rightfully his as the positive spokesman of England's youth. Humphrey would have written this in all humility to Spender as no-one was more in awe of Auden's genius. He would probably have felt that Spender was the man to write to, both because he was Auden's close friend and also because his own poetic work so often lives up to Humphrey's more romantic criterion. As we have seen Humphrey felt very drawn to Spender, through his writings and all that he stood for. He wrote at this time in his journal of Spender: 'The temptation to seek out this sun creature is very strong but it must however be resisted.'

Meanwhile a letter that Humphrey wrote to Martin Wight who was at Oxford probably gives the best insight into his state of mind and his feeling of crisis at this time. It tells us much too of that intense heartfelt bond of communal love at Bradfield that was the seedbed of his homosexual feeling and which has left him in suffering isolation at Dauntsey's. Here is the letter:

Dear Martin,

I wrote you a letter some time ago, but I did not send it, as I hardly saw that it mattered to you. But today something awful has gone snap, some last facade of stucco has rolled. I visited Bradfield after a year's absence. In five minutes I was acutely miserable. Since I left Cambridge my egotistical defence mechanism has fallen off and I have ended up in a state of desperation. The old loves well up again. Is it so contemnable to love a place like Bradfield? Haven't I lived long enough to know my own mind? Could I have been so utterly deceived at Bradfield as to have thought it worth throwing my all into it? Wasn't there an indescribable atmosphere, a true ideal which everyone knew was holy? (You remember Beloe said: 'Bradfield will be your religion'). Wasn't the resentment against Whitworth a fear for an ideal, a turning of the priests' heads askance to view the approaching desecrator? Think of the flowers you strewed before the House God. Think of the Gods themselves. Think how the most dusty Erics and Wiggins were somehow drawn into the tangle of holiness – and the masters were not outside it. When Bellamy and I were throwing everything into the ideal of Bradfield we were drawn together by a tie of a sort above love, approaching religion. My contacts with people like Bellamy were something I have never experienced since. They were the sweet countenance of a living tradition and the blossom on the bough every year. I have guarded myself against nostalgia for Bradfield for long, but now I know – I do love Bradfield and it is the only healing for the scab of cynicism. I shall not be afraid to acknowledge that love. I would do anything, everything for that place. I have come back here thoroughly discontented. That last night at camp you remember how I cried my eyes out, I see now it was not only for the people, it was also for the intangible divinity that was in Bradfield the place. It was a real wrench. Now I can let the scales fall from my eyes and worship again. Rupert Brooke – he was right – why have I suppressed my feelings for Bradfield and Bradfield people now for this whole year? Because I truly love it, and still wanted to be there. Oh if only I could get a post there. It is the only place I could be happy. A place which heals the distorted vision. Bradfield may not always turn out Grade A citizens but it gave a boy a spark which lifts him to the threshold of the ultimate mysteries. Life anywhere else would be a dry shell.

You remember at Bradfield I preached the spiritual love as being the highest action. I have come back to that. Why did I despise my Bradfield self who appeared priggish? That Bradfield self was right. I see it so clearly at last. All the happiness I have experienced has been due to that place.

Now I go on looking out for someone to love totally (i.e. spiritually) – but alas he is not.

Tuus

HJM'

After his two terms as a trainee teacher at Dauntsey's Humphrey secured a post as assistant biology master at no less a school than Shrewsbury. He had suffered inwardly at Dauntsey's. He was still very doubtful whether he would come into any public school port after his utopian experience of Bradfield, but his teaching and his natural history pursuits had in fact gone well at Dauntsey's. The school was well pleased with him even if it had not particularly well understood him. Despite his doubts, he had many reasons to feel encouraged.

SHREWSBURY

Humphrey approached the venerable institution of Shrewsbury with some trepidation. He knew that he must go there to better himself from the career point of view, but he had misgivings. He realised that the role of a kind of public school Orwell that he felt called to play out would be far from an easy one; and from things that he had heard about the school he feared that this time he might even be letting himself in for unbearable strife. He wrote in his diary: 'If Shrewsbury is as I fear, it will be necessary to move on. Oh for a life of action. It is a sad sight a bought spirit that has consumed merely books, blunting itself against an uninterested smooth wall of complacency.' He was aware that he was moving into an established outpost of the British Empire and the bourgeoisie; and so he arrived at Shrewsbury with the ambivalent feelings of one who knew that he was both by birth and background a member of that bourgeoisie and yet felt a compulsive personal mission to be a 'corrosive' member of his class at that point of time.

When Humphrey arrived at Shrewsbury at Michaelmas 1936 he was at a crucial stage of self discovery and self affirmation. He knew that he lacked sufficient self confidence to play his role of bourgeois radical as fully and effectively as he would wish. What he needed above all at Shrewsbury was a friend, one who would be be an understanding and kindred spirit, and ideally one whom he could also look up to as counsellor and guide. He felt that at all costs he must avoid the danger of isolationism and a negative wincing away from life that lack of understanding had recently occasioned. The consequence of that he knew would be a failure to bring the latent seeds of the spirit to fruition. For he felt that he was truly waiting to break into life.

Destiny had the friend that he needed waiting for him. The time spirit had prepared him for his meeting with Frank McEachran. In his first entry in his Shrewsbury journal he wrote: 'I anticipate the arrival of McEachran, who apparently found Auden as his pupil – O ye Gods. What does this portend? H . . . l extols him greatly, as a man in a thousand whose appreciation and opinion are worth having'. McEachran had indeed been an important influence on Auden at Greshams School Holt, and something of a father figure to the emergent poet as well. From information given to me by Dr John Auden, the poet's brother, it seems very likely that McEachran and Auden's friendship had begun before their time together at Greshams. It was from McEachran's influence that among other things Auden's concepts of 'the lords of limit' (those mythical patrons of the Independent schools) and, connected with them, 'the witnesses', had originated. McEachran had incidentally also influenced

Benjamin Britten at Greshams – facts that were known only at Greshams and afterwards at Shrewsbury at that time. McEachran was to be a lifelong friend of Auden. It is highly probable that when McEachran left Greshams he chose to teach at Shrewsbury because of the Auden connection with the school. For as many as seven members of Auden's family had been at Shrewsbury.

Largely through Frank McEachran's friendship the break into life was to come for Humphrey. McEachran, or 'Kek' as he was known to most of his friends, was everything that Humphrey wished for and more. Their friendship was to be for both men one of the most important in their lives; and they were to look back at their time together at Shrewsbury, despite the difficulties that Humphrey encountered, as one of the very happiest periods of their lives. They were both public school rebels and nonconformists, 'in' the public schools rather than 'of' them – though they shared a certain kind of idealistic public school philosophy. They wanted the public schools to be less exclusively for the rich, but they wanted them to continue to be bastions of middle-class freedom and to continue to represent a more personally enriching kind of communal ideal than is generally found in the increasingly collectivist world outside. Humphrey soon began to find new happiness in his friendship with Kek and a growing confidence in his burgeoning powers. Strife would, nevertheless, dog his outward steps.

Being thirteen years older than Humphrey, Kek fulfilled something of the role of a father figure to him. He was a classicist as was Humphrey's father. Kek moreover was already the author of several books and many published articles. Theirs was to be a close and warm friendship, as much like that between two brothers as that between a father and a son; there is, nevertheless, a sense in which Kek in part at any rate and just for a time took Humphrey under his wing. Kek was the guide Humphrey sought as well as the friend with whom to share his private life.

Humphrey at first lived in 'Kingsland House' with Kek and another colleague, Alec Peterson (later Headmaster of Dover College), alongside the Headmaster, H.H. Hardy, before he and Kek moved to another house 'Eversley', which they shared with V.A.L. Hill. It is very likely that it was prior to the move, at the beginning of his time at Shrewsbury, when the first intimations of a personality clash between Humphrey and Hardy were felt. The house Humphrey and Kek moved to, 'Eversley', soon became known as quite a radical place. It was a merry and an enlightened household where many of the younger kindred spirits on the staff, mainly leftward in politics, gathered together.

Humphrey's intellectual excitement when he and Kek befriended one another is clearly seen in his notebooks of the time. Soon after they moved into 'Eversley' he recorded: 'All my time up to now has been concerned with delight in the divine average.' Now at last he had found some equals and kindred spirits. He need not fear the isolation of the uniquely gifted teacher or the dominating society of dullards in the staff room. It is exhilarating to see in Humphrey's notebooks the great range of subjects that he and Kek discussed. As one would expect from the fact of his befriending the man who had almost certainly introduced Auden to Dante's poetry and had probably also influenced Eliot's discovery of it, the poet Dante was an important discovery for Humphrey at this time. He wrote to B.W.H. Coulson: 'I am now completely under the literary thumb of a truly medieval genius Dante, whom I read in Italian every Friday evening, under the tutelage of a man who knows what is what in literature.' He wrote an essay on A.E. Housman. He also began a treatise on Auden – the notes for which survive. He was beginning to blossom in his spirit and he was even beginning to come to terms with some of his emotional class ambivalence.

Humphrey loved and idolised Kek. He used to tell many wonderful stories in later life about Kek. 'He's a great man' he would always say. Kek was undoubtedly one of Humphrey's 'larger than life' characters, one who was to take on an almost mythical significance for countless boys who were later told about him. In Kek's case the stories needed no embroidery to give them this significance. As well as being a teacher of genius, he was a wonderfully free, uninhibited and joyful man. He had a rare quality of blitheness; he could be both serious and yet light. He was at heart a deeply religious man; and his serenity and joy emanated from his Christian/humanist monistic world view. He had an underlying awareness of a final unity in all things. His Christian monism had developed from and in a sense transcended, while still drawing inspiration from, the dualistic Greek tragic sense of life in which he had been nurtured, but he never abandoned the classical human ideal and continued all his life to oppose the shallow progressivism of so much of the modern world. He was an old style liberal individualist through and through, entirely lacking in 'public spirit' – as he was the first to admit – but he had the common touch. Humphrey used to tell how Kek would enter pubs, hand round sheets of poetry and would 'set the yokels and toughs chanting like children'. For as well as the ability to get on well with ordinary people he possessed an almost child-like quality of innocent fearlessness. He saw people fearlessly for what they are. He delighted in all sorts and conditions of humanity. He abominated only the pompous and the hypocritical.

For his friends Kek had a personal wisdom to impart. At Shrewsbury his philosophy of 'anarchy', or 'natural order' as he frequently called it, won Humphrey over completely. This was the philosophy that at Greshams had so influenced Auden. When Kek introduced Humphrey to this fervently liberal philosophy, Humphrey found himself in it. It was an articulation of what he himself had long felt. He slipped into it naturally. With Kek he knew that he was breathing his native spiritual air. He was soon won over also by Kek's advocacy of the Georgist economic philosophy.

Kek and Humphrey were aware of what was happening in the cultural and social world at large. They could see the larger import of Modernism, surrealism, symbolism – and too of communism. They felt indeed at the time that in many ways they were living through the decadence and the last throes of the bourgeois domination of the past. In this situation they felt that they understood the true position of the public schools better than most. Despite ultra-conservative establishments like Shrewsbury, they knew that history was moving dangerously and excitingly forward. They tried to bring a wider and more inspiring awareness of this to individual Shrewsbury boys. They taught that 'the enemy', as in Auden's contemporary work, were the maladjusted – all those who represented false values, vested interests and dead convention, as opposed to the living spirit of change and growth. It was the duty of the truly aware to be subversive of 'the enemy' – the main methods being satire and laughter. All phoney authoritarian figures were to be unmasked. The bureaucratic state (embodying monopoly interests) and all the connected forms of 'power politics' are inimical to freedom, which is the only true human end, and are to be seen as perversions of the natural law. Society exists for the free individual who in a normal world naturally wishes to be co-operative and who is the source of all true wealth (material and spiritual), all true power, and in whom alone the moral life exists. Prior to all the unnatural economic and psychological perversions of the collective unfree modern world, the private life (which includes of course its natural public dimensions) of the free individual under natural law (the true and divine limit to his freedom) is the real life of humanity for which all should strive. Humphrey and Kek kept together 'a handbook of anarchy' in which they made satirical notes about the actual contemporary scene.

Kek's stimulus now rekindled Humphrey's poetry. He began to write again, having written only a little while he was at Dauntsey's. Kek's doctrine gave him as it were an intellectual framework upon which to weave his expressions of reverence for living nature and his sense of the vital oneness of man with nature and with God. The influence of Kek's old style liberalism moreover enabled him to keep to a mainly a-political individualistic line – something quite rare for a writer in the Thirties. Kek in fact was the main stimulus, following that of The Merry Meeting in Cambridge, in forming Humphrey as a poet; but funnily enough, his stimulus on Humphrey as a creative writer was effected unbeknown to him. For Humphrey kept the fact that he wrote poetry largely a secret at Shrewsbury.

It was while he was at Shrewsbury and inspired by Kek that Humphrey produced the first and only collection of his poems to be published in his lifetime. This was a collection of thirty poems which he entitled 'The Romantic Residue' or 'Filoplumes'. Typewritten copies were circulated to his friends outside the school.

In his turn Humphrey also influenced Kek. He influenced Kek increasingly in the direction of a romanticism of the heart and feelings, by which Kek modified some of the extremes of his underlying classicism. Humphrey's romanticism was a stimulus for Kek towards the expansion and publication of his earlier thesis on Herder. It led also to the propagation among the boys at Shrewsbury of what Kek and Humphrey called 'Spells' – i.e. poetry of a magical or concentrated incantatory power which has especial reference to the contemporary world. Kek was apparently already using the word in this way at Greshams, and the book *Spells*, written for the boys of Shrewsbury School, was greatly inspired by Kek and Humphrey's shared sense of the revitalisation of the English poetic tradi-

Frank McEachran ('Kek') teaching at Shrewsbury.
Kek was the friend and guide under whose influence Humphrey talents as
teacher and poet began to flourish in the late-1930s.
Photograph lent by Laurence Le Quesne.

tion by Auden and Eliot (who Kek also knew personally, being a frequent contributor to *The Criterion*).

Early in 1937 Kek brought about a coup for Shrewsbury School. He persuaded his friend Auden to come to the school to talk on the subject of 'The Spanish Civil War'. Kek especially wanted Humphrey to have the opportunity to meet Auden. The visit was a momentous event for Humphrey. It took place, perhaps significantly, in the Science building. It was the only time when Humphrey personally met the man whom he as well as Kek acknowledged as the finest poet of the age, and whom they both envisaged as England's emergent spiritual leader. The personal impression that Auden made on Humphrey was, like that of his poetry, indelible. All who knew Humphrey as well as Kek realised their personal and primary commitment to the great teacher poet of the twentieth century. Among so many at the time, they were I believe two of Auden's chief disciples in the English public schools. It was shortly after this visit that Humphrey and Kek heard with considerable anxiety the news that Auden was himself going out to Spain to assist the Republican cause.

In his school work at Shrewsbury Humphrey found himself alongside a master who had been at Greshams with Kek, and who had also taught Auden there. This was Frank McArthey. As well as being the Chaplain at Shrewsbury he was also in charge of biology. He later became Chaplain of All Souls College, Oxford. Humphrey and McArthey cooperated in encouraging a natural history society at the school – Humphrey contributing especially to its ornithological section. It was good that Humphrey and McArthey got on well for a further reason: they soon got involved in running the Scouts together. McArthey saw very much eye to eye with Hardy, but Humphrey's good relationship with McArthey unfortunately could not help to overcome the mutual antipathy that was developing between Humphrey and the Headmaster.

Before very long, despite his love of the countryside around the school, it was beginning to become apparent that Humphrey's premonitions about how he would fit into Shrewsbury the establishment were proving to be only too true. For, with the exception of McArthey, Humphrey does not appear to have been a hit with any of the real powers that be. He did not make friends among the older serving members of the staff. The main reason for this apparently was that his attitude was felt to be too informal and his gift for making personal friends among the boys was resented and met with hostility. For Humphrey had an almost unprecedented way of treating the boys he taught as his friends and equals. The Old Guard felt that he did not make sufficient effort to fit into the overall esprit de corps. Humphrey admitted to friends that he found the school too large and administratively centralised – and he also found it very difficult to teach biology without a lab – but his class teaching was always excellent, and as well as helping to run the Scouts, he also organised an unofficial but eagerly supported Geological Society for the boys. In the nature of the case, however, his personal gifts could best be bestowed on individuals.

As a proof of how greatly in this sense his personal friendship was valued and was an influence for good several of his later indebted friends will bear witness. Special among these must be the writer, Francis King. More than half a century later, time had not dimmed the feelings of Francis King for Humphrey. He wrote in one letter to me:

Of all the masters at Shrewsbury, Humphrey Moore had more influence on me than any other. It was he who first introduced me to the work of Auden (the poet whom he then – and perhaps all through his life? – admired most) and it was he who chiefly encouraged me in my own writing (at that time poetry for the Salopian – the school magazine, of which I eventually became one of the editors). Moore shared a house with some other masters. I used to visit him there with another boy, from another House, called Dennis Russell. Russell and I were up at Oxford together, then I lost touch with him. He became a clergyman. Rather dear, with a disproportionately large head, he had great charm. Moore was very fond of him.

Moore used to mock at some of my literary enthusiasms of that time: for the early Yeats, for example and Charlotte Mew. But he always did so with kindness. He took immense pains with any of my own poems which I showed him. I felt that he was treating me as *a real writer*.

I wish now that I had kept in touch with him.

I loved Moore's poems and always wondered why they were never published. Somewhere, in some trunk in the attic, I think that I may still have one or two. One poem that I particularly liked was about 'the pippit's piping song'.

I think of him with nothing but affection and gratitude. I felt that the Headmaster and my own Housemaster disapproved of him – the latter not caring that I should so often go over to see someone who was not even one of my masters. But whether hearing him read or talk, or listening to music with him, I felt that rare sympathy which emanates from the few people who are truly born teachers'.

In another letter Francis wrote:

Having written to you yesterday, I lay awake in the early hours of this morning and thought about HM. Other things then came back to me.

He used to call me 'Roy' (Roi – King?) and he gave himself the nickname 'Jynx', by which I used to call him. The Jynx, as you will probably know, is the wryneck – an allusion to his affliction.

The odd thing is that I no longer remember how I first came to visit HM. He did not teach me, and he had nothing to do with my house. It must, I imagine, have been through the music society. (It was in fact through the Scouts that Francis and Dennis Russell first came to meet Humphrey, as Francis later recalled.)

My father died during my first term at Shrewsbury. I think that I came to look on HM as a surrogate. In total innocence, without any thought of sex – it is difficult to think of any teenage boy being so innocent today – I suppose that I loved him. One hears so much now of the perils of homosexual teachers. But almost all the finest educators, male or female, of the young whom I have come across have been homosexuals, with total dedication to, and sympathy with, their charges.

Francis King has told me also that both Humphrey and Kek, partly because of their disregard for dress and partly because of their rebellious behaviour, were regarded by some of the boys as somewhat eccentric, but, most boys being natural anarchists at heart, they were both very much liked by the boys at large. Another friend who knew them both at this time has told me that they spent a great deal of their time together in fits of laughter observing the contemporary scene and sharing an eagle eye for 'enemy' traits at the school and in other walks of life.

Humphrey's doom at Shrewsbury was in fact sealed from the start. He clashed completely with the Headmaster. H.H. Hardy was a pillar of the establishment; and Humphrey dared to question that primary tenet of the old public school system, unquestioning obedience to authority. Humphrey pitted himself against the power nexus – with inevitable results – but there were further interrelated reasons for the ensuing clash. Hardy was very much for the school Cadet Corps. Humphrey was still a convinced Pacifist at this time and he simply could not accept that the Cadet Corps could be a priority pursuit of a school like Shrewsbury. (A little bit inconsistent as this may seem prima facie in relation to Humphrey's school days.) Francis King has told me that Humphrey actually encouraged him *not* to join the Officer Training Corps.

There is another underlying reason behind Humphrey's clash with Hardy. Humphrey had heard all about Hardy's having given the young poet Cecil Day Lewis a hard time when Day Lewis was teaching at Cheltenham College, where Hardy had been Headmaster before he moved to Shrewsbury. The humiliation of Day Lewis by Hardy is recorded in Day Lewis' autobiography *The Buried Day* and was well known about at the time in public school circles. Day Lewis describes Hardy as 'the regimental type of Headmaster' who was very wary of him from the start as a possibly subversive young man who 'had committed poetry'. Whatever the reasons for Hardy's harsh treatment of him, Day Lewis as we have seen, was a hero of Humphrey's and someone he revered. Rightly or wrongly Humphrey decided for this reason from the outset that he was resolutely 'against' Hardy. Hardy was for him a leading representative of the forces of 'The Enemy' – a power to be resisted.

In fairness to Hardy, Francis King and others have presented a counterbalancing view. Hardy *was* a strict disciplinarian, even a 'martinet' – 'we were all frightened of him,' Francis has told me, but despite this, he liked Hardy as a man. There was another side to him. 'He was sensitive and intelligent underneath.' Many others have said similar things to me, and we must remember that Shrewsbury at that time was much stricter than any public school is today. Hardy was an excellent teacher and he also was musical and had his own tastes in poetry – good reasons why Hardy and Humphrey *could* have got on well together. Francis believes that Hardy looked upon Humphrey's way of treating boys as his friends and equals as demoralising – and this was perhaps partly understandable in those unliberated days. In Headmaster Hardy's eyes such an attitude singled Humphrey out as a potentially subversive rebel.

Humphrey unfortunately was unable to react to his situation with political expediency. He could not conform when his innermost being was in rebellion;

nor could he hide his antagonism for Hardy. The fiercely ad hominem nature of the collision soon became apparent to his colleagues, though not to the school at large. Even Kek could not come to Humphrey's rescue in this respect. Many are the tales of Kek's good-natured teasing of Hardy in his own inimitable style; but he and Hardy did not really get on together. Kek at this stage was not yet the institution of Shrewsbury that he was later to become. Humphrey found himself, notwithstanding the individual friendships he had made, a misfit at Shrewsbury.

His undoing came when the boys were organising a strike in connection with PT. Hardy had got a new gymnasium built at Shrewsbury; and it figured largely in school life. Like others, he saw the war coming and was keen to present fit boys to the services. Thus in 1938 he planned to increase the time that boys spent on PT. There was to be PT in the break in the morning for all boys. This was felt by many to be an invasion of free time. There was much murmuring and some of the boys planned a protest. They had pamphlets printed which began 'A spectre is haunting Shrewsbury . . .' and which invited boys to protest in a strike. The rebel boys were found to be frequenters of 'Eversley'. For quite contrary to the custom of the school at that time Humphrey used to allow the boys to use his room for music and reading, and it appears that they used his typewriter to print their strike notices. I am unable to say whether Humphrey knew that they were using his typewriter for this purpose or not. One can't help wondering whether the rebel in him couldn't resist this small sign of sympathy with fellow rebels. In any case the typewriter that had been used, an old and very idiosyncratic model, was traced by Hardy and his sleuths. This episode ended Humphrey's period as Assistant Master at Shrewsbury at the end of his fifth term.

Humphrey does not record in any notebook his reaction to his dismissal; but perhaps the following extract written not long before, when it was imminent, gives one a pretty good idea of the state of fury, no doubt reciprocated by the Headmaster, that his relationship with Hardy had reached: 'While I am studying Mozart', he wrote, 'intelligence reaches me from H.H.H. that he is in two minds about keeping me on because:

1) There is sometimes a gap between my pullover and trousers
2) I am grubby
3) I don't shave often enough (once a day apparently sufficeth not)
4) I go about with a puckered expression
5) When I speak to him I look as if I meant what I said

This forms the rating valuation of the Chairman of the Headmasters Conference! He is not concerned with what is in a man's head and heart: but judges him by the efficacy of his braces.'

He then adds Blake's aphorism: 'Damn braces, bless relaxes' and decides that he will wear braces: 'Orange Ones'. I can well imagine that another of Blake's aphorisms was also going through Humphrey's head at this time – one that he refers to many times around this period of his life. It makes one realise that, painful as his departure was, Humphrey no doubt saw it as inevitable and probably even accepted it finally with great relief. He noted from Blake: 'One must urge one's way *through* the gates of wrath', and he added, 'not try to bypass them.'

Humphrey knew that there are no short cuts to becoming what you truly are. You have to take responsibility for your own life and grow through the struggles that ensue from that responsibility. He had followed the promptings of his own geist. It may be that, because of his ultra-conservative parents, he had certain difficulties with authority figures as such, but at the same time he saw Hardy as an embodiment of what in his view was holding the public schools back, a leading representative of the repressive bourgeoisie with their formalised tables of the Law. His clash with Hardy lost him his job at one of Britain's most prestigious public schools, but he saw it as a necessary, if painful, step on his highly personal mission of being a corrosive member of his own class and thereby in his own way helping to bring something new to birth.

He would launch out into the destructive element with faith that the deep sea would buoy him up. He had certainly not come into port yet.

CLAYESMORE

Humphrey now had the immediate problem of getting another job without a glowing reference; and after the experience of Shrewsbury he must have been pondering very hard as to what kind of job he should apply for. He seriously considered the possibility of applying for Stowe. He knew that he had to think his whole position through carefully.

He had rebelled at Shrewsbury. He was not an Establishment man. His own individuality was far too strong for him to be content to carve a secondary niche at such a school. What he wanted was a smaller public school where he could mould the ethos more effectively to his own style; where the leader and the showman in him as well as the poet could make its mark. I believe too that he had realised that in the long run he wanted to be in the country.

He realised also something of central importance for the ensuing pattern of his life: that he felt a calling to help socially less privileged boys. He had something very special to give to them that would shine and express itself better in a setting in which he could be more free. Perhaps in such a setting in a sense he could be a 'leveller up' of privilege, making his own distinctive contribution to what was acknowledged to be the most advanced thinking in the vanguard of public school life. In such a school perhaps too, a bit like Cavafy, he would be able to stand as he would like more at an angle to the conventional universe.

Fortune smiled on him at this crucial moment of decision. There were not many public schools that would perfectly meet his requirements. Possibly one only at that time met his requirements in every way. Everything was leading him to Clayesmore in Dorset, one of the most progressive of the 'new' and also in many ways one of the most elite public schools, founded just before the turn of the century. By the most extraordinary coincidence the post of master in charge of biology fell vacant there at just this moment. He visited Clayesmore in the summer of 1938, as soon as he knew that he was leaving Shrewsbury. He fell in love with the school on his first visit. He applied for the post and was immediately accepted. For one thing the sheer natural beauty of

Clayesmore's setting captivated him instantly. Actually Humphrey used to say that there were two things that decided him in accepting his appointment at Clayesmore. These were, in the words of John Appleby, who was Junior Housemaster at the time and was to become one of his main friends: 'his interview with the Headmaster sitting behind his big desk and apparently wearing nothing (his white shorts being invisible) and on a tour of the school finding the Director of Geography conducting his class in bathing kit by the swimming pool. He had a deep love for the unconventional, the free, the informal, the nonsensical.'

Humphrey found too that most of the masters were of a similar age and generation who gelled together – and he himself belonged to this same generation. They were mostly from comfortable middle-class backgrounds like himself. They were all devoting their lives to Clayesmore, its ideals and values, with a special kind of heartfelt devotion. Humphrey knew with a sure instinct that here, at Clayesmore, he would carve his name. He rejoiced to have found the school where he sensed right from the start that he belonged.

The somewhat battered but just as ardent idealist had at last found a very special school with ideals to which he could completely dedicate his life: a child-centred education in an unregimented, friendly, and informal atmosphere among sympathetic colleagues. And this in the west country terrain that, for all his place loves, he had sensed from his childhood was his real spiritual homeland. All around in the midst of the luscious rolling green landscape were many of England's other most interesting medium-sized public schools, with many of which he was to forge links: Bryanston, Canford, Sherborne, Monckton Combe, Dauntsey's (which of course he knew) and Milton Abbey. He was back in the countryside of his heart, in the summer lands of Wessex where he was indeed to spend the summer of his life.

SALZBURG AND MUNICH 1938

Humphrey was able to go abroad in the summer of 1938 with a lighter heart – if lighter can be the right word in view of where he was going, but he was professionally anchored at last. His holiday had been prearranged while he was still at Shrewsbury. It was to be a visit to Salzburg and Munich – in the very year that Hitler had annexed Austria to his Reich. Humphrey had fallen in love with Salzburg on a family visit in the summer of 1936. It was the magnetism of the two places, Salzburg and Munich, and their music – for the holiday was planned as a music tour to the Salzburg and Munich festivals – that were the main reasons why he chose to go there rather than the desire to see the ominous events that were overtaking these countries, but inevitably his curiosity about the events was keen. Humphrey went with a friend called John Day who I have not been able to certainly identify: but John Day could well have been a young man who Humphrey is known to have befriended from the City of Shrewsbury. Humphrey had desperately wanted to return to Salzburg since his first tantalising visit there with his family when he had only been a sightseer of its beauties. This time he resolved that he would be sure to fully take in the music as well, which his diary proves that he did.

When Humphrey returned home to England he went first to 'Byams' where there was a long letter waiting for him from Alan Poole Gardiner of Bradfield – a delightful homecoming surprise. Yes, he was still in touch with Sniffers and he stayed in touch with him until Sniffers died in 1951. He had written to tell his dear teacher friend the story of his dismissal from Shrewsbury. Sniffers' letter, as Humphrey records: 'Commiserated with my affairs at Salop' and concluded in quintessential Sniffers style with the delightful tension-easing, humour releasing phrase: 'You ultra musical chumps always were a bit jumpy!' No doubt for Humphrey this very welcome letter, coming after his extraordinary musical holiday with John Day, helped to heal the smarting wound of his departure from Shrewsbury, as did also the prospect, which he was relishing, of beginning to teach at Clayesmore,.

CLAYESMORE AND ITS IDEALS

Founded in 1896 by Alexander Devine at Enfield, after two moves Clayesmore had come finally in 1933 to its present location adjoining the village of Iwerne Minster near to Blandford, at the eastern end of the vale of Blackmoor and to the west of Cranborne Chase, in Dorset. 'Lex', the founder, was a remarkable personality: an innovator, a hater of orthodoxy and endowed with an irrepressible sense of humour. He was devoted to youth – especially to those boys who had experienced any kind of a raw deal in life – and he was loved by the boys he taught. His watchwords were individualism and self reliance. Soon after the turn of the century Abbotsholme, Bedales and Clayesmore were said to constitute the ABC of modern educational ideas in public schools. They pioneered ideals of freedom, tolerance and individuality which are now mostly accepted without question. All these three 'New' schools were signs of the revolt against the until then unquestioned sense of tradition for which the public schools stood. For while making the best of the public school tradition their own, these schools were explicitly inspired by other educational ideals and were all to bear the 'Progressive' label with distinction. They were inspired by a variety of radical thought which included the child-centred educational views of Rousseau, the Christian anarchism of Tolstoy, the forward-looking pragmatic views of the teacher/child partnership in education pioneered by Dewey – and the utopian views of Edward Carpenter were also a formative inspiration. Clayesmore has always stood specifically for both tradition and liberty. The more humane public school system which Roxburgh instituted at Stowe between the wars is in many ways comparable. Like Roxburgh, the 'New' schools too started from the premise: 'Liberty itself is the best teacher. . . . If we learn from our liberty it will be a blessing to us: if not, it will be a curse.' All three schools purposely restricted the number of their pupils in order to give individuality every opportunity to shine while also allowing every opportunity to the staff to study individuals. Academic work, though seen as highly important, was not to be always put first on the agenda. Cultural activities, the pursuit of the arts and manual work in the open air were to be afforded their proper place in the curriculum. The Officer Training Corps was to be largely voluntary, and indeed Clayesmore had no Officer Training Corps until the Second World War. Bedales (whence had come several of

Rupert Brooke's main friends, both male and female) was coeducational from the very beginning, and Abbotsholme soon followed, although Clayesmore was not until 1973.

One further characteristic feature of Clayesmore which distinguished it from the great majority of public schools was its House system. The Clayesmore system had been initiated by 'Lex' and continued with one intermission until the 1970s. The Clayesmorian progressed through three houses, Juniors, Middles and Seniors. The great advantage of this was that he was not set in one little tribal society for all his time at the school; each Housemaster got to know him as well as he them. Furthermore there were no rituals connected with competition in games between Houses, something which in many public schools plagues the less games-minded.

All of this was guaranteed to evoke Humphrey's enthusiasm. This was no phalanx of the Establishment. The power struggle ethos would surely not blight this smaller republic. Here the individual would be valued for what he himself is and allowed to develop in his own way. Clearly the whole basis of the school's educational method depended on a closer, more friendly and 'family' relationship between masters and boys. They were to be more like friends engaged in a joint enterprise than people on separate and distinct levels – which was indeed what Humphrey had always believed that they should be. It was the foundation on which his unique gifts could build.

Not very long after Humphrey arrived at Clayesmore, when Britain had entered the Second World War, Alec Brown the writer and translator, who was at that time teaching at Clayesmore, wrote in an editorial to *The Clayesmorian* the following bold words: 'One may compare the part played by certain monasteries in the Dark Ages – such a stronghold of enlightenment and individual thought Clayesmore is to be in the coming years. It was for work in this very world of 1941, hostile to the individual, that this school was founded, fifty years ago by Alex Devine. Set in a world which is steadily congealing into a rigid shape, Clayesmore by its very soul is bound to draw on every source of individual strength and inspiration, and to take on still more vigorous life. . . . All we know is that Clayesmore will go on, and the Clayesmore spirit one day will triumph.'

Humphrey joined Clayesmore in December 1938. He lived at first in a room on the top floor of the main building among the dormitories of the Juniors. He was delighted to find that he was assigned his own fag to help to meet some of his everyday needs. Humphrey wrote to B.W.H. Coulson: 'I live in a minute but pleasant room. A boy has to bring logs to my room, and I have a private fag who acts as a very efficient and amiable valet. You see masters matter!' These were the days when all masters were resident, and masters' doors were open to those interested to visit them. The boys very quickly began to discover how extraordinarily varied and profound Humphrey's interests were; and very soon boys were in and our of his room all the time. As a result it was not long before he began to make many friends. Among those whom he influenced especially at this time Clive Balch (later Director of the National Institute for Research in Dairying at Shinfield, Reading) and George Brookbank stand out.

Now that he had the job he wanted, Humphrey's immediate task was to build up enthusiasm and facilities for natural history and biology at Clayesmore. He had a new biology laboratory when he started – as he said in *The Clayesmorian* 'a fresh stimulus to the biology already done in the school previous to this term'. The biology laboratory and also the Natural History Club room under his impetus quickly began to be stocked with all kinds of interesting and unusual collections, specimens and finds. He revived the somewhat flagging Natural History Society (which had several specialist branches) and made it one of the most thriving societies in the school. The boys responded eagerly and soon they were not only combing the highly rewarding grounds of Clayesmore but they were also setting off in parties to go all over the county and beyond. One new branch, The Clayesmore Bird Club, quickly attracted a very large number of eager boys to set up and mind traps for catching the birds which would then be ringed and whose flights to all parts of the world would be enthusiastically monitored. Something of the excitement of this fresh enterprise in natural history is reflected in an article that Humphrey wrote for *The Clayesmorian* in July 1939 on the 'Biology Laboratory'.

Scientific work must always remain largely anonymous. The key discovery may be made by one original genius, but the body of work on which he had made his deduction, and which has suggested to him his experiments, together with the subsequent testing out and elaboration of the new advance is made by the mass of his fellow scientists, sometimes contemptuously referred to as the spade-workers, and to them posterity owes it benefits. The spade itself was a big invention. So, with our own local patch of activity, to name all those who have assisted in the development of the Biology Lab. would probably entail most of the school list. This is satisfactory, because it shows that Biology is becoming the interest and activity of the society, rather than the peculiar rapture of the manic bug-hunter, the intent Arachnologist, or the fervent bird lover. A society who can endure a 'Zoo man' on the radio, has become aware of a new influence, and is growing a new respect for life in all its forms. It is only right that this activity should be given full scope in a modern educational programme. In the dust of the classroom, and the wilderness of a Latin nomenclature, it is possible to forget that one is learning to sweep the dust off a window. One is polishing a lens to look out onto a world of absolute natural beauty, the organic world of fern and firefly. Auden writes:

> And the investigator peers through his instruments
> At the inhuman provinces, the virile bacillus
>   Or enormous Jupiter finished:
> But the lives of my friends. I inquire. I inquire.

True, science does study the inhuman; but curiosity and wonder are human qualities, and their development is part of man's natural bent. This term we have bred the Fairy shrimp in our aquarium and we have studied the mouth parts of the Grasshopper. Maps have been made,

Humphrey setting off on a natural history expedition.
Botany and entomology, birds, mammals, butterflies and moths
were all passionate interests.

and specimens collected and labelled. Even the spider has now been raised to the dignity of the Glider (and, too, the Geometrical Rider), and visitors to the Arachnological Institute will learn that all widows are not Black. Out of doors, nests have been watched (and sometimes robbed). Trees have been mapped, and mosquitoes 'controlled'. An expedition to Studland brought back the rare Sand Lizard, while the colour of the swimming pool was traced to sources other than Dead Beagle (no insinuations!). Like a growing infant we are constantly stretching out our hands for more essential equipment: and the gift of Specimens and reference books will always be welcome. Our motto for all occasions must be: 'Let the good citizen here find natural marvels.'

Humphrey quickly found that he had much in common with several of the Clayesmore staff. He began to share his enthusiasm for poetry with John Appleby, the senior English master, a man with a quality of deep personal tranquillity who always seemed to be a bit detached from the hurly burly of school life. He was known to the boys as 'Apples'. John Appleby had come to Clayesmore from King's College, Cambridge. Humphrey also established a firm friendship with Carl Verrinder, an Oxford man, who was in charge of chemistry, and who like himself was a scientist of wide cultural interests. Verrinder ran Clayesmore's Dramatic Society. Humphrey made friends with two further Cambridge men, David Spinney, a naval historian, in charge of history, and Reginald Sessions, who had also been to the Royal College of Music, and was Clayesmore's Director of Music, and an Oxford man, Peter Burke, who was in charge of French and German.

Not all that long after Humphrey arrived at Clayesmore another colleague who was to be a friend and who was also to be completely devoted to the school joined the staff. In January 1940 the Rev. Norris Scadding, priest and doctor of medicine, became school chaplain and also master in charge of art.

In these first years at Clayesmore Humphrey's closest friend on the staff was John Simpson. John, of a similar age to Humphrey and from a similar upper middle-class background, arrived a term later. One of the things that had drawn him to Clayesmore was the fact that at that time it had no Officer Training Corps. After doing extremely well at Cambridge, where he was an Exhibitioner of Emmanuel College, Clayesmore was his first teaching job. He was a brilliant teacher of maths at Clayesmore – there were distinguished scientists among his ancestors – although in fact his main subject and training was in physics. John like Humphrey was by temperament an idealist and a nonconformist – he later became a Quaker. John shared too with Humphrey a kind of idealism of the child. He was to become Research Associate at the Department of Applied Mathematics and Theoretical Physics at the University of Cambridge. Until the war Humphrey and John were practically inseparable. When they weren't in each other's rooms or in the biology laboratory following up their joint natural history research, they would be together with Alec Brown and other members of staff at Carl's house in the village where regular entertaining meetings were held on two or three evenings a week.

John tells me that it was at one of these good times at Carl's house that

'Prodnose' was invented. It was Eileen Verrinder, Carl's wife, who in fact first suggested the idea which was then quickly developed by Humphrey and John. Apparently the name was invented soon afterwards by a Clayesmore boy called Portal. Prodnose became the personal symbol of Humphrey and John. Cards and letters to them from friends would invariably be decorated with it. Both Humphrey and John soon had Prodnose ties made for themselves. During the war, when John was an ambulance driver in China, Prodnose became something of an insignia for the 'Friends Ambulance Unit' there. The Chinese came to recognise it well, and John actually carved Prodnose on the Great Wall of China. Both Humphrey and John also discovered that Prodnose was very useful in all kinds of situations for getting the attention of boys. Prodnose always faces left and looks like this:

He is a near relative of the Shrewsbury Gnome, at whose birth and subsequent promulgation Humphrey had also assisted – the embryo of Private Eye's 'Lord Gnome', who is of course based on Frank McEachran.

It was John who introduced Humphrey to what were to be for him the very great pleasures of photography. Humphrey's photographic collection now spans three decades of Clayesmore life as well as including his own holiday photographs. Humphrey and John began their collections of rare hats, to which friends sometimes contributed. Both Humphrey and John were adept at clowning for the benefit of the boys when they felt the occasion was right, the showman in them both often dazzled and amused the boys. I recall for example that on several occasions in the depth of a snowbound winter in the 1950s Humphrey walked from the Middles to staff tea and back in a huge complete bearskin that he had brought back from Canada.

John's other particular love, probably his main one, was gliding. As an undergraduate he had been chief instructor of the Cambridge University Gliding Club, and he was one of the pioneers of gliding in this country. One year he was joint national gliding champion. While at Clayesmore John pursued this interest. Humphrey often used to help by towing him in his car to a suitable site, but I do not know whether he also flew.

This close and joyous friendship of Humphrey and John was celebrated by Clayesmore's second master, Alister McKenzie, in a poem in *The Clayesmorian* in July 1939. The poem which reveals I think quite a buried talent in Alister McKenzie was written to accompany a cartoon, also extremely well executed, of Humphrey and John surrounded by some of the many objects of their interests. The cartoon was drawn by another member of Clayesmore's staff, Clive Richardson. Here is the poem in full:

> Here you may study the effect
> Of beetles on the intellect,
> Or trace the strange and mystic strings
> Uniting souls in ponds and things,
> The rapture, the madhattery
> That blooms from being up a tree
> Or down a drain or in a ditch

And cares not greatly which is which,
That hither thither like a bullet
Roars to find a weed and pull it,
Crams in bottles bugs to gloat on,
Hunts for Fairy shrimps in Shroton.
One snuffs the wind and takes a glider
Up where views of gnats are wider:
T'other on the terrain sits
Pulling bits of things to bits.

Some say that far from being divided
In their deaths they simply glided
Changing fashion as they went
In spirals through the firmament
To flit among the sharps and flats
Of heaven, inseparable bats:
And frequently on frosty nights
There glitter among lesser lights,
Apotheosised into stars,
Their busy bright Binoculars.

Or we may think of them as come
And comfy in Elysium,
Greeting among its ghostly trees
Catullus' sparrow, Virgil's bees:
Or paddling with a mild surmise
Among the pools of Paradise.

I have kept to last Humphrey and John's other chief enthusiasm. This was their devotion to Auden. John like Humphrey had discovered Auden while at Cambridge. He had attended there one of the earliest productions in the country of *The Ascent of F6* and both Humphrey and John assisted Carl Verrinder in a production of *The Ascent of F6* at Clayesmore in 1940. Like Humphrey, John had been purchasing every Auden book as it first appeared. They often used to read his poems aloud together at 'The Talbot', Iwerne Minster's one pub. There must have been many a bemused Iwerne local who was familiar with such spells as:

On your left and on your right,
In the day and in the night,
We are watching you,

and many other parts of 'The Witnesses' which they used to chant together in menacing singsong voices, as well as other early Auden poems.

Humphrey had fallen on his feet at Clayesmore. He joined the school choir in which he was to sing for the rest of his life – until 1957 under the direction of Reginald Sessions and then until 1964 under that of Ronald Smith. Once every week he was given the entire sixth form for lessons in general culture. Poetry too positively flourished at the school. This was largely due to the

Cartoon of Humphrey and John Simpson by Clive Richardson,
from *The Clayesmorian*, 1939.

extraordinary gifts as a teacher of John Appleby. It is possible, even probable, that at no other public school in the kingdom did poetry flourish to the same extent. This may have been assisted by the fact that the poet Walter de la Mare was at this time a member of the Clayesmore Council. The achievement of placing poetry in the forefront of many of the boys' educational experience was, however, effected largely through John Appleby's patient and inspired work. He had encouraged the formation of a Poetry Club in 1935, which after the war became The Arts Society. Here the boys' own verse as well as professional verse was read aloud. Being also in charge of the school print shop, John Appleby had then encouraged other boys to draw illustrations for the best of Clayesmore verse and had the results printed at regular intervals. All of this greatly promoted the writing of poetry at the school. So also did the institution of an annual prize for verse. Not only the annual productions of *Clayesmore Verse* but also *The Clayesmorian*, and from 1948 *The Clayesmore Miscellany*, all bear witness to the remarkable amount of poetry, as well as other artistic creativity, at the school.

John Appleby was well aware of the unconventional nature of his enterprise in a public school. He believed, however, that his creative initiative more truly expressed the English liberal tradition in education than did the more conventional activities of many of the more celebrated public schools. The following quotation from an article by him in *The Clayesmorian* Jubilee Number 1946', where he presents his apologia, gives a good idea of his viewpoint. After stating the salutary truth that: 'A poet can write satisfactorily only in a creative social environment: in a society of which he approves, and of which he is, in part at least, the mouthpiece', he goes on to rebuke the, in this respect, false social environment and attitude engendered by many public schools in which a boy's verse 'may reveal cleverness – real or spurious – but it will not reveal feeling. Normally public schools are such societies; they do not foster the expression of the more private feelings, their values are faulty, their gods are of tin.'

John Appleby told me that although Humphrey was not directly involved in the production of 'Clayesmore Verse' his influence was an inspiration behind the venture. From the moment he arrived at Clayesmore Humphrey joined in the meetings of the Poetry Club. Humphrey gave encouragement to every boy who attempted his own creative work. It was always noticeable to anyone who knew what excellent poetry Humphrey could write how, when on rare occasions he was induced to read some of his own verse, in his generosity of spirit he never showed his best work in case this might be to the detriment of the budding efforts of the young.

How very much this environment stimulated his own creative writing will be obvious to anyone who looks at Humphrey's poetry. He loved to write of the countryside around the school, just as the boys so frequently did: and he tried to awaken boys to a love of the superlative beauty on their doorstep. His poetry writing, though it was largely a secret in the school, becomes the real account of his inner spiritual life at Clayesmore. It is his real celebration and thanksgiving for the wonderfully congenial environment in which he now found himself.

In Clayesmore Humphrey found, after his two false starts, what he had always been looking for: the true successor to Bradfield. Now at last Bradfield could recede naturally into his past. He would never forget Bradfield of course, it would never cease to be an inspiration, but he would no longer deprecate an insufficient present in relation to its halcyon past. Special it would always be, but it could now become a memory for him. He would give his all to Clayesmore.

Hardly had he begun to settle down to enjoy Clayesmore, however, when he was whisked away from his good fortune to play his part in the Second World War. He had been inwardly fearing for some time that any happiness that he could achieve might be thus interrupted. He had to bear another disappointment too just before the war.

POETRY LONDON

News reached Humphrey at Clayesmore of the founding by Anthony and Tambimuttu of *Poetry London*. As none of his own poems had ever been published, except those in Cambridge literary magazines and a few under pseudonyms in 'The Salopian' and those in typescript in 'The Romantic Residue', he saw that this must surely be his opportunity to begin to communicate his work to a wider public. The enterprise was after all especially linked with his two best friends from Cambridge. Accordingly in the April of 1939 he submitted a small sheaf of poems, written mostly around the time that he was at Shrewsbury, to *Poetry London*. After a few weeks he received a letter from Anthony telling him that, much as he personally liked the poems, Tambi who was the literary editor had decided not to publish them. This was a bitter blow for somebody whose innermost life had consisted in a devotion to poetry since childhood. I believe that it wounded Humphrey deeply and in fact deterred him from again offering his poems for publication. He never told me about this rejection. It was obviously something he never wanted to talk about. It did not, however, shake his own essential belief in his poetry. Rather it settled more surely in him the determination to find his own literary salvation unaffected by the changes and chances of the literary scene. This may sometimes not be a bad thing for a poet. It probably worked for good in Humphrey's case. After all, he had his Clayesmore world now, although temporarily severed from it by the war; and the rejection may well have led to a greater originality in the long run, but at the time it was deeply painful.

Of course all writers have their work turned down on occasions and it may seem that Humphrey's reaction to this was excessive, but it was in a way the particular circumstances that made the blow a bitter one. I believe too that just as influential on his decision not to attempt to publish in future was his own kind of puritanical self-denying idealism. For in a sense he saw even the seeking of publicity and fame as a kind of impurity and a falling away from the highest ideal – that of absolute personal sincerity. He knew that his poetry was sincere and that it issued from a sincere poetic life. Moreover, he knew that much of what he had already written would be a credit to any literary magazine, and indeed, John Lehmann told me in 1974 that had Humphrey's work been submitted to his periodicals he would certainly have published it.

Anthony later told me that had the decision been his alone he would have published some of the poems, but he said that the poems submitted were not of Humphrey's best. It is certainly true that at this stage Humphrey did not always take sufficient time off from an often hectically active life to revise them. Tambi in a sense made it up to Humphrey through much subsequent kindness to me and in the encouragement he gave me to have Humphrey's poetry published. After he had seen my 1974 booklet, Tambi wrote to tell Anthony that he would now want to publish Humphrey's work. In fact both Tambi and Anthony, as well as Laurence and Gavin Ewart, all encouraged me to get it published.

A great deal of the problem in 1939 I believe was the fact that when Humphrey went to teach at Clayesmore he was no longer able to be in close contact with his Cambridge friends who were now a thriving part of the literary world in London. He was already going his own way and in future he decided more than ever to go it alone. He was becoming confirmed in the habit; and he went on writing. It was an act of faith.

FIRST VISIT TO GREECE

Just before the outbreak of the Second World War, in the Spring of 1939, in the company of B.W.H. Coulson and R.B. Sibson, Humphrey went on his first visit to Greece. They travelled with Anglo Hellenic Cruises. Humphrey realised of course that this might be his last chance to fulfil one of the central aims of his life. It was a momentous occasion for him for which he had waited a long time. He kept a diary entitled 'Mediterranean Travellers' which is a depiction of all the places visited during the cruise with an account of their natural history – among them, Athens, Delphi, Olympia, Istanbul, Crete and many of the Aegean Islands. He found the Greek people, particularly those in the country regions, pleasantly anarchic and positive and very welcoming indeed to visitors, always smiling and proffering the flowers which are everywhere abundant on the land. Their ship did in fact land at Skyros, but passengers were prevented from leaving the tourist paths; and, extremely frustrating for Humphrey, Rupert Brooke's grave was at the end of the island to which they were not allowed to go. The fact that the war was imminent was probably what restricted their freedom of access. His longing to stand by Brooke's grave in tribute was not yet to be fulfilled. After lovingly describing the parts of Skyros which they saw, Humphrey concluded with a classical restraint: 'We thought it a suitable place for the Georgian to have chosen.' Apart from the restrictions on Skyros and a few minor incidents, they saw very few signs of the coming war during their visit. And Humphrey rejoiced that before the war could lay its claim on him he had reached the mythical land which from the time of his childhood had been at the centre of his imaginative life.

Anthony Dickins and Tambimuttu at the offices of *Poetry London*
which they founded in 1938. Anthony was Humphrey's
closest friend at Cambridge.

Wartime Service

Humphrey registered as a Conscientious Objector almost as soon as Britain declared war, and very many of his close friends in fact did likewise, but before he came to the point of attending a tribunal he suddenly decided to withdraw his application. Humphrey did not find it easy to explain the cause of his decision – it was one of several fundamental changes in his self commitment during his life – but basically he realised that his pacifism was a complex psychological matter. 'The faith called pacifism in my case', he wrote in his journal 'grew out of the self critical, inhibitory, cautionary instinct which was always checking up on my beliefs, and qualifying the intense drive of my beliefs', but, he adds, 'my nature is active and forward'. The central reason why he withdrew his application was that 'a decision had taken hold of me and determined to real action'.

Clayesmore bade good-bye to Humphrey in December of 1940. While he was away his teaching was taken over by Douglas Hillier, but Humphrey was in fact still able to keep in contact with Clayesmore for some while from the west country barracks where he was first stationed. He entered the Army feeling that it would be 'death to all my life of books, music and wild nature, as also the deceptive comfort of juvenile hero-worship by one's pupils', but he also knew that it would mean 'action, the possibility of giving myself to a social ideal, greater experience' and he hopes 'the surmounting of certain fears', by which he probably means both the fear of active participation in war itself and also his own peculiar kind of apprehension of mixing for the first time with 'the proletariat' and perhaps encountering 'the grim hand of the class struggle'. He has never up until now had the opportunity to get to know anything about ordinary working-class people at close quarters. He approaches the prospect as a kind of fascinating adventure and a new frontier for him to cross.

At first Humphrey found himself polishing buttons on Salisbury Plain in the Royal Corps of Signals alongside another Clayesmore master, Peter Burke, who after the war would be his Headmaster at Clayesmore. They both went into training together. In the words of Oliver: 'they cavorted around Salisbury Plain on motorbicycles learning to be despatch riders. They also did a good deal of square bashing and learnt morse.' After a time they also qualified as radio operators.

Humphrey soon noted in his diary his reactions to his working-class comrades in the barracks: 'The Army has as it were given me a carte d'entrée to that cherished land, the proletariat. And what dull, worthy chaps they are on the whole. They are bodily alive, but seem to lack cerebral tissue – the cerebellum being more developed.' 'Actually', he goes on, 'I could never accept the doctrine of the proletariat being perfect. And now I meet some of them they seem to me to have the same proportion of dullards and selfishes as any other class.' But this initiation does, as he thought it would, keep his left-wing sympathies simmering and resurfacing. Indeed he seems to have been near to some sort of a communist commitment at this point: 'If I throw in my lot with the communists, one of the previous barriers that prevented me from being more active is removed. I used to feel that, having no knowledge of the working-class I couldn't very well tell them how to run their lives.' But now 'the chances of a "Dog beneath the Skin" existence from within the Army' began to develop. He could, he thinks, under the cloak of the Army become a kind of leader in disguise like Francis, finding therein a kind of release of power – or perhaps become a kind of embodiment of a mysterious 'witness', seeing all that is going on and interpreting it to his working-class comrades, in particular interpreting to them the vast impersonal sweep of the dialectic that will he feels inevitably alter all the bourgeois dominance of the past and bring about the downfall of capitalism.

At this stage, however, this is all purely theoretical fantasising. He was feeling far too alien to Army life to be able to put such ideas into practice. He was feeling miserable at heart and hating the ludicrous life of the Army. One day Humphrey let it out that he had modern languages, including modern Greek. This fact soon reached the ears of his commanding officer. As a result he was immediately transferred to the Intelligence Corps based at Winchester. He now had to do all his basic training over again. After this he was sent for specialist training in security duties. It was here that he first met Geoffrey Arthur who became a close friend.

Early in 1941 Humphrey was called to the War Office and interviewed for intelligence work in Greece. He had now moved to Trowbridge in Wiltshire and was fledged as a Lance Corporal. He passed the interview and had 'the ideals of the Foreign Service' explained to him, but despite the fact that intelligence work in Greece could materialise at any time he described his first months at Trowbridge as 'a nightmare'. He was feeling above all the anguish of utter isolation in a crowd, plus the feeling of being penned in continuously and cut off from free access to nature. He found the unnaturalness of the life they were living almost unbearable. 'It is amazing,' he observes, 'the way they try to suppress anarchy here. Every day negative regulations are being restressed. Every day the natural thing is forbidden.' He longs for any chance to get away to the fields and the hills and the open spaces. 'It is not the hardship that bothers one in the Army', he notes, 'we haven't really touched anything in that line – but inconvenience arising directly out of stupidity affects one every time one puts ones left foot forward.' But, he also notes, the officers are suffering just as much in their own way as the men.

Frequently time has to be filled in, 'so we are given idiotic jobs to pass the time, for example on a Sunday morning we were shown a field of grass and told to pull the grass with our hands till it was all level'. 'Lovely,' Humphrey comments, 'all the roots of course were left underground – a little life and dried tubers,' and he adds: 'I am a dried tuber here – and I am thus a constant danger as I may spring up anarchic foliage without warning. And however much they may dry me up I still have my food reserves inside,' and he comments: 'However much they shout at you, you just glitter back at them like a smart crystal on parade.' He finds great comfort all the time in Auden and in the assurance that as the bullies shout and curse 'inside and outside and everywhere the sweet dialectic is driving forward on the flood of history. And their hands are already "charred": if indeed history held one moment burns the hand.'

In February 1941 Humphrey discovered what lay in store for him during the war. He noted, 'I am about to join the Field Security branch of the Intelligence Corps; and he added, relishing the irony, 'I discover that my activities will be as much to check up on Communists, pacifists and Agents Provocateurs as on enemy agents! So is man caught in his own destiny.' By this time Humphrey was an Acting Sergeant. He was beginning to relax more with the other men. Comradeship develops fast in Army circumstances and soon he found himself identifying with all of his working-class colleagues, but sympathising too with the remote and awkward lives of the officers. 'No, they are not the enemy. They are just as much puppets in this sinister process as we are.' More and more he feels that they are all of them, officers and men, Germans and English, part of a macabre apocalyptic process, but despite his apocalyptic boding he was actually able to begin to unwind and to appreciate the humour of his situation. His notebooks are full of ludicrous and grotesquely funny episodes and sayings from these months at Trowbridge.

One day Humphrey was called into his commanding officer's room. According to Oliver's recollection the conversation went as follows: 'What language have you been pulled in for?' 'Greek.' 'A bit late now,' said the commanding officer, 'Greece is lost. Let's see, there is a job on Basra airport. Iraq is somewhere near Greece isn't it?'

So that was that. Humphrey's wartime field of operations was decided. It was perhaps a strange coincidence that one of his Bradfield heroes was Lawrence of Arabia. In September 1941 Humphrey set sail for the Gulf on H.M.S. Devonshire. On board with him was Geoffrey Arthur, and they kept one another constantly amused, Geoffrey particularly enjoying Humphrey's vein of fantasy.

In October they landed at Aberdan in Persia. When they arrived by staff car at Basra they were not at first allowed in 'owing to sikh rough house'. So Humphrey therefore immediately began to study the birds and the wildlife of the area.

The background to the situation in Iraq when Humphrey arrived there was as follows. Iraq had been theoretically independent since 1932 when it became a member of the United Nations. On the outbreak of the Second World War it was a non belligerent on the side of the British, whose influence had been strong since the time of its military control at the end of the First World War, but in the Spring of 1941, not all that long before Humphrey arrived, Raschid Ali broke with the Anglo-Iraq treaty of 1930 and took Baghdad with assistance from the Germans. There followed the thirty days Anglo-Iraq war when the British crushed the rebellion and restored constitutional government under the child King Faisal II. The new British Ambassador Sir Kinahan Cornwallis started the idea of having 'Assistant Political Advisers' who reported to the ambassador at the British Embassy rather than to the military authorities, though they did have military rank. They were administered overall by the Combined Intelligence Centre, Iraq.

On Basra airport Humphrey was given the job of Acting Sergeant doing Field Security Police Duties. It was soon after he started this work that Humphrey met Charles Boswell, Professor of Biology at Baghdad University. Charles has told me of the manner of their meeting: 'I had just returned from Kashmir where I had been allowed to fetch my family back after their evacuation in the Spring of 1941. I called in at the college office to collect the key of my department and was informed that an English Sergeant had been waiting to see me. He had been several times during the last few weeks. I was surprised when I went into my lab to find a khaki-clad figure sitting in my chair with his feet on my desk! It took only a few minutes to dispel the brief feeling of anger and I invited him to dinner that night. This was the beginning of a firm friendship and he came to stay with us whenever he could get time off from his duties in Field Security. We spent many evenings listening to Mozart, Beethoven and Bach on what would seem an indifferent player. During daylight hours we used to go out bird watching. In desert country one could drive almost anywhere. I well remember Humphrey's delight one day when I was able to show him Bee-eaters and Rollers in our own garden.'

Humphrey spent the Winter and Christmas of 1941-2 with Geoffrey Arthur at Khoramshah on the Iraq/Persian frontier. Iraqi relations with Persia had deteriorated just before World War II, but had been composed by a pact in 1937. In the delicate relationship between the two countries Humphrey and Geoffrey's work on the frontier was of diplomatic importance. Geoffrey's widow, Lady Margaret Arthur, has told me: 'Geoffrey and Humphrey lived in extremely primitive conditions during a winter of exceptional severity. They were alone examining documents and refugees and personnel crossing between Iraq/Persia and Persia/Iraq. For this reason they were probably closer than the galaxy of Intelligence Officers scattered around Iraq for the rest of the war.' Humphrey and Geoffrey undoubtedly became very close friends and they kept in touch throughout the war. After the war, Geoffrey became the last British Ambassador in Bahrain. Soon afterwards he was knighted and later became the Master of Pembroke College, Oxford, until his death in 1984.

Humphrey soon acquired a very good working knowledge of Arabic. This brought him to the attention of Lt. Col. Charles Aston, the chief Political Adviser for central and southern Iraq. Charles Boswell has told me, 'Humphrey was one of the very few Britishers who spoke Arabic and we all had to depend greatly on his ability with the language.' In 1943 Charles Aston secured for Humphrey the post of Political Adviser in Kut-Al-Imara. In effect Humphrey now left the Army Intelligence Corps to do political work, but the two were still closely interlinked as previously explained. In fact Humphrey entered the political sphere at exactly the right moment since in early 1943 the final blunting of the German menace from the Caucasus absolved the Xth Army from a fighting role. The role of the British Army in Iraq then rapidly diminished.

Charles Aston has told me: 'Humphrey came to me as a Deputy Assistant

Political Adviser (DAPA). We were a sort of liaison between the British forces in Iraq and Persia (PAIFORCE) and the Iraq government. I immediately accepted him and posted him to Kut division. Kut was important as the river port where supplies for the Russians in Persia were unloaded from the barges and river steamers for onward transit by road (or rail and road). Humphrey became my eyes and ears, and eyes and ears too for the Army and the British Embassy.'

As he set to work Humphrey discovered a great accord with the Arabs. He began to make many friends. He became very friendly with Amir Rabia and his brother Abdulla, extremely wealthy sheikhs and leaders of the Roubiah tribe. Amir Rabia lived in an incredible palace to which Humphrey was made continually welcome. Amir also lent Humphrey a piano which was a great joy to him. Amir and Abdulla showered Humphrey with gifts. The Arabs had definitely taken to him. He was the kind of man's man, yet unworldly, humorous and sensitive, to whom the Arabs most respond. In later years Humphrey would have many tales to tell of the Arabs, and their ways and customs. He had very many really quite romantic sagas to tell of his adventures among them; and his room was always adorned with Arab mementoes.

I wonder how often during these years he thought of his boyhood hero, T.E. Lawrence. Like Lawrence, he understood the Arabs' passionate desire for independence, their proud unworldly faith and their fundamental dislike of authority. Humphrey carried forward and was in his way a part of the same essential hundred years British love affair with the noble Arabs.

As well as being a useful Political Officer, Humphrey found time to be a keen naturalist. Charles Boswell has told me of the first time that he visited him in Kut: 'I well recall my first visit to him at Kut. He was sitting at his desk with a Guinea Fowl sitting on his shoulder! During his time at Kut we had some wonderful bird watching for a week or so on the Har Suwaicha, a huge shallow marshy lake.' Very shortly after this Humphrey and Charles had the idea of conferring together on a study of the birds of Iraq. This was indeed a brilliant idea. There was a lack of work done in this field and Iraq is a marvellous area for birds. They began by collating the work that had already been done by other ornithologists during the Second World War. Then with great enthusiasm they set to work, keeping their own assiduous notes on every bird seen and the whereabouts of its sighting throughout their war years – pursuing this work in every spare moment away from their official duties.

After a bout of malaria in Baghdad in 1944 Humphrey asked to be allowed to move to Northern Iraq. This may seem surprising when one considers how well he had established himself in his work at Kut. Col. Aston has wondered whether some affair of the heart may have been connected with his request to move, but Professor Boswell has told me that he thinks it is much more likely that Humphrey asked to move in order to be able to pursue his natural history even more keenly. Southern Iraq is mainly featureless desert, whereas Northern Iraq has the most marvellous mountainous country and a more temperate climate.

In September 1944 his request was granted. He now became DAPA first at

Humphrey's photograph of the Mulla Mustafa of Barzan.
Mustafa, the father of Kurdistan, became a friend of Humphrey's.

Kirkuk and then at Mosul, both in Kurdistan. He was now under the command of Lt. Col. W.A. Lyons. Before leaving Kut Humphrey initiated John (now Sir John) Richmond, his successor, into the work there. They became good friends. After the war, John like Geoffrey Arthur, entered the consular service. He became British Ambassador in Kuwait and then a diplomat in England.

In Kurdistan Humphrey soon became friendly with Baba Ali, son of the well-known Kurdish leader, Sheikh Mahmud, a British protégé who led several insurrections against the Arab government. Then as now the Iraqi government gave the hill people a very raw deal. Since the ending of the British mandate in 1932 the Kurds resented more than ever control by the Arab majority. Sheikh Mahmud was always fighting for an independent Kurdistan. While Humphrey was in Kurdistan Sheikh Mahmud was succeeded by the great Mulla Mustafa of Barzan, the most remarkable leader of the Kurds in modern times, and the man who is esteemed now by the Iraqi Kurds as 'the father of the nation'. I recall Humphrey telling me that on several occasions he had to leave Mosul in the dead of night for important secret meetings with Mulla Mustafa in the hills. Humphrey was involved above all in the efforts to suppress Mulla Mustafa's rebellion against the Baghdad government, but luckily for Humphrey he got on extremely well with them both. He quickly became a leading figure in the Baghdad government's attempt to placate the Barzanis. Mulla Mustafa had officially been in exile since a rebellion in 1938, but during a serious famine in Kurdistan in 1943 he slipped back to Barzan with his brother Ahmed to rally the tribes. The Barzanis had shown communist leanings during their exile and in the eyes of the West the entire Kurdish movement at this time had a reddish colouring. No doubt Humphrey's own leanings in that direction formed another point of understanding. For without doubt Humphrey became a personal friend of Mulla Mustafa and he felt, as did very many of the British, a great deal of sympathy for the Kurds as a whole. They had suffered centuries of oppression and had on several occasions come very close to having their own independent country. After the war Humphrey always kept one of his own photographs of Mulla Mustafa on a table next to the chair where he sat in his study. Incidentally, Mulla Mustafa was still stirring rebellion in Kurdistan well into the 1970s. His treaty with the Shah of Iran in 1974 and then the subsequent reversal when the Shah cut a deal with Saddam Hussein, leading to the Kurds' support for Iran in the Iran/Iraq war in the Eighties is the immediate political background to the whole tragic situation of the Kurds after the Gulf war of 1991. While Humphrey was in Iraq, he had managed to his great credit to keep Mulla Mustafa happy and loyal to the Allies, but, much as he loved the Kurds, it is probable that the continuous insurrectionary plottings with which he had to deal were a factor in his growing disillusionment with the Left.

After his time in Mosul Humphrey was returned to Baghdad to become A.D.C. to the newly arrived British Ambassador, Sir Stonehewer Bird, whom, Charles Boswell says, Humphrey 'immediately began to refer to as Sir Woodpecker Fish'. Humphrey had really done first-class work with the Kurds. It was even felt at this time that Mulla Mustafa and the Kurdish rebels should be granted an amnesty. This was in March 1945 just after Humphrey had left Kurdistan, but the Kurds, possibly needing or missing Humphrey's restraining influence, unwisely resumed fighting.

As A.D.C. to the British Ambassador Humphrey was now fledged with the rank of Major and this was to be his rank for the rest of the war. Now that he was in Baghdad, he was able to spend a good deal of time with the Boswell family enjoying the cultural life of the city. Charles remembers the first time Humphrey came to stay with his family: 'Humphrey was on his motorcycle and had tied a small can containing his telescope and scarlet pyjamas on to this carrier with a string. When he arrived it wasn't there. He was in many ways very haphazard about that sort of thing.'

A friend from those days in Baghdad was the distinguished classicist and historian, Stewart Perowne, who at this time was 'Oriental Secretary' to the ambassador, while Humphrey had the official title of 'Oriental Counsellor', so they saw a great deal of one another. Perowne was a close personal friend of Freya Stark who at that time was organising her 'Brotherhood of Freedom' in Iraq. Humphrey vividly recalled to me later an occasion when he accompanied Stark around Baghdad. Stewart Perowne and Freya Stark in fact were in due course married.

During his time in Iraq Humphrey corresponded frequently with Francis King who, being a Conscientious Objector, was working on the land, first in Essex and then in Surrey. Francis has told me that he remembers vividly Humphrey's long letters that he received during the war: they were often written on lined school paper and joined together with a piece of string. Ever since their close friendship at Shrewsbury Humphrey had hoped that Francis would become a professional writer, and he was delighted to learn that Francis was beginning to have his work published.

Humphrey flourished in Iraq. Of course he hated the war itself, and of course he was missing England and Clayesmore, but the camaraderie, the activity in a cause and the dedication to the task in hand had released something in his personality. He had not been so introspective or inwardly divided in those years. It is surely significant that he stopped keeping a self-analytic notebook from this period onwards. He had gained in knowledge of the world. He had increased in confidence and maturity, and he continued to write poetry.

Professor Boswell did the final preparations for the press of the joint book that he and Humphrey had written on the birds of Iraq. In 1953 he was asked to return to Iraq for a time and this was an excellent opportunity to do them. The final preparations turned out to be quite an undertaking. Both he and Humphrey wanted the book to be published in the 'Journal of the Iraq Natural History Museum' Baghdad, but it wasn't until 1956 that the book finally appeared under that imprint. It was entitled 'Field Observations on the Birds of Iraq' and it was published in three parts. (It was one of the first books on the birds of Iraq to be translated into Arabic.) All their hard work had finally been rewarded. Their book, like very many high-class original natural-history works, is now usually found listed in natural history catalogues as 'very scarce'. It was a pioneering and important work in its field and is now nearly always referred to by later authorities: and it was a tangible fruit of the authors' friendship and their years together in Iraq.

While at Baghdad just before the end of the war Humphrey was offered a Vice Consulship in the Diplomatic Corps; the very job to which both Geoffrey Arthur and John Richmond had moved after their work in DAPA, and incidentally the same job that the poet Elroy Flecker, whose poetry Humphrey loved, had done before the First World War in the Middle East, but Humphrey declined the offer. He wanted to return to his beloved Clayesmore. Did he perhaps feel a bit, in the Forsterian sense, that he was avoiding being netted by the Establishment? Or did he perhaps feel like Michael Ransom that he was renouncing the demon of government for his monastery in the Wessex vales? Maybe he also obscurely felt that, like the later T.E. Lawrence, he was setting aside further opportunities for self-elevation in favour of a more truly and relevantly modern free choice of service? In any case since 1938 his heart had been set on Clayesmore. His heart was now set on returning to Clayesmore and the greater degree of individual freedom that he believed he would find there. He had opted for the private life and for boys.

Clayesmore after the War

Humphrey returned to Clayesmore in January 1946. By a happy coincidence it was Clayesmore's Jubilee year. A Jubilee year by ancient tradition is a year of emancipation and restoration. Many of the staff were returning from the Forces and there were also two important retirements. Evelyn King was retiring from the Headmastership to enter the arena of Labour politics – though he continued as 'The Warden' living a good deal of the time at the school until 1950. Peter Burke, Conservative candidate for West Dorset, became the new Master (the word Clayesmore used at that time instead of Headmaster), David Spinney Seniors Housemaster in his place and John Appleby, Acting Master during the War, became Juniors Housemaster. Alister McKenzie was forced to retire through ill health. At Michaelmas 1947 Humphrey was appointed to be the new Middles Housemaster. This entailed having charge of some eighty boys in transition between the Junior and the Senior Houses.

He was going to have his hands full as Middles Housemaster as well as being in charge of biology throughout the school, but he was ready to take on this increased responsibility. He was allotted two separate rooms in the Middles: a bedroom and a study, and the private use too of his own bathroom. The location of his rooms in the Middles brought him into close proximity with Mr E.S. Daniels, the Junior physics master, who had a room nearby. They became good friends. His study was over the Middles arch, at the centre front of the building. On the ground floor beside the arch his biology lab was conveniently situated. The study commanded a wonderful view of the countryside to the west, including Hambledon Hill, and of the modern classroom block and the comings and goings of the boys there.

As a Housemaster Humphrey was to demand high standards. He became in fact quite renowned for his strictness but he cared for all those in his house, and took a real interest in his charges. He insisted that boys work hard, not least at biology. He insisted too that the boys in his House maintain an expected code of behaviour. To this end he tackled difficult or unruly boys with firm discipline, and it was doubly important that he did so with boys at this stage of development: one-third of their way through their school careers, with examinations looming and adolescence in full flight. As John Appleby said: it was very important that he 'never allowed the Bold Bad Barons to rule the roost'.

It was generally recognised at Clayesmore that boys were let in fairly gently in the Juniors with John Appleby and were not so in need of discipline by the time they gained the calmer waters of David Spinney's Seniors. So the Middles gained the reputation of being the most demanding and difficult part of a Clayesmorian's passage through the school. Better for Humphrey to begin if anything too strictly and then be able to relax his grip later. He set out to demand the respect of his House and he earned it. His more seasoned maturity now facilitated the exercise of his authority, and he was determined too that his best and more private gifts could be sufficiently devoted to those who could most profit from them. So here he was with his own House. He had come through the war and he had a mission towards individual boys to fulfil. He was in the prime of life and was well set up for the life he wanted to lead. No troublesome boys were going to be allowed to disturb his well ordered ship of state. I think too that he probably nursed in the old public school mould the unspoken ambition to make his the best House in the school.

But, having renounced the more worldly temptations, as he saw it, of a career in the Colonial Service, he was nevertheless on the slopes of his own particular F6. Schoolmastering in its own way has a lot to do with power: control over a House, control over classes, control over groups. He had become in a limited sphere one of those who govern, but like Ransom he was both a man of action and a poet. Would he discover, like Ransom, that, even if he understands the dangers of power, the necessity of exercising it will condemn him to suffer in a particular way? Humphrey saw his power over his House as a distinct and separate sphere from the world of individual personal relations. In the former he was bound to act by the nature of his public duty – the duty that he owed to the parents of his charges and the duty that he owed to the boys' own social ambitions. In the latter he knew only the pure freedom of loving influence. The two worlds would be separate but they existed in connection. Could he live successfully in both worlds keeping them in connection? He would attempt it: by working to build 'the Just City' in his House while also initiating individual boys into the realms of culture. It was his version of living, in Auden's words, as a 'double man'.

These two aspects of Humphrey's life at Clayesmore would also be reflected in another way – his attitude to sport. Both of these aspects of his life in a sense reflected the two aspects of his personality. Though not himself particularly adept on the sports field, he had enjoyed soccer at Bradfield, and he took an interest in sport at Clayesmore. He admired the 'Grecian' ideal of the athlete and aesthete combined in the public schoolboy. He had met it at Bradfield but not very often since. In fact in the actual situation of most of the public schools that he had known since Bradfield he tended to see a somewhat philistine dichotomy between the tougher sports-minded young and the more sensitive arts-minded young. This dichotomy was really there but it was notably absent from Clayesmore in the pre-War period, according to David Spinney's *Clayesmore: A School History*. Since the resurgence of the public schools in the second half of the nineteenth century it had had an effect on the ethos of the ancient British universities as well. As a Housemaster and for the sake of the sports-minded in the school Humphrey kept up a strong masculine persona; while always underneath was the more secret and sensitive aspect of his personality which found expression in his deeper relationships and in his poetry. He had a tendency also sometimes to hide the depth of his feelings and his sensitivity from the school at large behind what he called 'the clown's protective mask'.

The new Headmaster, Peter Burke, a genial Irishman, had a very sympathetic, urbane and relaxed manner that did much to settle the tone of Clayesmore for nearly two decades after the war. He had great success in

charming the allegiance of parents on all occasions. Humphrey enjoyed a cor-
dial and understanding relationship with him. Though very different from Beloe,
he admirably met the requirements of Clayesmore at this moment of its his-
tory. Burke rarely needed to lean on his authority as the Master. With the boys
he was able to be unaloof and friendly and with the staff primus inter pares.

John Appleby and David Spinney with Humphrey, the new Housemasters,
though of very different personalities, were three bachelors of a very similar
age and backgrounds. They complemented one another very well in personal-
ity and approach, and they were all devoted to Clayesmore. With Peter Burke
they gave to the school a tone of genuine enlightenment.

Humphrey, the pre-War libertarian with his leftist ideals, had returned to a
Britain that had considerably altered; and he himself had altered. Oliver says
that he and the Moore family noticed a big change in Humphrey when he came
back from the war. Oliver wrote to me: 'One thing that we, as a family, noticed
when he came back from Arabia was that he had done a political volte face.
No longer was his outlook Left, he had become in fact a very blue Tory. I think
that the war and his particular experience in Arabia had shown him that much
as the leftist or freedom-seeking ways of the Left were an attractive dream,
they simply fouled everything up in actual practice, in a real world with real
and very imperfect people.'

I don't think that Humphrey saw it in quite that way, but there is a basic
truth in what Oliver says. Moreover the world had changed. Britain had lost
her glorious Empire and thereby most of her pre-eminent position in the world.
The pre-war left-wing euphoria and the belief in the coming of the millennium
had gone. The pre-war socialists had to face the strong probability that capi-
talism was not decaying after all. The dream of dialectical materialism was
being replaced by the reality of egotistical materialism. All of Humphrey's
pre-war thinking had been inspired by a kind of utopianism and an essential
belief in the goodness of man which after the war had all but disappeared –
though in his friendships with the young he would gain hold of it again at
important moments – but the idealist had become more of a realist. It was now
clear to him that the exercise of power and authority is a regrettable but a
morally necessary aspect of all attempts at human government. His own class,
however, was no longer in the driving seat. The great men, like Churchill
whom he had revered in pre-war days, were no longer in control. The British
people had come of age and had come to political power, inaugurating nothing
short of a revolution in British life. Imperial greatness was now giving way to
the building up of the welfare state. There was to be greater social justice but
it was gained at the cost of a lowering of much of the individual quality of life.
The culture of liberal individualism was being replaced by a mass culture in
the hands of the mass media, and emphasising entertainment above service
and education. The pre-war cultural 'gentleman' ideal and the gentility princi-
ple had been well-nigh destroyed. It was not even possible to say that the war
confirmed his fundamentally tragic view of life: though, in truth he had never
abandoned this. For everything had been undeniably diminished, and for men of
Humphrey's generation and outlook the particular tone of the post-war planned

and rather mundane materialistic social order evoked little echo in the heart. They felt that the spark and excitement had gone out of it.

His own class had become practically marginalised. History had evolved in a way they had not foreseen. Humphrey knew where his loyalty now lay. He saw the greatness of a great tradition under threat. He knew that in the changed circumstances he must identify with the rulers. The rebel had become a leader. From now on he consciously upheld the best of the aristocratic gentleman tradition in education rather than talking of bourgeois decadence, and he accompanied this in his professional life by a more traditional belief in and exercise of his authority. By the greatest of ironies Humphrey had undergone a change of character and had become a strong and sometimes feared disciplinarian reminiscent in this respect of Hardy at Shrewsbury.

The changes in the world at large were reflected in the changes that took place in the public schools. Butler's Education Act of 1944 was a recognition of the changed circumstances in the field of education. Henceforward the state schools would be the mainstream of the country's secondary education and the public schools a tributary. The post-war world was to be a fraught new era of 'all out egalitarian reform'. The old ethos – 'the self sufficient and inward looking ethos, cultivating the manners and the morality of a governing elite' – would from now on be increasingly challenged, indeed it seemed to very many to be founded on a delusion. As a result the public schools were for a time fighting for their survival, but the growing prosperity and aspirations of the business sector of the middle class ensured that numbers did not in fact fall dramatically; more boys at public schools were now to be from the expanding business sector of the middle classes – far less were the sons of professional men.

The public schools may have become a tributary of the main stream of education after the war, but Humphrey for one would uphold the best of the tradition that he had inherited. His mandate was clear. Something uniquely valuable had to be kept alive. At Clayesmore he could try to harmonise the best of the great English public school tradition that had always been the very lifeblood in his veins with the best of the new world that had come into being. For he saw change as most meaningful when part of a living tradition, like a tree putting out new branches. His idealism and his utopianism could in a sense live on, despite the widespread disillusionment that the war had caused. They could live on at Clayesmore, where, with so many enlightened colleagues, in the enclosed and liberal school community in its lovely West Country setting, he could attempt to hand on the torch of a great heritage to certain chosen 'children of light'.

He was, however, determined not to become a reactionary. He would attempt to move with the times and maybe even influence change in his own sphere. Deep down his idealism still burned. He still longed for love and beauty and freedom – for the realisation of that vision of a lasting good both in and yet beyond time on which his religious sense of life depended – for all that as a poet he had always called 'perfection', but he would seek it now primarily in individuals. He saw that mainly in individuals and in personal relationships would these qualities now live on, but beauty he knew was all around him too in nature.

After the war Humphrey re-embraced the Dorset countryside with the rapture of a vision. He returned to it with a deepened spiritual awareness and love. It was now a paradise regained. His poetry from now onwards will be mainly about human love and about the loveliness of the countryside around him. Interwoven with this more consciously is a dialectical striving for Christian faith.

There was always to be an element of utopianism in Humphrey's special feelings for Clayesmore. His wartime experience had brought a greater sense of realism and self knowledge, both of which hastened his return to Christian faith. He had learnt too in the course of time better to accept and, if possible, transfigure what is ordinary in human life, but his romanticism had not diminished. He returned to Clayesmore after the war believing that there the innate wholeness and affirmation of his poet's vision could be restored and healed. His utopia he believed could be here and now in Clayesmore. Clayesmore could heal the distorted vision.

In order for this to be completely true, however, Humphrey would need a close friend, and after the war John Simpson unfortunately did not return to Clayesmore because he was dissatisfied with the governing body of the school. He went on to teach at a leading Quaker school. When he arrived at Clayesmore in 1938 John had seemed set to be the Clayesmore friend that Humphrey really needed. After the war John always remained in touch, but inevitably their meetings now became infrequent and Humphrey missed him terribly. Humphrey tried to keep many of his links with other friends too, but distances were prohibitive.

Humphrey often visited his parents at Byams – taking over the years very many boys there with him. His parents were ageing but still very sprightly. He and they remained very close. In a way I believe he needed them as well as loved them. Monty was retired now. He and Amy still entertained a lot, went to Sunday morning service at Bagborough, enjoyed the countryside and loved to spend long hours reading to one another from the great English novelists. All their sons had come through the war. They had much cause for rejoicing. Of the three, they saw by far the most of Humphrey, and he was able to perform many helpful tasks for them as they got older.

When Humphrey returned to Clayesmore he was thirty-three years old, still very boyish in spirit, although more mature, but just beginning to approach middle age. For many reasons, some biological and some psychological, he had made the definite decision not to marry, though I know that had he proposed there would not have been a lack of takers, but with the exception of his mother, women were really rather a foreign land to him. He had never seriously considered marriage. So what can an ageing bachelor teacher do with the approach of age? Humphrey could never have settled down into a increasingly mellowing twilight like an ageing Mr Chips. He had far too burning and indefatigable a life force within him for that.

With his rugged idealism and independence from convention Humphrey determined that he would keep closer than ever to the young, thereby keeping

Amy Moore in the drawing room at Byams in about 1940.
Photograph: Oliver Moore

his own spirit young and stealing as it were a march on the ageing process. Above all he would keep his own inner attitude young. By keeping ceaselessly active he would be constantly rejuvenated. Tucked away in the depths of the Dorset countryside he would live a fairly rarefied kind of life, while maintaining contact with the larger world. By the sheer energising wealth of his many links, in natural history and music especially, all around the West Country and beyond he would prevent the danger of any stagnation; his inner spirit would flourish. Shortly after arriving back at Clayesmore he wrote in a notebook: 'The more that one allows oneself to burn away on the current of activity, the temporal event, the deeper within one smiles the fire – though one must not in fact confuse the everyday immediate activity with the eternal activity (= process = fire).' Ceaselessly travelling, ceaselessly exploring, constantly rejuvenated by the young, what need would there be to acknowledge the onset of middle age? He would try to preserve untarnished Rupert Brooke's ageless vision of youth, but for all of this to be possible he needed a loving friend with whom to share the vision and with whom to keep the vision rekindled. Moreover he felt that, notwithstanding all the wonderful friends that he had made, he had not yet found the real bosom friend of his life.

MICHAEL RIDDALL AND ANDRÉ TSCHAIKOVSKY

Humphrey was to take many boys under his wing at Clayesmore after the war, and some seemed destined to be moulded by his influence. He formed with them a close friendship in which he was able best to transmit the riches that he had to offer. His room in the Middles was open house to boys who wished to pursue their interests, particularly in music and literature, in a congenial and quiet atmosphere. It was only a small room, with a framed reproduction of Stanley Spencer's 'Magnolias' over the hearth, and mainly filled by the grand piano on permanent loan from his American aunt, otherwise crammed with books and music, pictures painted by Clayesmorians and his Arab memen-

Montague Moore, from the same period, at Byams.
Photograph: Oliver Moore

toes, but over the years countless boys either singly or in small groups were constantly drawn there in leisure hours. Humphrey welcomed this opportunity to get to know them better as individuals. He had an almost uncanny understanding of boys and an incomparable ability to inspire the gifts within them. Boys knew instinctively that with him they were with one of life's rare adult child spirits. He was always giving of himself to all the boys who came within his orbit. At this time and shortly afterwards he particularly influenced, to name just a few, such boys as Jock Beesley, Derek Bendall, David Birt, Peter Down, Christopher Fettes, Roderick Fisher (later senior lecturer in Zoology at University College, London), Bobby Hill, Roger Kingwill, Larry Liermann, John Nightingale and Julian Rathbone, all of whom became his friends. To attempt to list all of the boys he influenced would be impossible, there were so many. In these circumstances it may seem invidious to speak of his influence on certain boys in particular, but this is inevitable in a few cases, so deep and abidingly significant was the relationship formed.

Given his lack of a close friend after the war, it is not surprising that on some occasions Humphrey found the loving friend he needed among his charges. I believe that on the occasions when this happened the charge too had need of his friendship. Humphrey was a man who was both unusually attracted by boys and also unusually attractive to boys. He inspired a platonic love, and this occurred invariably after some kind of deep kinship of sharing in music or poetry had been established. He had tried many times to erect defences against the establishment of such a deep rapport with his pupils. Like Auden he did not approve of the sexual element in his feelings for boys. Homosexuality as such was for him always a 'decadent' affliction, and if put into practice very definitely a sin, but the interchange of deep platonic love, though he worried about its possible implications, was at times inevitable for him.

Soon after he returned to Clayesmore Humphrey without any doubt actually fell in love. The boy was Michael Riddall. Michael, or 'Mickey', as

Humphrey frequently called him, came to his room to listen to music. There was something about the boy's nature, a shining sincerity and a depth to his understanding of music that swept Humphrey off his feet, but Michael for a long time had little or no idea of the reaction he had caused. He treated Humphrey with the utmost politeness, always calling him 'Sir', and he remained largely oblivious of Humphrey's feeling for him.

Michael could hardly know the special depth of feeling that he had evoked. He has told me that he lacked a positive father figure in his family background. He did not have an easy relationship with either of his parents. His was in fact a family in which his qualities could not shine, but as he began to realise Humphrey's devotion to him and what Humphrey could give to him he began to come into his own as a person. Humphrey's poetry manifests a more than usual care for Michael, his welfare and his future. The tender solicitude of the poems that Humphrey wrote for him is very moving. A parent could hardly wish better for a child. Humphrey encouraged him both as a musician and as a natural historian/biologist. With Roderick Fisher Michael became the star pupil of his time in Humphrey's Biology Sixth.

Michael went from Clayesmore to Sidney Sussex College, Cambridge, to study medicine. When he left Cambridge he met the young Polish international concert pianist and composer, André Tschaikovsky, who had recently come to live in England. During the Nazi occupation of Poland André, who was Jewish, had lost his mother and most of his close relatives. Michael was by now a practising doctor and psychiatrist, but he became for a time André's private secretary and companion. Soon after they met they set up home together in Michael's flat in north London. After a while André moved to the flat of a married couple who were involved in the world of professional music, but until he married Michael remained an important part of André's private life. During all this time Michael kept in touch with Humphrey. He now knew and understood the depth of Humphrey's feelings for him. When André gave his Dorset debut concert at Dorchester, quite near to Clayesmore, I had the privilege of going with Humphrey to the concert. André, as is well known, was a captivating romantic pianist. His playing of Chopin was especially unforgettable. Virtuosi pianists were in any case for Humphrey always a type of the romantic hero, and here was clearly a very notable one. Michael and André came back to Clayesmore after the concert. This was the beginning of Humphrey's friendship with André: a friendship that, like that with Michael, was to last for the rest of his life.

Michael had brought together two most gifted people who shared some similarities in their world view. André loved poetry as well as music. He also had a curiously self-defeating strain within an otherwise overflowing, magical and larger than life personality. They were very fond of one another. Humphrey travelled long distances from Clayesmore on many occasions to hear André play in different parts of Britain. I think that he recognised, as did very many famous musicians, the very special but almost fated quality of genius in André, a quality that never fully realised the fruits of which it was inherently capable but which burned none the less brightly in the man for all that.

When André died in 1982 he was only forty-seven years old. He left behind him a few very remarkable compositions, which are alas all too rarely performed, but by which, even more than by his wonderful piano playing, he would wish to be remembered. Michael and André visited Clayesmore on several other occasions. On the last occasion that Michael visited Clayesmore with André, not all that long before Humphrey died, André gave an informal and deeply moving concert for Humphrey and a few other close friends in Clayesmore's drawing room.

GREECE AND BANYULS

Hardly had Humphrey returned from the war than he determined to realise straightaway a central longing of his war years: to visit Greece alone. He would celebrate coming through the war alive by going on his own to that country where he believed life to be at its most affirmative. It is very likely that he formed the determination to go immediately back to Greece after the war during his first visit there just before the war began. The sacred land of Greece was to be both the last place he visited before the war and the first place he visited as soon as the war was over. In the Spring of 1946 he went there; and he gave thanks. For him this was a pilgrimage of which he had dreamed during the dark years of the war – a pilgrimage of affirmation and self-renewal at the birthplace of western civilisation – but political problems had in fact been rife in Greece in the aftermath of the war. There had been civil war in 1944 and later in 1946 hostilities resumed. The Spring of 1946, however, was unaffected by this. On this second visit he was unhampered by either wartime or tourist restrictions. He would savour the experience to the utmost. The pilgrim from the darkness of a death-laden Europe would bask in the glorious undying light of Greece – the undying legendary as well as the actual light that despite wars and political problems shines on. He knew that now at last the time was ripe for his pilgrimage to Skyros. First of all he went to pay his homage at Rupert Brooke's grave. For Rupert, he always said, is in Greece with the gods. Then in the town of Skyros he saw the heroic nude bronze statue gazing out to sea, 'the statue of immortal poetry'. He talked with the people of Skyros, discovering with joy that Rupert was still the islanders' own cherished hero. Then he visited Delos, the birthplace of Apollo, and many of the other islands. Next he went inland to Delphi and Olympia, and, as always in the places he visited, he studied also the natural history. He recorded this visit the following year in 'Hellas 1947' – a poem written from a truly resonant heart.

In the Summer of 1947 Humphrey was again beside the Mediterranean. This time he went with two Clayesmore colleagues, John Appleby and the Rev. Norris Scadding, to Banyuls on the south coast of France. It was an idyllic time. Norris Scadding painted in the harbour. John Appleby spent his days reading *The Fairie Queen* in preparation for his A level class, and for Humphrey the holiday really did release a new creativity. At first it was a creativity that centred around one essential dialectic, summed up in his journal as follows: 'There are two elements: the sleep which attracts, ensnares

with its beauty and murmurs in our ears that all effort is wasted and that it is better to sit still. Of such attraction are the sea, church bells on a fine evening, much poetry and music, and Rupert with his rout of dream fancies and pillowed act. Then there is Fire or Life which pushes this away from it, laughs at sleep and runs leaping over the dew of grass in the crystal morning. It is quicksilver yet more of a vapour, being unconfirmed. Organisms have this life. It consists in the unified motion, which keeps an organism from being swallowed up by the occasion – it is maintenance energy, that keeps an object sufficiently discrete, to be regarded, more or less, in a different breath from the environment.'
The Mediterranean meant for Humphrey the archaic, classic world of sensuous warmth and colour: the feminine world of pure being. It was always associated with what he called 'true ancient ease', and it constantly lured him towards sleep, dreams and fancies. He truly loved it but he had to as it were constantly assert his northern vigour and his masculinity in the face of it in order not to be swallowed up by it.

We can picture him at Banyuls rejoicing in the prime of his life, relaxed but active, achieving a truly harmonious balance of his personality and his powers. He is poised creatively between the Mediterranean pull of the sea drawing him towards ease and sleep and an inner force which, like that of the migrating swallows he depicts on the seashore, resists the static pull with the assertion of an inner fire and energy. Humphrey wrote several poems on this holiday and several more in the same year when he was back in England. In a sense something in him needed the archaic classical affirmation of the south. His holiday in Banyuls heralded a year when a new harvest of poetry was beginning to be gathered in.

JEREMY

The barriers that Humphrey had erected to prevent the engagement of his deeper susceptibilities again crumbled in 1950. Michael had recently left Clayesmore. Humphrey was feeling inwardly desolate in his emotional being. This was, however, certainly not apparent to most people at the school. To all outward appearances he was flourishing. He was on top of his responsibilities, his House and his teaching. More and more boys were passing O level biology and an increasing number were being prepared for A level. He was having scholarship successes too – one of whom, Balliol Scholar Robert Mash, became a friend and eventually his successor as Master in charge of biology. An increasing number of boys were profiting from his tireless interest in them and his efforts on their behalf. Several of these boys became his friends – Bill Beesley, Roger Bromley, Richard Hayward, Bruce Ingham, Robert Meadley, Dara Khadjeh Nouri, Ian Pond and Nicholas Robinson, to name just a few, stand out in this period. On top of all of this he was increasingly making his name all around the West Country and beyond as a distinguished naturalist.

Into the midst of his crowded active life and burgeoning achievement in the latter part of 1950 came Jeremy, and Humphrey realised that despite all his activities he was hiding a frozen gulf in his emotional self. He did not feel happy or fulfilled in what was the most meaningful sense for him. He had nobody really close to him with whom to share all this overflowing life. He could fight and resist his need; even become to all outward appearance a paragon of self-sufficient dutiful hardworking normality, but it was all no good. The truth was that he was not happy unless he had someone to love. The world could blame him if it would, but who by willing can alter his true nature?

Jeremy was a boy of outstanding and somewhat haunted good looks. I have since learnt that he suffered an unsatisfactory relationship with his father and felt keenly the lack of a positive father figure in his familial background, but in any case there was something egregious about the charm of his personality. He quickly established himself as Clayesmore Dramatic Society's star actor. Indeed from 1950 for several years Jeremy held most of the school captive with his annual succession of performances in leading dramatic roles.

Humphrey was especially captivated. Jeremy was a star for him too. In fact Humphrey became, unbeknown to Clayesmore at large, quite besotted by Jeremy and almost emotionally dependent on him. At first, when most of the school was applauding Jeremy's thespian prowess, Humphrey's rapidly increasing admiration was hardly noticed among the rest, and so for the most part the situation brought little difficulty to either Humphrey or Jeremy in its earlier stages.

Humphrey had gone overboard for Jeremy in his emotional life. He found Jeremy's mixture of innocent joy and seriousness irresistible. Jeremy had reinvoked the whole world of goodness and beauty that he believed in but had largely hidden away because of the philistines, until he feared that he had lost it forever. He saw in Jeremy's wondering eyes, as he had in Michael's, the symbol of the secret source of the beauty that he followed. Soon his emotions were in danger of running away with him. He began to feel an almost pathetic need for Jeremy's approbation and emotional accord. He wrote many passionate but tormented poems for him. He began to take Jeremy on splendid holidays. They went mountaineering in the Austrian Alps and skiing in the Swiss Alps. He had gone on organised holidays with boys before this – term and holiday were never really for him two separate entities – but Jeremy, and later myself, were I think the only boys who Humphrey took on holiday on our own. This was really the beginning of what became a pretty well non-stop extension of his school life into his holidays until the time when I left the school.

In 1954, the final accolade, Humphrey took Jeremy to Salzburg and the Salzkammergut: the inner sanctum of his spiritual topography. I think that by this time there was much envy felt among Jeremy's contemporaries at Clayesmore. There were many who would have wished to be in Jeremy's place, on such a kind of romantic quest with one who reverenced the vision and the spark of youth and enabled a boy to realise the very best that was in him. I think that there were a few at the school who out of envy tried to misrepresent the relationship, but Jeremy was totally unaware of being in any sense an object of desire. He knew what he was being given. Humphrey moreover seems to have reached a watershed in his determination to resist powerfully those who would deny, pull down, and besmirch the kind of platonic love that he and Jeremy were living out in the face of the world.

Jeremy has told me that during all those years with Humphrey the very thought of the possibility of a sexual relationship did not even enter his mind. Yes, he was on a romantic quest, but at the same time Humphrey was always stretching his capabilities, studying his development, setting further goals and aims which he was determined should be reached. Jeremy was aware of being chosen to strive for a high ideal. It was the strenuous quest to realise nothing less than the perfecting of his potential. It was not easy in this respect to be singled out by Humphrey, but Humphrey would move heaven and earth to get the best for a boy he loved, once he had singled him out.

Humphrey thought for a time that he had found his Rupert Brooke. Jeremy was initiated into the poetry, the music and all the good and sacred places: the whole legend. Jeremy indeed cared for it all deeply, but somehow it wasn't quite to be the fulfilment that Humphrey initially believed it would be. It very nearly was. I think that by about the end of 1954 Humphrey found that his feelings were as much infatuation as love. As Jeremy matured and grew up Humphrey began gradually to come round from his feeling of dependence. He would never cease to care for Jeremy, or any to whom he had once opened his heart. The relationship ended in a warm and ingenuous friendship on both sides when Jeremy left Clayesmore.

Humphrey's influence was to remain the central inspiration of Jeremy's ensuing life. After a period of schoolteaching, during which time he married and started a family, he went on to become a lay Canon and a leading light in the life of the Church of England in Cornwall.

NATURAL HISTORY

After the war Humphrey rapidly gained in reputation as a naturalist. He was known all over Dorset and the West Country for his many discoveries and scientific studies as well as for his regular county reports, especially those on birds, butterflies and moths. As an ornithologist he was becoming known nationally, and he was to achieve national fame for a special study that he undertook at Clayesmore after the war. This was his great study on the migration of toads.

Since before the war, in fact since his arrival at Clayesmore in 1938, Humphrey had his curiosity aroused by the movement of toads at and near the school. At certain times of the year very large numbers of them could be found squashed on the roadway beside the school. Why, he wondered, were there so very many? Where were they coming from and where were they going to? He decided to plot scientifically all the facts about their movements. All of this was to lead eventually to entirely new knowledge about toad migration. He discovered that the toads were migrating annually in two phases: to the Clayesmore lake where they were breeding and thence to the school swimming pool about half a mile away, travelling a good deal of the way by the public road which lay between the two. In the early Spring they were assembling from very many sources over a wide area for breeding in the Clayesmore lake. Then in the late Summer and Autumn the newly bred young toads were migrating to the swimming pool. Humphrey went on studying their migration well into the 1950s, that is until he had assembled and collated all his scientific findings. He was in touch during all this time with one of the leading British herpetological experts, Dr Malcolm Smith.

Eventually his findings were published. *The British Journal of Herpetology* gave over an entire issue to this work (Vol. 1 No. II December 1954). It was entitled 'Some observations on the migration of the common toad (Bufo bufo bufo)'. The article covers over thirty pages with eight maps and graphs. Humphrey began the article characteristically by saying: 'The work has been accomplished largely through the enthusiastic help of the boys at Clayesmore school, in particular the members of the Natural History Society, and I wish to express my gratitude to them for their readiness to help study toads at any time of the day or night under almost any weather conditions'. Humphrey's work was a breakthrough in establishing a good deal of convincing evidence about the traditionalist habits of these secretive and mainly nocturnal creatures.

The herpetological events at Clayesmore were soon reported in the local dailies, and then in early 1955 news of Humphrey's discoveries reached the national press. It happened in this way. Prince Philip when he was passing Clayesmore said: 'Clayesmore: That's where the toads wear trousers.' Prince Philip's remark was immediately reported in the national press, and Humphrey's discoveries were soon known about all over the nation. What Prince Philip had referred to was the fact that at times Humphrey gave the migrating toads little pairs of coloured trousers made of yellow or red elastic. (Carl told me however that they promptly lost them on some occasions.) Prior to that he had marked the migrating toads with a spot of dye (made in the chemistry lab with Carl's assistance), but in fact the 'ringing' or tagging of the toads, which he had begun in the Summer of 1951, proved to be his better method of study. The publicity following Prince Philip's remark put Clayesmore very much on the map nation-wide at that time, and I can remember vividly the School Speech Day of 1955 when Prince Philip's reference to Clayesmore and to Humphrey's work and the national press reportage were worthily celebrated and with just pride.

Humphrey's work on toads attracted a lot of attention in scientific circles as well. He was invited to become a member of the British Herpetological Union and soon he was giving talks around the country on his discoveries. In March 1959, he gave a fascinating talk about his discoveries in the Naturalist's Hour on the radio. He spoke at many university conferences. I recall that in July 1961 he talked at the International Conference on Animal Behaviour held at Cambridge University. Toads are not as abundant as they once were. Some types of toad are even endangered species. This makes Humphrey's work all the more valuable. An offshoot of it has been the attempts to secure for toads their migratory routes.

Humphrey's energy seemed boundless. No sooner had he completed his work on toads than he immediately resumed another study which was likewise a big undertaking. This was his study over many years of the housemartins at Clayesmore, in particular the migrations of those housemartins that nest annually under the eaves around the Middles House. Indeed the housemartins had some of their principal nests right around the windows of Humphrey's study. He had begun taking notes and observations of their movements in 1948. Then in 1958 he did a giant indexing of all the notes he had taken, getting out headings under which to summarise his findings. His aim was a book, but unfortunately he was not able to find sufficient time to pursue this aim to its conclusion.

Humphrey had been a member of the British Ornithological Union since the Thirties. Birds were always a principal study and one about which he was extraordinarily knowledgeable. He completed a study of the roosting of starlings at Clayesmore soon after the war, and in 1953 with a group of Clayesmore naturalists he captured a live buzzard in the snow. To capture a live buzzard is really quite a rare occurrence and Humphrey presented it to the London zoo where it lived for twenty four years, until near the end of 1977.

There were other scientific investigations that Humphrey completed at Clayesmore after the war. One of these, undertaken with the co-operation of the school's Natural History Society, was an intensive study over several years of the rival vegetations in the school lake. Humphrey also made sure that members of his biology sixth form and members of the Natural History Society had every opportunity to pursue their studies with visits to, and sometimes courses at, such special centres in the West of England as, for example, the Wildfowl Trust at Slimbridge and the Plymouth Marine Biological Station.

One other main field of Humphrey's constant scientific study must be mentioned: that is, moths and butterflies. He had enormous collections of both, set out painstakingly in collecting drawers. His moth trap with its hypnotising steel blue light would be placed on the lawn opposite the Middles during most nights in the Summer. The following morning he would go through the catch making a record of it. On summer afternoons he would scour the expanses of sequestered meadows for butterflies in many parts of the West Country with a silken net, assisted by similarly equipped Clayesmore boys. He would faithfully write up all his findings and then make an annual report for the Dorset County Records of all moths and butterflies caught at Clayesmore or by Clayesmorians. In the course of this work he discovered moths quite new to the county.

In all these undertakings Humphrey involved Clayesmore boys a great deal. These were the days before videos and television when school societies and extra-curricular activities really flourished. Nearly all of the boys in those days were actively involved in at least one school society, and the Natural History Society at Clayesmore was I believe at the peak of its activity under Humphrey's leadership. As Carl has said with regard to Clayesmorians generally, 'in all these activities he could kindle fires in boys one would expect to be far below flash point'. As in the arts so in the sciences Humphrey catalysed the young with his enthusiasm.

THE BRITISH SCHOOLS EXPLORING SOCIETY

The British Schools Exploring Society leads exciting expeditions to some of the wildest and most inaccessible areas of the globe. It was founded in 1932 specifically to fulfil this purpose for public school boys and their teachers. Up until 1948 it was know as the Public Schools Exploring Society. Thus it existed prior to the foundation of Gordonstoun and Kurt Hahn's powerful inspiration behind the Outward Bound Schools – which were in a sense attempting to give to boys and girls from less privileged backgrounds the same kind of opportunities as already existed for public school boys and their teachers.

On each of the British Schools Exploring Society expeditions a resident biologist/naturalist was required. He would be subsidised by the Society for the whole venture. In 1951 Humphrey's application to be resident biologist on an expedition to Iceland was accepted. Carl Verrinder applied to go on this same expedition but the Society could not subsidise a chemist. Humphrey and Carl, however, with groups of Clayesmore boys, enjoyed two skiing holidays together doing hut-to-hut tours over Austrian glaciers in the early 1950s. In 1951 Humphrey was in fact chosen as assistant leader of the Society's expedition to Iceland.

Humphrey had wanted to visit Iceland for a very long time, especially since he discovered that Auden was of Icelandic descent, and like Auden, he understood the magnetism of its ascetic refuge to the overindulged and the 'pale' of Europe. Interestingly enough, Auden's own first visit to Iceland in 1937 had originated from an expedition planned by a teacher friend and a group of boys from Bryanston school, near Clayesmore. In 1937 while teaching at Shrewsbury Humphrey had read the newly published *Letters from Iceland*. Humphrey was asked at the time if he liked the book. He had noted in his journal that to say that he liked it would be too feeble a statement: 'It is a budding genius, a fruit with seed. How can I extol all the clear-leafed phanarogasus of the mind that will grow from it? How do you like protoplasm? Though I have no formulas to pronounce: the book has affected my sensibility. I feel as if my structure were altered, as if certain lenses had been cleaned and polished, as if certain wheels were running for the first time since the womb and the darkness.'

In 1952 and 1953 Humphrey was again chosen as resident biologist for two further expeditions (in 1952 again he was assistant leader): the first to Arctic Norway and the second, on which he was accompanied by a Clayesmorian, John Grebby, to the remote and dense wild forests of British Columbia. For the expedition to British Columbia a highly skilled team of scientists had been assembled. Except for one, of which he was co-author, Humphrey wrote all the four Natural History sections for the Annual Report of the Society. All the botanical and entomological specimens collected on the expedition were pressed for the Natural History Museum.

As well as revealing an otherwise unknown world of natural marvels full of extraordinary scientific interest, these expeditions were also rugged tests of strength and courage. They expressed the urge to take the human body and spirit to the limit; to test manhood; to learn to live as a team under harsh conditions; to experience at first hand the balance between people and a fragile environment; and to open up new and untapped areas of those reserves of human endurance and resource which lie dormant in the midst of the softer, cushioned comfort of our twentieth-century lives. They were also temporary liberations from the enclosed community and opportunities for the teacher to see his life in a wider perspective.

Humphrey saw much of the meaning of these expeditions in terms of his self-identification with Auden and to some extent in relation to T.E. Lawrence. These two heroes for him provided their spiritual background. As a kind of public schoolmaster saga hero among schoolboys, Humphrey knew that the pedestal he was on could be dangerous one. He was now a housemaster with power over and responsibility for eighty young lives. Would he through self discipline deserve the position of leadership in which he was placed? Would he be able to keep at bay the dangers of the self delusions of hubris? He knew the need to overcome the menacing accusations of Auden's repressive 'witnesses' by living adventurously with a group under deliberately chosen severe conditions. Being a man of action as well as a poet, he felt overall the need to chasten his will and pride by actively acknowledging what Auden termed 'The Lords of Limit' – a complex concept (to which of course 'the witnesses' are closely related), which Auden had originally derived from Frank McEachran's influence at Greshams. In early Auden 'The Lords of Limit' represent a mythological version of God or Fate. They were the feared genii of borders emanating from the divided self. They represented in general the means of civilised restraint that keeps the basic human will to power in check. As his early work became less exclusively private, they became significantly the patrons of the settled, free and integrated communities of the independent schools. In this sense, the one that mattered most to Humphrey, 'The Lords of Limit' ensure that the somewhat precarious but precious freedom enjoyed in the independent schools never turns into undisciplined freedom.

Ever since the 1930s Humphrey had been attracted by Auden's concept of 'the truly strong man'. It showed him a kind of ideal that could both appeal to his sense of the heroic while at the same time qualifying it in a self-disciplined way relevant to an unheroic age. Going on these expeditions was for Humphrey all part of the quest to become 'the truly strong man'. The expeditions were for him not so much heroic as ascetic tests, and here the influence of T.E. Lawrence was also strong. Though on one level I think for Humphrey, as for Ransom on the mountain, the expeditions represented a means of asserting his manhood in order to come to terms with the overpowering influence of his mother; thereby proving himself to her who had always held up his elder military brother as a paragon of virtue. In the main they were ways of recognising and dealing with his urge to dominate, his wild impulses and the weaknesses that he knew to be inherent in his reverence for the heroic ideal. For, as Auden had taught with T.E. Lawrence in mind, weakness can be turned into strength through the ascetic rejection of twentieth-century decadence, 'the process of decay', with its characteristic egotistical, aggressive lust for power, and it is surely significant that in one of his notebooks from the 1930s Humphrey summarised the main theme of *The Ascent of F6* as being 'the assertive man's quest for gentleness'. He knew that in the modern world there is more relevant heroism in acts of endurance than in acts of bravery. Indeed the realisation and endurance of human weakness in forms of ascetic test, life style or service is in fact probably the most relevantly modern form of heroism.

In contrast to the side of his personality which opened like a flower beside the Mediterranean – the unrepressed Southern classical ideal that expressed the more rooted, archaic and sensuous part of his being (the feminine strength of pure being) that took pleasure in life without feeling the need to prove itself – in the wilds of the far North, a beckoning, difficult and in a sense more dislocated realm of peculiar relevance to the modern man's existential quest, the man who would be 'truly strong' and would give wise leadership to the young puts himself in the weaker camp in order to learn a more patient and humble strength. He discovers that in our weakness lies much of our true strength. In his deliberately chosen ascetism he discovers the strength to transform weakness and to be open to possibility and thereby he is able to seek in our more alienated culture for the autonomous life of his authentic self.

The aim ultimately is the attainment of a rare elemental spiritual freedom. As Humphrey put it in a poem written in Iceland in 1951, it is a 'sampling of a tired triumph over death/By living harder, cleaner, with each moist breath'. It is the spirit's desire to be rooted in and united with life actively realised in an elemental setting, and it brings for Humphrey a temporary victory over his predominantly romantic conception of personality – the sense of the divided self which can only find wholeness and freedom in death. The word 'cleaner' points also to a kind of puritanism in these expeditions. It was a puritanism which was far from uncommon among the men of Humphrey's generation of public school teachers who frequently felt that their semi-monastic school re-publics represented a higher and purer ideal than that of the more collectivised world outside the school gates. For men such as Humphrey there was some-thing almost religious behind these arduous self testings in places far remote from the tainted comforts of the 'public' world in which our modern lives are now increasingly lived.

JOHN BRIDGEN

It seemed at the time as if I first got to know Humphrey by chance. From the time that I arrived at Clayesmore I had been primarily under the influence of my Housemaster, John Appleby. Then a friend of mine in the Middles House, David Munro, was asked by Humphrey to go to a concert at the Bath Festival with another boy. The other boy couldn't go through illness and David suggested that I should go in his place. I had recently taken up the oboe and was beginning to be recognised as a musical boy. I had arrived at Clayesmore only a few months before from Clayesmore Prep School where stories about Humphrey had reached us all. I was somewhat in awe of him and when I heard that he had accepted the idea of my coming to the concert I felt a thrill of expectancy that I could hardly explain. The feeling was more than amply justified by the friendship which began on the day of the concert, a friendship which was to alter my whole life. What a baptism for our new friendship that concert was! It was Bach's Matthew Passion performed at the Abbey as a chief highlight of the 1954 Bath Festival. The experience for me came indeed like a religious revelation. As with so many of Humphrey's friendships, it was music that first brought us together.

The ensuing weeks quickly increased my feeling that something of the greatest importance for me was happening in my life. Now Humphrey wanted to spend more and more time with me; he took me to more concerts; he talked to me about literature and music. I found that he was really interested in what I had to say. Nobody in my family had taken such a positive interest in me; with one exception. At the age of six I had lost my mother. Until that time she had been my world; I had adored her. When my mother died my father struggled to cope with a child on his own. He had been dependent on my mother. He did his best, but he was not helped by relatives. An only child, I frequently felt little understood among what family I had, but I knew Humphrey was a man who actually valued a child as a child. I needed his friendship and, to my initial surprise, he appeared to need mine. The feeling of a kind of destiny in our befriending one another began to grow within me to an inward conviction. It was as if something that was in a sense beyond both of us had drawn us together.

But that Humphrey, this egregiously cultured man, should take so much interest in me at first I could hardly believe. Despite some mostly faint praise, I knew that whatever achievements I had earned in my young life were not really appreciated at home. Soon after the death of my mother I was sent away to Clayesmore Preparatory School. There I did well and eventually won the top scholarship to Clayesmore School. I had an innate desire to learn and to do well. Meanwhile my father, alas, was making a poor job of managing a child on his own. On the positive side he did encourage me to learn, but in general our affairs were drifting from bad to worse. I had to live through a painful rift that took place between my father and my uncle, and I think in retrospect that some others of my father's side of the family were trying to single me out as a scapegoat for their own misfortunes. I couldn't comprehend what was happening at the time, but I feel sure now that there were family jealousies involved. There were no relatives on my mother's side. Since the loss of my mother my father increasingly retreated from life into melancholia and fecklessness. His response to anything I did was invariably: why had I not done better? He was more interested in his own problems than in mine. I strove to succeed, but it is hardly surprising that a certain amount of guilt feelings became a part of my makeup.

My father was from a working-class background. By dint of native intelligence and application to his work as a British Railways Clerk he had become a part of the lower middle classes. My mother's father had been an Army musician. My mother had provided us with a very fine house in Fulham in which at first we had lived. When she died my father immediately sold the Fulham house for a very small sum and farmed me out to friends while he moved to his mother's very old and semi-decaying house in a poorer quarter of Sloane Square – where I later joined him. When a Compulsory Purchase Order pulled that house down, shortly after I arrived at Clayesmore School, without consulting me, my father found us a cramped flat on a sprawling soulless housing estate in Surrey. The shock of this it has taken me a long time to get over. He had uprooted me from central London and isolated me in indigence while I was still materially and in many ways emotionally dependent on him. I felt that for some obscure and strange reason he had trapped and victimised me. I think now that it was all part of his attempt to retain possessive control of my life, and maybe also to placate jealous relatives. In any case the incommensurability between my schooling and my home background caused at that time a mentally schizoid tendency. My experience was that of trying to live in two disparate worlds. I was like a personification of The Two Nations. Shame feelings as well as a good deal of suppressed anger were now added to my feelings of guilt. I soon realised that all my hopes lay through my boarding school educational opportunities.

Humphrey above all was bringing me my liberation from my familial limitations. For he was becoming like a surrogate father to me – my father in the spirit, but the truth was that he had fallen completely in love with me – although I didn't understand this at the time. I learnt later that he had fallen in love with me more completely than with anyone else. What mattered to me was that he was taking me under his wing and caring for me. We hardly ever talked about my home background, but he was answering my need in a positive way. He expanded my horizons. He manifestly showered all his many gifts upon me. He blessed me with his intellect and understanding, and, though I think he was always aware of who I was, he began to form me in his own pattern and to mould me after his own image. Above all, he gave me love. The abused innocent was being recompensed for his pains and neglect. I soon realised that I was indeed being given something special and privileged. The spiritual riches of Humphrey's life were being poured into my lap abundantly. All I had to do was to receive them and to say yes to them.

With Humphrey I emerged, during term time and when we were together on holiday at any rate, from a past of much frightened and cloistered unhappiness into a new awareness of a world of youthful delight and freedom. Under his aegis the inimicable threat of home problems and of the past would recede and I could rejoice in the precious inheritance of my youth that was opening up before me.

Humphrey supplied all the warmth and encouragement and enthusiasm that, as he retreated from life, my father was failing to supply. Indeed in a sense at that time Humphrey supplied my want of both father and mother. For he kindled my nascent being. He warmed me into growing confidence. He fed all my enthusiasms and brought forth new ones. Under his fostering care my awareness began to grow richer and more hopeful, and although Humphrey could not eradicate my home problems, he helped to build up in me the inner resources to do so myself. He never ceased to believe in me; and this enabled me in time to find my way through to the better life I enjoy today.

I soon sensed that Humphrey also had a great need. When we met he had once again no real friend, and he was now beginning to enter middle age. Above all I felt admiration for him, but I also felt a kind of compassion. For the fellow feeling that grew up between us had also somehow to do with our sufferings. We had here a kind of complementary understanding to offer one another. I had little support at home, and I was elegaic for my loss of my mother and my consequent suffering. Humphrey was elegaic for his own youth and for something lost in his past. Our happiness was to be found through the healing that we could give to one another. We were both loners seeking for 'love the beloved republic'. We were on a quest to discover through one another a whole new life. This new life depended on each other absolutely. Humphrey had found in me the person to love completely. My father had in a sense disinherited me. Humphrey had reinherited me. He was to give me my inheritance. Indeed he was himself to be my inheritance and the foundation of my future.

I discovered that for Humphrey I was his Rupert Brooke – a somewhat deraciné, post-war Rupert Brooke from a poorer background, a Rupert Brooke who was experiencing some of life's most ugly and depressing as well as some of life's most lovely and ennobling experiences – but nevertheless I became for him a very incarnation of Rupert Brooke. He told me that I was the Rupert Brooke for whom he had sought all his life. We took to reading Rupert's poems together in the Dorset countryside. He truly breathed the spirit of Rupert into me. As I grew he tried to ensure that I knew as much as possible of that range of felicitously opening experience that had characterised Rupert's charmed life. Under Humphrey's influence I even began to look a bit like Rupert Brooke. I ran the risk of course of an appalling vanity, but the truth was that Humphrey's devotion was so sincere that I was at that time truly filled with Rupert's youthful spirit, and soon I was worshipping at the same shrine with Humphrey.

In the Summer of 1955 I played the Cimarosa oboe concerto with the Clayesmore school orchestra. Humphrey greeted this performance with rapture. It was a kind of confirmation of his belief in me. I discovered that as well as being his Rupert Brooke, because of my oboe playing I was also his 'merry guide', after the figure in A.E. Housman's poem – furthermore as his poetry shows, he thought of me as Endymion. There followed four Summers, from 1955-1958, that we spent in a state of near perfection. Although I was in the second half of my teens, being a late developer, I was still virtually a child. The wonder of those years for me is almost past telling. We explored every avenue and aspect of beauty, natural and artistic. I really feel that we lived every waking hour by an hellenic equation of beauty with truth. We walked in the woodlands and over the downlands of Dorset in a state of near ecstasy. We toured Britain delighting in the inheritance of its natural beauty and celebrating the associated geniuses who hallow each region; we felt that the spirit of Thomas Hardy presided over all our Wessex explorations.

As we explored the beauties of Britain, we would explore the works of the English poets – frequently popping into country bookshops to glean some new treasures as we went. Always we took our copies of Rupert Brooke's *Collected Poems*, the *Collected Shorter Poems* of Auden and the *Oxford Book of English Verse*. We would also at different times take copies of *The Orators*, Auden and Isherwood's plays, *A Shropshire Lad*, Keats, Shelley, Wordsworth, Coleridge, Arnold, Tennyson, Shakespeare's Sonnets, Marvell, Herbert, Milton, Blake, Hopkins, Yeats, Hardy, Edward Thomas, Dylan

John Bridgen, photographed by Humphrey at Clayesmore in 1955.

Thomas, Spender, Day Lewis, Betjeman, De La Mare, Flecker – to name just some of our favourite reading. For the rest of my life I have associated certain poems that we read with places that we visited and frequently with some features of the natural history of those places as well.

I sometimes think that we were like two twentieth-century scholar gypsies, two 'truant boys' roaming the countryside and 'nursing our project in unclouded joy'. Yes, we had 'one aim, one business, one desire': and that aim and business and desire was to wander like two vagabonds among the beauties of nature reading the works of the English poets and thereby keeping our spirits pristine and hopeful. We lived in a state of constantly joyful hero worship. It seemed to me then as if indeed the spark from heaven had fallen. Like the scholar gypsy too we both felt that if we ever surrendered and gave in to 'the world', the uncomprehending armies of the philistines, then too our 'glad perennial youth would fade'.

Then Humphrey took me to Europe. He took me to many of the great music festivals – Salzburg, Munich, Vienna and Bayreuth – where we steeped ourselves above all in the world of opera. We had holidays with Gudrun and Gusti at Winterthur and a walking tour in Tuscany. Everywhere Humphrey helped me to deepen my understanding of what we were witnessing. Always we took books with us – poetry, and also certain favourite novelists like Isherwood and Thomas Mann, and books too relating to the places where we were travelling. The learning process with Humphrey was nothing but joy. In France we read French poetry, in Germany German. Everywhere laughter and fun shone around us, and under Humphrey's guidance these holidays in Europe became for me like an extended European Grand Tour.

It was also in the Summer of 1955 that Kek came down from Shrewsbury to visit Clayesmore at Humphrey's invitation. He gave a talk to Clayesmore's Arts Society on English poetry. His visit was heralded by Humphrey as a great event, the chance for all at Clayesmore who had heard so much about this remarkable man to meet him in person and hear him talk. 1955 was in fact the year in which he published his best loved book, *Spells*, and we were treated to a preview. John Appleby's room, where all Arts Society meetings were held, was on this occasion overflowing with boys. Kek was himself a spellbinder. He spoke of the native genius of our language, its latinate and germanic contrasts, and how often great English poetry manifests it. He spoke also of Auden and of his contemporary revitalisation of the English poetic tradition. He recited from memory great passages of English poetry in his unique way. Humphrey's joy was patent. He was reunited for a few blest hours with the bosom friend and mentor of his younger teaching days and the friend whom he idolised beyond all others. This occasion was more like a visitation than a visit from Kek. After this Humphrey began to suggest to me, rather than to state, his knowledge about the special relationship between Kek and Auden, but later on he told me certain things about it more directly. I well remember too that soon after Kek's visit a copy of *Spells* arrived for Humphrey sent through the post on Kek's instructions from Blackwells in Oxford.

I was soon taken to meet Monty and Amy at Byams – the first of many memorable visits. I rejoiced that Humphrey's parents had taken to me warmly. We visited Oliver who had returned from the sea and was living with his wife, Theo, and family fairly near to Clayesmore in a large rambling country house in the village of Kington Magna. Then we travelled to meet the Paines, the Boswells (Humphrey was now godfather to their younger son, James) and many of Humphrey's other long standing family friends. Humphrey and I also began to make some new friends. We first met George and Win Burger in the Clayesmore drawing room at the refreshments after the concert in which I had played the Cimarosa oboe concerto. The Burgers were very frequent visitors to the school for all school occasions. George, a Jewish retired administrative Civil Servant, and a pupil of Gilbert Murray at Oxford, offered to give me extra tuition with my Latin at their home in the village; and Win invited me to have tea with them after each weekly session. Humphrey and I then on several occasions went to dinner with them; and we all became firm friends. George and Win adored Humphrey's humorous 'sagas' about life at Clayesmore. Inveterate walkers, they planned some of our holidays in the 1950s with us, and it was they who introduced us to what became our shared passion for Lieder. Being ardent feminists, the Burgers exercised what I now see to have been a very salutary influence on me, a boy almost entirely without feminine influence, in the constant praise, admiration and concern for women that they expressed to me. Before long Humphrey and I met Win's sister, Marion Milner, the writer, and on one occasion their brother the Cambridge Nobel prize winning physicist, Patrick, Lord Blackett. We learnt with fascination of George and Win's connection with Auden whom they had known when they lived in London. William Coldstream, a family friend, had painted portraits of both Auden and Win. Win's portrait, now in the Tate Gallery, hung then in the sitting room of their cottage where we used to have tea. I think that both Marion and Win were a bit in love with Humphrey. When George died in 1959 Win turned increasingly to Humphrey as well as to Marion for support.

One summer's day after we had been reading Rupert in the depths of the Dorset countryside Humphrey and I went to a concert in Salisbury Cathedral. As we were leaving the Cathedral after the concert, we were suddenly accosted by an elderly gentleman with a very kind, open and I though professorial sort of face. He asked us if we had enjoyed the concert, which we certainly had. He then launched into a recitation of a speech from a Greek play, which Humphrey immediately recognised from Bradfield days and joined in with. The man was impressed by this, but he didn't seem in the least surprised. He then proceeded to greet us like two long lost brothers, shaking our hands, embracing us and beaming on us with delight. Soon we discovered that he had been at King's College, Cambridge, and had been a friend of Rupert Brooke. His name was Swofield. He and Rupert, he told us, were contemporaries at Cambridge. He told us that he and Rupert frequently used to bathe together at Grantchester. He talked of his past lovingly and nostalgically, and before we parted he urged me strongly to make sure that I got to King's. That is the place he said to which I *must* go. Then with a final farewell, he was gone. This was the kind of amazing encounter that seemed to happen to us when Humphrey and I were together.

Ever since the beginning of our friendship Humphrey had affected me with his reverence for both Auden and for Benjamin Britten. I remember him saying to me once that for one such as himself Auden and Benjamin Britten were the two greatest joy givers that he returned to after the war. He, of course, had a peculiarly strong link with them both, not only through personal temperament and through the private school milieu that formed them all, but also through Kek who had taught them both. Although Auden and Britten had to all intents and purposes gone their separate ways since 1942, for Humphrey they remained the twin beacons and guides in poetry and music for his generation, and just as we sought out Britten and Peter Pears on all possible occasions for concerts, so we sought out Auden when he made his rare public appearances.

An experience of the greatest importance for me I will now relate. In 1957 Humphrey took me to hear Auden lecture. Auden had the year before been appointed Professor of Poetry at Oxford. Humphrey had heard him talk on at least three occasions in the 1930s. Just as in May 1959 he motored to Oxford, this time on his own, to hear Auden lecture on 'Translating Opera Libretti', but for me it was to be the first time that I saw Auden in person and heard him talk.

We motored up from Dorset with two other Clayesmore boys, preparing all the way for the great occasion. I can hardly describe the state of suspended excitement that I experienced all that day as we drove to Oxford. When Auden entered the lecture hall I could hardly believe that it was actually him standing in front of us. I felt that I knew him so well – in my childlike way. Yet he knew nothing of me. Did he know of the reverence in which Humphrey sitting there before him in the audience held him? After the Shrewsbury meeting, maybe he did, but for me it was as if a figure of mythology had stepped from the Pantheon into the hall in front of us, and I was surprised almost to see that he had a mortal as well as a legendary existence. Knowing so perfectly, as I felt then, what he meant to Humphrey, there was also a strange sensation as of suddenly seeing Humphrey's alter ego there embodied in front of us. I always thought of Humphrey's relationship to Auden in such terms. He was actually, I always felt, more like Auden personally than most of Auden's friends, but I can see now in retrospect that Auden was equally Humphrey's counterbalancing ego. Auden was the leader and the mentor that he needed as well as a kindred spirit. Auden lectured on Shakespeare's history plays. I must confess, however, that, for all the intellectual power of his theme, I was taking in the man more than what he said. Auden's tallness and full vigour of delivery were impressive. He seemed like a man at the height of his powers. He spoke loudly enough for everybody in the hall to be able to hear him, and his face at this time was very strong. It had not yet got the dramatic lines that seemed to develop so suddenly in the early 1960s.

April 1958 really was a pilgrimage for Humphrey, and he made it one for me. We went on a two week Swan's Hellenic cruise to Greece and Turkey. Many most distinguished hellenists had been assembled to deliver lectures on board the ship and at all the places we were to visit. The star, whom we were privileged to befriend, was Sir Maurice Bowra. We were honoured by the fact that he took to us and even appeared to seek us out during the cruise. He was a most wonderful raconteur and Humphrey and I avidly enjoyed his tales of the great writers who had been his friends. Bowra appeared to take it for granted from the outset that we were both poets. He offered excellent advice on poetic technique. His stories of Yeats were especially vivid, and it soon became apparent that all three of us shared Yeats' 'religion of poetry'. We were particularly enthralled by Bowra's account of his meeting with Henry James and Rupert Brooke. He seemed to be challenging us with regard to Rupert. He spoke almost with awe of James while referring to Rupert as 'a nice prefect'. We met the challenge and reminded him of James' own very special feeling for Rupert. Bowra seemed well pleased with what we said. We joined him for a magnificent meal in Istanbul. Before the end of the cruise I sounded him on his views on Auden, whom I had heard he did not particularly admire. 'A great genius' he said to me 'and one who has matured consistently since he first set off his youthful fireworks at Oxford in the 1930s'. When we parted at Venice, Humphrey and I both knew that we had made a very special friend.

After the cruise we learnt that I had secured an unprovisional place at King's College, Cambridge, to read English. Mr Swofield's prediction had come true. Humphrey and I danced for joy when we heard the news. Three years at Rupert's own college reading English Literature! Forster was there in residence at the College! And so many of the other great Cambridge men who Humphrey had told me about were still at the University! Our hopes were working out.

The friendship between Humphrey and I while I was at Clayesmore had been difficult for both of us. In those years when our friendship was blossoming there were many murmurs among the boys. I suffered especially among my peers for the favour shown to me by Humphrey. At times I was sent to Coventry; I had to endure frequent quips and insults; and at times I even felt almost stigmatised into isolation among most of the other boys. Humphrey taught me to understand that ours was a friendship for which in the nature of things we would both have to suffer. I accepted this, and I should add that, despite all that I went through in this respect, I am sure that it would have been far worse at most other public schools.

As soon as I left Clayesmore Humphrey began to miss me very sorely indeed. In the first of his frequent letters he wrote: 'I know in my bones that there will never be anyone else in my teaching days who will understand so exactly the way we looked at music and poetry and nature. For years I sealed that side of me off from the philistines and now I must do so again.' Humphrey immediately began to grow lonelier at Clayesmore. To partially console himself he bought his first fast sports car. He still had a series of other friends among the boys, but, important though all of these friends were to him – such friends as Lindsay Burn, Henry Dryden, Roger Green, Gerald Stoner and Mark Wilton stand out, and there were also others – it was not the same.

Soon after I left there seemed to him to be an new generation of

Clayesmorians. Though the friends mentioned above, with others, were exceptions, something in the attitude of this new generation and in their amenability to what he had to offer, he felt, had changed. They were a somewhat tougher post-war generation who mainly wanted to get through their school days as a necessary prelude to earning their living and required their teachers mainly to dispense their professional wares. Humphrey's pupils always got excellent exam results, but this kind of approach to education was anathema to him. He wanted to light inward fires in the young that would burn for life. The new generation seemed to mature so much faster and to be so much more worldly wise. Many of them seemed to lack something in deference to experience. Some of them resented his autocracy in the Middles.

Meanwhile I was being taken up into the whole new world of Cambridge. It was in vital connection with our life, but not having me at Clayesmore made all the difference to Humphrey. In my first year at King's I had the honour during a conversation on poetry of a 'bless you dear boy' from Sir John Sheppard – Rupert's friend, his classics tutor and his literary trustee; one of my claims to inheriting the true anointing. I wrote to tell Humphrey straight away of course. I was also to enjoy several meetings with E.M. Forster, who had stopped writing by this time and was devoting himself to personally influencing the young. He was a kind of mentor in residence in our midst at King's. I knew that despite my home background, I was walking in the inner sanctum of spiritual privilege.

Was it coincidence or was there a deeper meaning in the fact that in my second year at King's I was awarded The Rupert Brooke Travel Scholarship by the college? This was part of The Rupert and Alfred Brooke Fund bequeathed to King's College by Mary Ruth Brooke, Rupert's mother. Did King's College know about Humphrey's and my years of virtual worship of Rupert? Perhaps the college did.

At Cambridge it began to come home to me forcibly just how attracted I am to the opposite sex. I began to go out with girls; although none of the relationships at this time was really serious. I had far too much sorting out of the complex emotional confusion connected with my home background to be ready for a serious heterosexual relationship, but it was on a holiday from Cambridge in the summer of my final year, and after I had reached the age of consent, that Humphrey first broached to me the suggestion of a homosexual relationship – in effect he was suggesting what would have been a permanent ongoing homosexual relationship. It was one of the most difficult things that I have ever had to do: to have to tell Humphrey that for all my undying love and gratitude towards him my nature is such that I could not enter into a homosexual relationship. I wanted our relationship to be what it always had been for me, platonic and spiritual. I had in fact gone through a romantic adolescent phase among my peers at Clayesmore, and had then experienced an ensuing period of bisexual turmoil, but I knew that to continue further down that path would be dishonest and retrograde. I considered that it was only fair to both of us to tell him the truth. I couldn't bear the thought of causing him pain or seeming to let him down, but what else could I do but tell him the truth?

I had little idea then of the course that my subsequent life would take, but I must set it down now, as I write, that I have found the fulfilment of my life in marriage – and that in general the chief happiness of my life since Humphrey's death has been to draw ever nearer to women in admiration, sympathy and friendship. If I had agreed to Humphrey's suggestion of an ongoing homo-sexual relationship I feel sure now that for me the sexual element in the long run would have led to personal inauthenticity.

I believe that Humphrey *was* deeply hurt, and for this reason I began to feel increasingly worried about him. His pleas to me at a distance became sadder, and this in a way was made worse by the fact that he was feeling more remote from the new generation at Clayesmore. He wrote to me in 1961: 'As one gets older and more isolated which is what lies in store for teachers, one needs to have one really good friend with whom to spend holidays and whose interests and future are one's own.' I was still this friend. We still went on holi-days together, but I couldn't make the physical commitment. I was plagued by the ambivalence of my situation and a feeling of disloyalty. In 1962 he wrote typically: 'O John, there isn't much that I can say. I have thousands of photo-graphs of you but no you.' It was around this time that Humphrey mentioned casually to me one day when I was visiting him in the Summer holidays that he was leaving his books, his poems and his records to me in his will. I felt very grateful and flattered but I didn't read anything into this at the time re-garding his sense of his own mortality.

When I left Cambridge I was at first uncertain as to what I should do. I had returned home where my father was exercising considerable negative influ-ence over me. Because of this and because of the circumstances in which I was living, I was for some time in a state near to depression and a prey to self doubt. I was however developing some relationships with girls. Humphrey still continued to give me his encouragement and every support that he could. I was probably a very difficult person for him to be with during much of this time. After debating long and hard about my future, I decided to enter the ministry of the Church of England. I began my theological training at Ripon Hall, Oxford, in 1966.

In the meantime at Clayesmore Humphrey's spirits had been temporarily revived by the arrival of two masters who were clearly exciting catalysts for him. First, in 1959, came Alistair Kaye, a giant sized Evelyn Waugh lookalike with a childlike zest for life – with whom he had a kind of last youthful 'fling' in middle age. After him, in 1961, a more serious figure, came Harrison Birtwistle, the burgeoning young composer, who was for a time, Clayesmore's director of music. Humphrey realised immediately that Birtwistle, who was shortly to begin publishing the music that has since been recognised as his breakthrough into his true originality, was a person very much out of the ordinary. He enthused to me about the exciting addition to Clayesmore's staff, and he en-couraged me greatly to visit the school as soon as possible to meet him. When I did so, I was rewarded by meeting a young man who was bursting with inspiration and with original ideas. Both Kaye and Birtwistle greatly rekindled Humphrey's spirits, but unfortunately neither of them stayed long at Clayesmore.

After this Humphrey began to feel lonelier and more remote from things again. I recall that around this time he advised me not to go into teaching. In his letters now he could be mocking and sometimes even scornful of the teacher's life he was leading. When a man has been as idealistic and youthful in his aims and hopes and in such close rapport with the young as Humphrey had been, there is always the danger of a disillusionment setting in with age. Humphrey's capacity for intensity of enjoyment had in a sense never been far removed from an obverse capacity for suffering. That was his nature, and now he suffered intensely as he began to feel for the first time in his life out of touch with many of the young.

From the early 1960s Humphrey began to be plagued by a persistent indigestion, and he seemed to be tiring more quickly as the terms went by, but he was still extremely active. In the Spring of 1963 he went to Greece with the school matron, Miss Ruth Dear – renewing his friendship on this holiday with Sir Maurice Bowra.

Then in early 1964 came a bolt from the blue. On the decision of the Clayesmore Council of Governors all of the housemasters were to be retired and replaced by younger men. They were to keep their teaching responsibilities; but their housemasterships were to be taken from them. Humphrey was the first to be relieved of his house, the reason being apparently that he had the largest house and was not in the best of health. This blow undoubtedly hit Humphrey hardest of all. He suspected that someone on the school governors had got it in for him – and information that I have recently learnt suggests that he was right. Nobody could have been more loyal or devoted to Clayesmore than he. Maybe the extent of his unconventionality had frightened some of the Council, but more likely someone was being vindictive. Humphrey smouldered with indignant wrath, and he was unable to hide his feelings. He wrote to me at this time: 'There is little in Clayesmore for me now, apart from the Dorset scenery in the hols.' He was truly devastated by the loss of his housemastership in his fiftieth year.

The situation was made even worse by the fact that Humphrey felt that the housemasters were being replaced by a new generation of 'career' teachers who had not the same kind of disinterested love and dedication to Clayesmore that he and Appleby and Spinney had. Times of course were changing. A more progressive breed of teacher was replacing those who held on more to the past and to tradition, but the traditional was an aspect of Clayesmore's life that Humphrey would fight all the way to preserve.

Later in the year Humphrey went with Charles Boswell to Malta – hoping no doubt to soothe the blow of his demotion, but his indigestion was becoming worse. He was beginning to have difficulty sometimes in keeping his meals down. When he returned to Clayesmore he learnt that his American aunt had bequeathed him a legacy; and this piece of good news seemed to give him for a time a slightly more solid feeling in facing the future.

In 1965 Humphrey and I went on a butterfly-hunting holiday to the Jura and Savoy. I learnt later that he was revisiting butterfly hunting scenes of his childhood and youth. He seemed determined not to let school problems diminish

William Coldstream's portrait of Win Burger.
Win and her husband George provided a ready audience for
Humphrey's tales of life at Clayesmore.
Photograph: Tate Gallery

his appetite for life. I was concerned by the state of his health. His stomach was frequently misbehaving. Admittedly, he had not now his responsibilities for a house, but he was not letting up in his other activities at all. Indeed he was a little obsessed with keeping routinely busy; and he seemed to be somewhat losing the knack of being able to relax, but he still talked as much as ever about Clayesmore and Old Clayesmorians – though in a sadder key.

I realised too from our conversations that Humphrey had mixed feelings about the changing world of the 1960s. It is true that a kind of revolution was going on. He was stirred by many of the changes in the direction of greater freedom – of which I can't help thinking that some aspects of his own life had been curiously prophetic. But he realised that the overall ethos of the time reflected the final disintegration of the old order in which he had been nurtured. British influence in world affairs was declining still further, and the British educational system was at the time in turmoil. The escalation of dangers in the cold war and modern weaponry hung over all, and the youth revolution in the 1960s was unlike the rebellions of his own youth in that now there was a throwing over of all traditional restraints. 'The Lords of Limit' were being transgressed. Humphrey felt that a sense of flux was beginning to supervene on the old sense of purposive history.

Amy and Monty both died towards the end of 1966 in quick succession. Humphrey had given them both constant love and care and he was with both of them up to the end. They had spent their last few years at Holnest Park House, near Sherborne – an old manor house that had been converted into several comfortable flats for the elderly gentry. This was the first time that Humphrey had lost any of those very nearest and dearest to him, except for certain friends in the war, but, as he had no family of his own, the loss of Amy and Monty was truly an incomparable loss to him.

A few months after his parents' death Humphrey suffered a haemorrhage, but nevertheless at Christmas 1966 he went, with Win Burger and Marion Milner, for the first time to Africa. They spent their Christmas in the bush exploring the natural history of Uganda. Humphrey's health held up fairly well during the holiday. He was able to do the driving in the game parks. In some sense not easy to define his visit to Africa was a kind of spiritual landmark for him.

Humphrey did not go away on holiday in 1967. He was extremely busy at Clayesmore on natural history notes and other work. He had a sixth form of thirty boys which entailed a tremendous amount of extra marking of essays on top of his routine work. He still however went to sing in the Salisbury Choral Society on Tuesday evenings and to Bournemouth for most of the Thursday symphony concerts – both of which weekly activities he had been doing regularly with groups of Clayesmore boys since the early 1950s.

Humphrey came up in the Summer to see me at Ripon Hall. He didn't seem quite his old self. He was almost a bit claustrophobic about his life at Clayesmore. Its problems were pressing in on him. I felt that because of this he had retired a bit from things and gone somewhat into himself. We had a long discussion about my decision to enter the church. He felt very much the seriousness of what I had decided. I think that he had expected me to take up a career in music. I told Humphrey that I was doing what I really felt I should be doing, and it was a decision that I had made myself.

When he returned to Clayesmore Humphrey began to plan a whole series of holidays for 1968. He was still assiduously training his Junior Colts Hockey team in the winter term – an additional activity assigned to him after his house was taken away from him. Late in 1967 a new headmaster, Roy McIsaac, was appointed to take Peter Burke's place. He took over at a very difficult time and he proved to have the necessary qualities to see Clayesmore through what was clearly a transition period. Humphrey liked McIsaac. During the winter term Humphrey was again extremely busy with his biology sixth. Suddenly during the winter holiday his stomach misbehaved badly, but this did not make him alter his holiday plans. He was seized by an urge and determination to revisit as many of his 'good' places in the coming year as he could, and he had a sudden spate of inspiration for poetry, writing at this time some of his most moving and nostalgic poems.

Meanwhile to everybody's surprise Humphrey had quite suddenly come to the decision to buy a house. His legacy from his American aunt would supply the basic capital, and for the rest he would save. He found a house in Shroton, a village nearby Clayesmore, and he threw himself enthusiastically into all the arrangements for the purchase. His friend, John Appleby, was actually already living in semi retirement in the same village.

In February he returned for one week to the Canford School of Music for a week of choral singing. In April he set off for Greece. He wrote to tell me: 'I am going on a cheap-rate Mediterranean cruise round some old haunts with Chandris line boat. Not the Grand Manner with the Hellenic Bowra-Bird!' He flew to Venice before sailing down the Adriatic. His holiday took him to the Greek islands, Athens, Delphi, Parnassus and many other of his most beloved places. He kept as usual a complete list of all the birds and butterflies and much other wild life that he saw during the cruise.

Final Illness and Death

I learnt later from Miss Dear that after this visit to Greece Humphrey told her that he made friends with some people on the boat who told him that they did not think he was looking very well and advised him to see his doctor when he got back to England. Humphrey wrote to me at the beginning of May from Clayesmore:

> The latter part of my cruise was wrecked by my tummy playing up. The gullet-tube (oesophagus) just where it enters the stomach won't let food through. After waiting ten days with only liquid foods, and they don't always go down, I was able to be seen by a specialist at Poole who said he will have a good inspection sometime next week at Southampton Hospital. I shall go in for three days and after that expect to have a big 'chop-up' either straight off, or at the end of term or whenever the National Health can get me a bed.

> In the meantime, he has told me to do no work. So I live a sort of half-life getting my forms to start on their own and then pop in at about 10 am for ½ hours teaching i.e. am doing about ½-time work for the really important forms, and *no marking at all*!

> Have lost a bit of weight I think and spend a lot of the day crouched over the fire asleep and listening to music too. . . .

> Once they have done this job, I hope to be a New Man.

> He's said to be one of the top chest surgeons in the country. Expect when they operate to be in for 3 weeks and then 2 weeks convalescence.

> Expect all at Southampton. If I get any definite news I will try and communicate with you.

> Bye,

> Good luck. Humph.

I was devastated to learn how ill Humphrey was. I was relieved to get a letter from him in June saying that he was convalescing in Wokingham at the home of a Clayesmorian friend. Could I pop over? I immediately did. He was looking quite a lot thinner, but taking all into account better than I thought he would look, but I was appalled when he showed me the operation scar; it went right from his shoulder to his hip. He had been opened right up for examination. He said he was feeling better but he wasn't absolutely sure that they wouldn't need to operate again. He was enjoying a pleasant recuperation. He told me that he was going to the Yorkshire Dales to stay with the Boswells for two weeks, after which he would go up to the West coast of Scotland. Further than that he didn't know his plans in detail, but he expected to be back at Clayesmore. If I was in any doubt about where he was, he said he could always be found through Oliver at Kington Magna. He also told me that he had set the wheels in motion for buying his house in Shroton.

I took all this as evidence of a recuperation. I did not think that he would be doing so much unless he were feeling that he was recovering. So the summer passed during which, as it happened, I was dealing with my father's illness and hospitalisation. I wrote to Humphrey asking him how he was. I had just begun to feel that my father was back on his feet again and was feeling reasonably confident that Humphrey was also when, at the beginning of December, I received a letter from Humphrey, which I shall come to. He was back at Southampton Chest Hospital.

Later I found out more about Humphrey's movements during this time. In his 'History of Clayesmore' David Spinney writes: 'Most of the summer term he was away sick. He sent a 'Good Luck' post card to all his examination candidates, as he had always done throughout his teaching career, and his last words to Roy McIsaac were 'Keep my job for me. . . .' He did reappear at the beginning of the Michaelmas term 1968 looking desperately ill but the effort was too much.' Miss Dear later told me that when he came back he was hardly recognisable. It was pitiable she said to see him struggling to keep up his normal routine. She told me that once he was coming round the corner of a corridor when a boy came running from the other side and not seeing him knocked him completely to the ground, but he was nevertheless determined to keep on teaching as long as he could still stand up.

When I received Humphrey's letter in December at first I didn't know what to make of it. I knew that a further operation was always on the cards, but his light-hearted tone in his letter still encouraged me to take an optimistic view of what was happening. He wrote from Ward G2:

Dear John,

Thanks for the letter. As some of the tests have run me down, they are postponing the big op. till next week – probably Monday, but one just can't prophesy.

If you feel like looking over, I suggest you ring Tuesday or Wed and ask when I will be suitable. I should then add a few days to that! especially as various people from Clayesmore and also Oliver will be over. In fact don't put yourself out, as I shall be in here for 2-3 weeks after the op. In any case I doubt if I shall return to Clayesmore this term. I am already plotting to spend the latter part of my convalescence at Treyarnon Bay, Cornwall.

Suppose you wouldn't be taking your holiday just then?

The last two days have been rather hellish, I have been aching all over and of course back to bed. On top of my month's semi-starvation, to have the last 48 hours without even a glass of water, and three enemas, just so they can photograph my gall-bladder – well, I ask you, chum, it's a bit rough!

Had a kind letter from Scad – Drinkall (Clayesmore's new Chaplain) was over here first. He's a great hospital man! – but indeed very kind – The Rev. Swale brought me Holy Communion this morning.

All around me are noisy painters – Incredible how little work they do and how many and eternal tea-intervals they have.

No one will tell me how long after leaving hospital before I shall be safe to drive!

Have you any paperback Anthony Powell? I am told he is lightish diet.

So far have read: – F. King 'The Man on the Rock', very well done – Then W. Faulkner 'The Wild Palms' – brutal, violent, poetical, but written in the most exhausting prose possible – no paragraphs for pages, like a tall yew hedge and about as impenetrable. Embarbed with enormous parentheses, often lasting over the page. Truly barbarous stuff and full of nightmares – Not quite the best hospital reading. Am now starting the same author's 'Requiem for a Nun', which looks easier reading. Then I have Uncle Aldous's 'Eyeless in Gaza' and 'After many a Summer' for my next fare. Clayesmore are bringing me over my late father's T. Hardy novels.

Well enough said.

Did I tell you I was in a private ward, but on the N.H.S.!!!

Best Wishes

Yours ever

Humph

A few weeks later came an early Christmas card sent from ward G2. It had depicted on it an elderly gentleman playing a flute. Humphrey had written on it:

After a series of illnesses, I was dragged off to Blandford Hospital on Friday (13th) in a wretched state. I took no book as I didn't even want to read. Tuesday I go back to Southampton Hospital, I hope for only a few days.

I am not to work next term. I was in the process of buying a house when all this happened.

I can't tell you my movements but c/o Cdr. O.R. Moore will get to me.

(on the other side of the card)

Best wishes to you and your father

Merry Christmas & a happy New Year

from Humphrey

Memories of Pickard Cambridge.

Two days before Christmas a note arrived from Carl saying: 'Humph is not at all well. I think you should see him as soon as possible'. I knew immediately that I had been deceiving myself about Humphrey's recuperation and indeed for a long time about how ill he was. I caught the first train to Southampton. When I reached the hospital I caught a glimpse of Humphrey as I passed by the window of his ward. I was instantly horrified by what I saw. Before I reached the ward I met Oliver who told me: 'There isn't the slightest hope of him recovering. Peter is sitting with him and talking with his visitors. That way he doesn't have to talk but he can hear everything that's being said. There has been a constant stream of visitors from Clayesmore. He's been asking to see you. He couldn't have known how ill he was because he was in the process of buying a house when this happened.' I went into the ward. As soon as I saw him I knew that he was dying. He was propped up by pillows, a skeletal small drooping figure with down-bent head and staring eyes that had no sign of life or expression in them. He was so desperately thin that he was scarcely recognisable. I noticed that there were fresh flowers in a vase beside the bed. He saw me immediately and showed his recognition by moving his head towards me. Peter who was sitting near the end of the bed motioned me to sit beside the bed. He began conversing with me. Humphrey did indeed look too weak to talk, but I was sure that he would communicate with me somehow. I took his right hand in mine. I sat down beside him. As I leant towards him Humphrey said in a just audible voice 'This is not really me.' Peter began to talk with me in the most generalised kind of way. I could see that Humphrey wanted to speak. I leant nearer to hear. He said with as much emphasis as he could muster 'Thank you' and he repeated it. I was over-whelmed but determined not to lose control of my emotions. I really felt that it should have been me thanking him. All I could reply was 'Thank *you*'. Peter resumed a conversation for a while. Then I could see that Humphrey again wanted to speak. I leant nearer again. He said 'I'm leaving you my books, my first editions and my poems.' I said 'I shall treasure them.' Peter now asked me what I was doing and what I hoped to do. When he asked me this I felt a bit embarrassed and said 'I feel certain that I will eventually be ordained to the Priesthood.' Humphrey at this moment moved his left hand to join his right hand that I was holding. He was making his hands form the posture of prayer. It was not easy for him even to move his hand, but I could see what he was doing.

By the comings and goings of a nurse I could tell that it was nearly time for me to leave. Humphrey again said to me just audibly several times 'Thank you'. Peter and I made a few final remarks. I rose to leave. I was holding myself in check. I knew that I would never see Humphrey again, but I would not break down in front of his relatives. I held his hand once more and looked at his face which was long past registering emotion and said 'Good-bye'. I walked to the door and turned for a last look. He had turned his head to follow me to the door.

When I got back to my father's flat my emotions broke. Grief began to shake my body in spasms and to stream from me in tears; I was full of self accusation. I thought of all the sadness and disappointment of his last years. I thought of all that life had meant to him – the incomparable riches of life that he of all men had showed me and so many others how to value and celebrate. I thought of all we had shared. I thought of how I had underestimated his illness, and maybe many others had too, as if I refused to see how he was suffering. Because he tried to keep active until the very last, because he made light as much as he could of his illness to spare us, how many of us had given the comfort or care that we could have done and should have done? Did I really understand his increasing loneliness and his fear of loneliness? How many ever understand the isolation and suffering of the homosexual? As I was wrestling with my own problems he was dying and I went on deceiving myself until I could no longer. I, the poor fool, knew the wound he carried. I had only got to the hospital just in time. Thank God for Carl's note. To have died at a mere fifty-five years old! How could that be? And yet, hadn't he always told us that he would not live to be old. Hadn't everything he had told us made it clear that he didn't want to be old or disillusioned with life? But why couldn't he have died when I was proving myself more, when I could begin to pay back something of all I owed to him? How feeble had been my last words to him. What did it all mean? Did it have any meaning at all? He died knowing that I was not yet independent or free, but I believe he knew that one day I would be free. I feared that he might have died feeling that he had failed, but at the same time I felt that more success, in the ordinary worldly sense, than he had known would probably have been boring to him. I thought of the terrible fate of being a lover of boys. All the boys he had loved and helped had grown older and left him, and I couldn't help putting myself in this category – although in truth I had not left him. The lover of boys is always aware that his way of life is something that the heterosexual world rarely forgives. The thought of the pathos of his last years I found almost unbearable. Had he lived perhaps too intensely from his heart? Had the wisdom he had found through beauty in the end led him to the abyss, as Plato had prophesied and as it did Aschenbach? And yet surely there had been something uniquely special and enduring about our relationship; and this must bear fruit. I knew that his love for me, far from decreasing, had only increased in his last years of life. I would bear the torch. Humphrey had always said 'have faith'. So I would have faith. There had to be a meaning in what had happened between us. Everything we had lived for and believed in could not come to nothing.

Next morning I rang Oliver. He and Theo were back at Dash Hayes as I expected they would be. Humphrey had died shortly after one o'clock that morning. He had died peacefully. He had not said much after I had gone. Oliver and Theo stayed with him to the end. The day on which he died was the day after the end of Clayesmore's term and it was Christmas Eve. Oliver, Theo and Peter had arranged an immediate cremation at Southampton which had taken place that morning. Oliver now had the ashes. He still hardly believed what had happened. 'We must arrange a suitable time when you can come down for scattering the ashes,' Oliver said. 'And we must go through his books too. He wanted me to have the scientific and travel books and all the rest he wanted to go to you. We'll do that when you come down as well.'

I telephoned Win Burger and Marion Wilner to tell them that Humphrey had died. Both were very sad indeed to hear the news. Marion said: 'He was a very gifted man. And he was like a father to you.' In the coming difficult years first Win and then Marion would both be like mother figures for me.

Shortly after Humphrey died I was ordained and I began the life of a parish priest; but my spirits had sunk to a low pitch. At first I felt terribly alone. My father had damaged my self esteem, and as I worked for my parishioners I was attempting to rise from a trough of depression. I who was so strong in so many ways when I had Humphrey was to discover the full extent of my weakness without him. Indeed I might have been a gonner but for Humphrey's faith in me. It was Humphrey's faith in me, allied to my Christian faith and my work in the Church, that sustained me through the darkness of the time after his death. I believed that there was a thread of meaning and purpose in my life running through my relationship with Humphrey and all that had happened between us and leading into the future. To my belief in that thread of meaning and purpose I held.

THE FAREWELL

Clayesmore held a Memorial Service for Humphrey in the School Chapel on 2 February 1969. The Chapel was filled to overflowing with family and friends from all stages of his life: Peter and Oliver and their families; and also with their families, the Paines from Bradfield days, the Boswells and Charles Aston from his days in Iraq; John Simpson and of course a multitude of Clayesmore friends past and present. Kek unfortunately was not well enough to travel. The Chaplain, the Rev. John Drinkall, took the service and the school choir, led by the Director of Music, Nicholas Zelle, sang the Introit from Mozart's Mass in B flat. Another Old Clayesmorian, Richard Ratcliffe, and myself sang 'Comfort Ye' and 'The Trumpet shall sound' from the Messiah. A complete performance of the whole of the Mozart Mass in B flat was given in Humphrey's honour later during the term.

The Memorial Service was a moving and unforgettable occasion. It helped many of us who were very close to Humphrey to begin to come to terms with our loss, and, though of course there are some who would consider even a controlled homosexuality to be a flaw, it was a fitting expression of the fact that Humphrey was an outstanding embodiment of the best that Clayesmore stood for, a kind of fulfilment indeed in his time of the Clayesmore spirit. It was a public acknowledgement by his friends of an essentially private man – a remarkable man who had made Clayesmore the centre of his life and his world. More than that, I think that many of us who knew him best felt that we were not only publicly acknowledging a private man but also paying tribute to one of the last of the romantics. He was one who had stood out among his friends and all those who had responded to his exceptional personal powers and qualities, and these included adults as well as schoolboys, for his many-sided gifts, his generosity of spirit, his infectious enthusiasm and his undisputed leadership. As far as we, his friends and followers, were concerned, within the limited community of the English public school he had trodden his own uniquely inspiring path and had lived his life, notwithstanding the whole tendency of the world at large, in a still recognisably heroic mould.

John Appleby said in his valediction in *The Clayesmorian* in 1968: 'It is characteristic of staff at Clayesmore that they feel the leaving of it very keenly indeed. Humphrey was spared this pang.' Yes, and neither did he have to endure the twilight dwindling years of physical severance from the school to which he had given his heart. It was so appropriate and an added testimony to the esteem in which Humphrey was held that during 1969 a new biology laboratory was dedicated at Clayesmore and named after him The Moore Laboratory. This would have deeply moved and pleased him.

Oliver and I had expected to scatter Humphrey's ashes in the summer of 1969, but we were forced to leave it until 1970 because it was impossible to fix a date in 1969 when we could both be in Dorset; leaving it until 1970 meant that I could perform this last office for Humphrey as an ordained man of that church with which, in its public school aspect especially, he was closely associated all his life. Meanwhile Humphrey's ashes sat in a cardboard box in a cupboard in Oliver and Theo's living room at Kington Magna. I didn't know until I arrived to stay with them that August where the scattering was to take place.

I then learned that in the last week of his life Humphrey had requested that his ashes be scattered on Hambledon Hill overlooking Clayesmore, the countryside which he loved better than any other in the world. It was Hambledon Hill of which he had such a wonderful view from his room over the Middles arch and which he saw every day of his life at Clayesmore, and when I heard of his request I remembered how Humphrey and I used to so often wander down Iwerne Hill on summer evenings, still breathing in the musk of summer after a day of exploring the woodlands and the countryside. We would look down over Hambledon and the vale of Blackmoor on our way back to school and he would intone to me:

Comrade look not on the west,
T'will have the heart out of your breast.

He had a great understanding of and love for A.E. Housman – a fellow teacher poet who, like himself, had loved those he taught, but with an unrequited and a hidden love. Housman was an anguished private man who had early lost the love of his life and who found healing in nature as well as in human love – a poet who, in Humphrey's view, had voiced one of the deepest and most passionate expressions of man's hunger for the spiritual universe: that eternal universe of beauty, order and final unity which transfigures the tragic in human experience. He was a poet, Humphrey once said, whose poems are 'the sap of larger spiritual life bleeding through into the material present'; and he 'saw in death the time when 'l'homme moyen sensuel' is called to account for his long neglect of the spiritual universe'.

Oliver, Theo and I performed the little ceremony of scattering Humphrey's ashes on the hilltop on a late August day of great beauty and calm. I said a few prayers from the Book of Common Prayer and then I read Rupert Brooke's poem 'Day that I have loved'. After that we took it in turns to scatter his ashes around the slope of the hill looking towards Clayesmore. Just the three of us on the hill with the vast expanse of the Dorsetshire countryside on every side, committing his remaining ashes to the earth he loved. We could see Clayesmore with its trees in the midst of the vale of Blackmoor. Some of his ashes would probably be blown to mingle with its earth. I felt the appropriateness of Rupert's words for one who had always felt man's essential loneliness in a largely uncomprehended and mysterious but supremely beautiful universe. I remembered something that he had written in one of his notebooks: 'All man's culture and learning seem like a mere protective robe when he feels his isolation in the wild universe which only his heart can warm to sympathetic harmony.' I felt that 'Day that I have loved' were the very words that Humphrey would have chosen for his valediction – expressing the essential child humility, the wonder, the mystery and the love which, like Rupert, he had shared with his friends, and were these words in any way inappropriate beside my spoken prayers to the one who said 'You must become as little children'?

As we said our farewell and I read from his sacred book of youth I thought of Humphrey's understanding love of Rupert Brooke, and I thought too of his loyalty to myself through thick and thin. The torch he had first lifted at Bradfield he had held high. He had managed to an unique extent to live by Rupert Brooke's spirit, to keep alive his spirit, right into the 1960s. He had never surrendered his youthful vision, and he had handed on the torch to others. He had combined the inspired and dedicated life of a teacher and a poet. His writing was known to only a few, but he was surely one of the last of the purely lyrical singers in English poetry. In the citadel of the middle-class public-school establishment, though a trained and active scientist, he had stood all his life, at times heroically against the odds, for the life of the spirit and the imagination. He had paid the price. In the end the world had broken him. In pursuing his vision he had driven his spirit and his body to the limit. He had taken the consequences of his own romanticism. He had taken the consequences of his love of boys. He had dared to live honestly by his gospel of beauty. In his poetry the love that dares not speak its name has spoken it out boldly and unequivocally and maybe it has spoken it out for the last time so boldly and unequivocally from the milieu of the English public schools.

As I read I thought too that we were saying farewell to a legend. I knew that Humphrey would become a school legend. I knew that subsequently no-one would come to Clayesmore who would not hear of this legend. Perhaps his legend will now be shared by some who never knew either him or Clayesmore. As Oliver, Theo and I said our farewell on the hilltop on that calm and beautiful day the sun shone warmly on all that we did. The three of us, through Rupert's words, were speaking to Humphrey as I read aloud:

> Tenderly, day that I have loved, I close your eyes,
>> And smooth your quiet brow, and fold your thin dead hands.
> The grey veils of the half-light deepen; colour dies.
>> I bear you, a light burden, to the shrouded sands,
>
> Where lies your waiting boat, by wreaths of the sea's making
>> Mist-garlanded, with all grey weeds of the water crowned.
> There you'll be laid, past fear of sleep or hope of waking;
>> And over the unmoving sea, without a sound,
>
> Faint hands will row you outward, out beyond our sight,
>> Us with stretched arms and empty eyes on the far-gleaming
> And marble sand. . . .
>> Beyond the shifting cold twilight
>> Further than laughter goes, or tears, further than dreaming,
>
> There'll be no port, no dawn-lit islands! But the drear

Waste darkening, and at length, flame ultimate on the deep.
Oh, the last fire – and you, unkissed, unfriended there!
    Oh, the lone way's red ending, and we not there to weep!

(We found you pale and quiet, and strangely crowned with flowers,
    Lovely and secret as a child. You came with us,
Came happily, hand in hand with the young dancing hours,
    High on the downs at dawn!) Void now and tenebrous,

The grey sands curve before me. . . .
    From the inland meadows,
Fragrant of June and clover, floats the dark, and fills
    The hollow sea's dead face with little creeping shadows,
And the white silence brims the hollow of the hills.

Close in the nest is folded every weary wing,
    Hushed all the joyful voices; and we, who held you dear,
Eastward we turn and homeward, alone, remembering. . . .
    Day that I have loved, day that I have loved, the Night is here!

EPILOGUE

Soon after I was ordained in March 1970 I felt a great desire to tell Auden about Humphrey. I felt that it was really right that Auden should know about a man whose whole life had been so peculiarly closely identified with his own – a man who had passed on something essential of the inner gnosis of Auden's life's work to so many young disciples. I didn't think for one moment that there was in fact the remotest chance of me actually being able to tell Auden about Humphrey, but I felt that I had to try. I therefore wrote a letter to Auden and sent it to Faber and Faber whom I asked to forward it. I thought it probably wouldn't reach Auden. Faber and Faber were probably deluged with letters from admirers of the great man, but what was the harm in trying?

I was at the time going carefully through all of Humphrey's manuscripts and notebooks, extracting all his poems and typing them. I was also taking a pride in the collection of Auden and other Thirties poets first editions that Humphrey had left to me – filling in gaps here and there by getting on the mailing lists of London bookshops.

As regards Humphrey's poetry, I was convinced that he should be published. Some poems were left unrevised, and a little work of revision was called for in places. Humphrey himself had said the same to me. I knew, however, that with poetry as individual as Humphrey's a taste has to some extent to be created, and when I spoke to literary friends and acquaintances in these early days after Humphrey had died most liked the poems that I showed them, but some spoke of the extreme difficulty of getting people interested in poetry these days.

I knew that for Humphrey there was indubitably one final court of appeal. There was one man as far as Humphrey and I were concerned whose opinion would be absolutely trustworthy. So in my boldness I told Auden in my letter that Humphrey Moore, one of his most fervent devotees, had recently died and as well as leaving me a marvellous collection of his works had also left me his own unpublished poems in his will.

I should be extremely grateful, I said, if Auden would please look at some of these unpublished poems and tell me his honest opinion about them, because I knew that his would be the opinion that Humphrey would value most. In fact I knew that it was the one opinion that Humphrey would not for one moment think of doubting or gainsaying. In short I knew that if I had Auden's view I needn't go on taking the poems around and showing them to so many different people and obtaining so many different points of view. I would then know about the poems.

To my delight and surprise early in January 1971 I received a letter from New York with Auden's name written on the edge of the envelope. I opened it. It was sent from 77 St Mark's Place, New York, on 6 January. It read:

Dear Father Bridgen
Your letter of Nov. 21st only reached me yesterday.
I shall be in England very briefly in June or July,
but the best time would be the last half of October.
Yours sincerely,
W H Auden.

I wrote back to Auden in New York immediately asking whereabouts in England I could contact him in the last half of October, and as I was moving parish at the time I told him what my new address would be. I knew that a meeting could still slip through my fingers unless I persevered. Auden would be very busy and doubtless seeing a lot of people, and he was getting quite old. It was possible he could forget about me. A good deal of time went by and I began to wonder if perhaps he had already forgotten about me. Then towards the end of September I received a second letter from Auden. This time he had written from 3062 Kirchstetten, Austria. The letter was dated 20 September and read:

Dear Mr. Bridgen,
Thank you for your letter. I shall be in England from October 7th to November 1st. I expect to be staying with Mr. Stephen Spender, 15 Loudoun Road, N W 8, but am still not quite certain.
Will let you know my whereabouts when I do.
Yours sincerely,
W H Auden.

My hopes were rising, but the whole arrangement could still possibly not come to fruition. As the days went by and October 7th passed I waited on tenterhooks to see whether there might be a further communication. As there wasn't, in the middle of October I wrote a short letter to Auden at Stephen Spender's house to see if he was there and to remind him of my hope of seeing him. The very next day my telephone rang and Auden himself was on the line. He said: 'This is Mr. Auden. Would you like to come to tea on Thursday afternoon at 4.30 at 15, Loudoun Road?' I could hardly believe that I had just spoken with him on the telephone. At last I was sure that I would see him.

When I arrived at Stephen Spender's house Auden remarked on the fact that I was not wearing my dog collar. He told me that he had just been writing a haiku and that he was fascinated by the form. He showed me into the front room in which I had already had a glimpse of him from outside through the window. We sat down and proceeded into a long and most fascinating conversation in which, needless to say, I did most of the listening. He succeeded in putting me at my ease. Auden was of course quite old by this time but his brilliance as a talker was in no way diminished. Later on we went downstairs to Stephen Spender's kitchen and Auden made us both some tea.

I told Auden about Humphrey. I told him that I really wanted to know whether the poems are good or not. Would he please look at a selection that I had brought, I asked, and let me know his honest opinion. I emphasised that I didn't want him to be polite because we had met. I really wanted to know the truth of what he thought of Humphrey's poetry. Auden took the selection and said that he would study the poems soon and would write to let me know what he thought.

I then told him something about Humphrey as a person. Auden listened intently to all that I told him. I can't help wondering now whether Kek had talked about Humphrey to him. Perhaps he already knew a little about Humphrey the man, and perhaps he had some recollection of their one meeting at Shrewsbury in 1937. I showed Auden some photos of Humphrey that I had brought. He particularly liked one of my own favourite photos of Humphrey taken at Clayesmore in the 1950s – it shows him alfresco with a cigarette. He said of it: 'Yes, very nice.' I told Auden of Humphrey's return in his post-war years to his Christian faith. I told him how ill Humphrey had been and how sad his last years were. Auden asked me several questions about this. Did Humphrey know that he had cancer? I told Auden that he never said so and several of us wondered whether he knew. Auden said we have a right to know about our death. He thought that Humphrey possibly did know especially as he was a biologist. (I have since learnt that Humphrey did in fact know the nature of his illness.) He asked whether Humphrey went rather suddenly? For how long had there been signs? I told him of the years when Humphrey used to talk about an ulcer, then the haemorrhage and then the many years when he couldn't digest food properly or sleep properly.

We talked on many subjects. Auden was particularly interested in the fact that I was a cleric who was also interested in Freud and psycho-analysis. He talked about Freud and sex and the church for a long time. We talked too about Christian doctrine. Auden told me that he held to one heresy – that of Patri Passionism. Here he had significantly shifted from what is known to have been his view in earlier life. He said that he could not believe that the Father was impassive while the Son suffered. Following on from this we talked about the differences in the conception of God

Humphrey on holiday in later life.
Long school holidays enabled Humphrey to travel extensively and
to pursue his interests in music, literature and natural history.

the Father in the Old and in the New Testaments and of how the differences have been viewed by certain major writers.

What chiefly impressed me about Auden personally, as well as his extraordinary intelligence of course, was his goodness. I do not think that it has been sufficiently generally realised that in the deepest sense Auden was a very loveable and a very *good* man. I felt this very strongly indeed.

Stephen Spender joined us after we had been together for about two hours. I was able to take this opportunity to tell Spender how much his life and work also had meant to Humphrey and myself. After we had all talked together for a while, Auden told me that he was returning to America next day. I was due back in the parish. So I thanked Auden very much indeed for his help and Stephen Spender for his hospitality before I left. I reminded Auden one last time about Humphrey's poems and he reassured me that he would write to me.

One week later Auden's letter arrived. As I opened it to learn his verdict as far as I was concerned the future was in the balance. The letter was dated 2 November and it was sent from 77 St. Mark's Place, New York. He wrote 'I find the poems both moving and most original.'

I think I know how Humphrey would have felt to read these words that Auden had written. I felt the same. The dawn was coming. I was convinced that now Humphrey, one of the most remarkable teachers of his time, would have a testimony to be remembered by, and it would also be a testimony by which to remember our days together. I had been with the great poet teacher of the twentieth century – the chief fount of the same educational spring that flowed and pulsed into so many young lives through Humphrey and Kek. Auden liked Humphrey's poetry and he had told me so. The circle was complete. I felt that destiny had performed an edict and completed a necessary pronouncement. I knew that when the time was right I should have to record it.

Though I am not in a parish now, the Church of England has helped me to put my life together again and find its pattern and key. I hope that I have given good service to it. I now live in Cambridge.

There was something prophetic in the words that Humphrey wrote in Cambridge in 1932:

> Oh you rocking atoms and you tireless spheres. . . . When I am
> gone, when all of me is dust, let this my gift be given unto some
> little child who'll bear it purely till it flower. For flower it must.
> Lead on, lead on, you processes of life. I'll hold aloft the torch.

A flowering was coming to pass despite all that might have prevented it. I was that child who would present Humphrey's poems to the public.

The name that Humphrey wanted more than any other in this life was the name of Poet. It was not to be granted to him by any recognition during his lifetime. May he be rewarded now, though he is not here to see it, with this name of which we see him dreaming in a poem that he wrote in 1958:

> The rain has been falling on the tender earth
> And in my heart at least the seeds give birth
> To fairy flowers in silvered groves of leaves.
> The rain has stopped. Now tender the night breathes
> Of Summer and all the oceans where the waves
> Fall on a marble shore and cover graves
> Of untried poets who must perforce be dumb
> Until the Antique Trumpet bids them come
> With Laurel crown and humble lyre to place
> Their simple offering in the hand of Grace,
> Who trust and believe that as the healing rain
> Falls on their husks of hope, such patient blooms
> Will not expand and flower this time in vain.

A Bradfield tag:

> Ου γ αρτι νυν γε κ(με) γφες
> 'ᾷλλα ποτηζη τᾷντᾷ

> Spirit of beauty, high eternity –
> The wind blows outside, fashions change
> But such things live for ever.

Collected Poems of
Humphrey Moore

Humphrey photographed in the grounds at Clayesmore in about 1950.

CAMBRIDGE, 1932-1935

For Michael Paine

Across England speeds the communicating Angel,
Like a telephone message sent for anxious ears;
Love and steel, poised on pistons going
Through the rotting shires.

To Ludlow where they were lately quacked about
Drew my Conquistador, as a purpose plainly
Come home. To offended heart a curt proposal
And drawing of cords together.

You and I, the steel and the stone in the tower,
Were born to an urgent errand, explicitly bound
For an expert climb together, when darkness falls
Upon the lighted town.

And climbing by mountain path beside the sea,
Scanning for truth the eye of the innocent stranger,
We shall impugn a horizontal motive
In the direct answer.

For they may not hold, the economic fingers
Pulling the expensive tweed from the back;
Will not harm, will not arm, indeed they will armour us
Perfect, for indistinct.

Atomic love is sung for, forces, moves,
And therein bound is brevity and life –
Life on one life long sentence for praise, Michael,
A triumph in your life.

To the Child of Sofia, Rupert Brooke
Though that I dearly loved you was my plight

You have stepped over the fountain's spray
Into the clear and final light of day;
And I have felt your love through my life sing
Till hand and head and heart for the dead must bring
To you the holiest tribute; I followed green ways
To Cambridge – there were your flowers, your friends, your bright days.
Along the river I spent the hours for you,
Hungering strangely among those from whom you flew.
They seemed not to know any more the joy that late
From their side was gone. O child of pardon,
So free from hate, born for laughter and tears
As a god-gift burden; Earth and tide did not wait,
But swiftly moved you out from the blissful garden
To become the firstborn of Youth's immortal years.

Postscript
Oh Rupert, the Sonnet that I wrote for you
Was but a poor comment in my heart.
There is only a single element, fortune,
That in different ages has put us apart.

Sonnet
To Denis Cooper

When I hear people praise a mortal face,
And make of their delight some sorry show,
Then fierce I hold within my heart your praise,
Feeling unworded knowledge the best to know.
But when the fearful scimitar of night
Calls each of us to our secluded cell,
My torrent hopes unloose and drown me quite
With unspoke tears distraught in lover's hell.
And then I think of you to slumber fared,
Quiet and cool, and thinking nought of me,
Your breathing body by all passion spared.
And I declare your pure divinity:
I train with words these lips, which fain would kiss,
And learn to utter my secret unknown bliss.

Untitled

Mad, mock, merry, mow,
We beseech you to consider;
The river's all in flood now,
Beseech you to consider.

Mad, mock, merry, mow,
Lord Jesus was a liver;
No dead dog floating in the river;
Mad, mock, merry, mow,
The river's in the blood now
And Jesus in the river.
Float swan, fly scum,
Jerusalem is golden.
God must now in heaven hide
And never can grow bolder.

Mad, mock, merry, mow,
We beseech you to consider;
The river's all in flood now,
Beseech you to consider.

Cambridge:
The Backs in Fog

Still
Loom through the
Boom through the
Fog, water dripped logs
Kintinkling, besprinkling
The tension. . . In suspension. . .
Till tension is gone
Pst!
As through the fog
The pale green
Swathed stream
Pool tributes
    droop drip
       drops
Drained from the urgent
Stomata.

The Birds
First published in 'Contemporaries', Cambridge 1935

As chaffinch hoard in flock for Winter gain
And scavenge the hoar frost hedge, on ridge of lane;
Gathering round, their special instincts choose,
Submit, and jointly fight the close-knit Winter noose.

From clear bright fields and frozen sky they chase
Along the hard fringe of copse; the warming face
Of lonely fields receives their chattering skein
Of tangled flocks, that light, and collect to spread again.

Rising as one to fly over sun-crouched stubble,
Seems monarch their heart, and but brittle their trouble;
The pinch of close adversity joins them now
For finding, and fending off hunger, united in popular vow.

But when Spring stains the first mild air with tonic,
These temperate robber-bands fade, quickly to astonish
In couples; their tuneful contention now gives pleasure
To man, who, seeing no cause of strife in the weather,
As he richly seeks contact with earth in the health of his leisure,
Sees not that the sound is the song of the sameness in fellow and feather.

Untitled

Thorns dance in my flesh a jig
When the yellow moon is three parts gone:
And barn-owls flop their way among
Black coated clerks and silver swans.
Dark splinters of the night, you tread
With consideration round my bed:
While in my head, my stupid head,
A song of sorrow outs its groove:
Oh away sticky phantoms, for the road is still wet
With the blood of a goggled motorist,
Who three parts gone,
Who three parts gone,
Putting aside panting, at last
Asked for the moon.

Flowers about my Room
Written in his room in King's Parade at Cambridge

Flowers about my room,
You ponder green philosophy;
And all the richness of your amber vase
Reflects your youth – and childishness.
Rose meets rose, astonished lips;
Whose blush envisions
Deep in the recess of ruby folds
Such youthful purity.
While far off on the bleak
And mountain side of time
Your vague incipient air will leave
The eternal stream of life
That flows harmonious
Round the universe –
Until upon a pale and lordly night
The cold and bloodless moon sails forth,
Queen of the night and ruler of the clouds;
Old moon, older than tender flower,
Old when craters rose
And grey wolves howled;
Old when man-beast fought his elements,
From the scarred deep
Summoning magic to his aid –
She will then to the throbbing wellkin tides
Draw you around her fantastic course
Till she again give you birth and stimulus
Venting through you rich chords of mighty harmony.
And all who hear are shaken deep
By the primordial sigh
Your course's chord proclaims
From star to star –
Flowers about my room.

Two Poems for Basil Gough
I

Armed with arrows, free and fine,
To you I'd give no deception.

You by the love alone have smiled
That has my nettled ways beguiled.

Swift your startling eyes to find
And help unloose the rope of mind.

Keen your trembling lips to say
That you and I will soon away.

And last your heart has sympathised
And stormed with me hopes unrealized.

II

Leaves stationary, leaves still,
Once stirred by the wind.
Put your hand on the bark,
Caller of christian name;
All these obey your will.

Down mossy rides, by willows,
The wind is across the waters.
Feel it tell the lie to the reeds,
Deceiving them still.

They yet talk of Summer.
Summer is gone, with my faith
At your eye, Caller of christian name.
What is your will?

A love's impertinence, perhaps,
Unrepentant – Oh let's away,
The leaves have roared for you and me today
And the moss has drunk its fill.

Lovely the wood in Autumn
That bravely dances;
But your heart not mine advances;
And here your eye,
O Caller of christian name,
Stops it still.

Adverbial Fair

Fair
Infinitely fair;
Yet not infinitely
Simply definitely
Finitely
Fair, oh
Fair!

Fair hair
Infinitely fine fair hair;
Yet not infinitely
Simply definitely
Wholly matchlessly
Fine, your
Hair.

'Lean out of the window, Golden Hair.'
Oh sweet stupidity:
Your silk, silly,
Fine silky
Fair hair!

Sane Man's Song

Hark the blue-bell, hark the swallow.
Folk will chatter, worse will follow.
In a nightmare world of sorrow
Trees grow red with blood tomorrow.

If the she-wolf make you howl,
And the heron make you prowl;
Let the knot remain untied.
Trouble not, who have not died.

When the magic casket's closed,
And your throat by night's exposed,
Never trouble when you rise
To take the spider by surprise.

Handkerchief, handkerchief, why do you weep?
I answered them all in healthy sleep.
My fears by cleverness were bound,
Now innocence will sleep quite sound.

In a Garden. Evening
First Published in 'Poems Read At The Merry Meeting'

Evening steals her way among the shades.
Children all go in as twilight fades;
While shadows twist the dying light's grimace,
Fearlessly falls padded
Faint foot of moth on to my blanching page.

A stranger scent now moves over subtle lawns.
It stirs quiet leaves in Summer's transient breath,
And it stirs the great wheel of man, his hopes and fears;
Rousing the night-gods, uneasy;
Till silhouette describes a new event.

Three Quarters Strike

Three quarters strike
Old woven time
A slumbrous woman
Croons to her child
An echoed lullaby.
. . . But no child there
And quiet is fled –
My heart would stride the firmament
If I could see you, boy.
But you're away
(In London's solemn night).
You rest at the silver peal
Fiercely ebbing on sleep's cool tides
To the land where life's redealt.
And I am left
Like an old fool
Who stumbles on in the dark,
Stick poking through the grime
On time's dull track.

On First Reading D.H. Lawrence

Man you have been asleep;
Not seen the liar go down
Stealthily into the deep
Recess of the heart you own.

A man produced this voice
Which calls you to be man;
Where you, by other choice,
Had followed other plan,

Pleased with a light success.
O Grace defend such art
From artifice confessed;
Send lightning to the heart.

Now is the land new ploughed
And you must find new life
Whose growth in you will be crowned
With glory through the strife

And deeds of vital truth –
Let others themselves decide
If they will conjure wrath
To entertain their pride.

O proud sun-singer, cry
Of the one new birth that we need,
Which we must soon descry
Or perish with our creed.

SHREWSBURY 1937-1938

Sketched in a 1930s notebook
Shortly after meeting Frank McEachran

Is it now
That your savage eye seeing all
Has pierced into a garden
Brushed by enveloping moist leaves?
Is it now
That you pierce into this darkness
Seeking for a person?
Oh pencil-eye, pointing at me again,
I'll no longer dodge your accusation.
Yes I had retreated
From admiration,
Yes I was defeated
Turning from your eye away
In my febrile wincing, my negation.
But now it is Pencil-Eye:
I shall suck paps of Destiny again
And sow on paper
     the new seed forest
Forever waiting.

Is it now? goes the whisper,
Is it now for the break into life?

For Frank McEachran

Shining steel, forth came the rose on the garden;
And the messengers, the rain, the hail,
The dying leaf's circling cry,
Have found in the rose life's pardon.

A new foliage, a conqueror, brought forth in pain,
Will survive and breathe out the air of Summer.
Though the sap is doomed to fall short
Of the eager vein.

This is the individual life, sun's toy,
Who winds and warms again to set it flowing;
But flowers in the firmament on high
Are joy's watersheds, a people knowing.

The flower falling, the streams run down to dark,
We in our mortal graves repeat
The repetition of our fathers,
The old streams' talk.

But I tell you this, the individual cycle
Is the divine moment upon itself,
And where time's evolution struggles
The individual goes, the tragic birth
Is borne, gives impetus to others,
Raising the earth's god with the earth.

Now no earth-death lies upon your efforts,
Fear you no friction in the void;
The eternal cycle is itself roaring
In fire on time's unprinted track,
Perfect within itself,
While none destroying.

The Young People Stroll on the Common
or Don't Go too Far

We stroll out on the common
Under the look of blue:
God's blue eye in heaven
Is studying me and you.

The church bells in the belfry
Ring wide across the plain:
From the red sandstone tower
He is watching us again.

Watching every movement
As we strip to bathe and swim:
Though the flicker of a minnow's tail
Is no mystery to him.

By the stream we meet a viper
Lying jewelled in the sun –
The stream that set our queries
On their long fantastic run.

A thin white line of poplars
Marks the limit of our world,
In an ordered row, umbrellas,
Unbroken, trim and furled.

Beyond, paths lead on for ever
Into fairy worlds of charm:
He sees us grow romantic
From the window of a farm.

'Do you think we should be turning?
I had quite forgot the time.'
Up above he spreads a clock face
Which the creeping shadows climb.

If the heavens started dripping,
We should turn to hurry back,
Schooled to think it frightful
To be caught without a mac.

And should we wander further
On the bramble-covered common,
He would surely send a swallow
To investigate and summon.

His climate of approval
Is predictable and sure
When we know our limitations
And reject the unfamiliar.

Journey from Austria, 1936

Yes, the mountains are gone.
Flat England lies supreme;
And our irritation at heights now passed
Sinks fossil in geological stream.

Where were the banners?
The European banners?
We saw only oxen who pull the maize in
Plodding below halo of clouds' dream.

The ringed mountains were above,
Masters sheathed in mist;
And political doctrines were as distant
As any latest newsrag scream.

Central Europe, dry heart;
There the people plod unmindful,
Under the dictatorship of mountain gods,
Like hands over their mouths, it would seem.

To rouse such a people, some say,
Were merely to blunt a fine tool;
There is nature in the raw, if you like,
And man before rock a fool.

He must live separate,
The mountaineer without machinery;
His open lungs and honest brow
Resemble the true Parnassian, observe.

We can know for holiday
The service of his creed,
But the dumb moments, those we do not know,
Those we may never know.

For only the foolish tourist
Blesses himself with toil
To revel in rocks and stamp on spurs,
Above the forgetful map of valleys.

And when the tourist goes, the native
Shrugging his shoulders, hides
Beneath wood and stone, holds on,
A limpet who waits for the mountain tides.

His winter, it is the dark cave.
But to lure men out to the light
Is no purpose for the plain man with plans
Who would help the farm to reorganize.

He knows the sun can vanish
And the valley's eye lie shut;
When the shaded spurs come arching over
And bury in snow his heart.

Yes, we are well away from the mountains;
They are snarling now with Nietzsche's word:
'Go away from these rich flowering slopes,
And the eagle echoes you have never heard.'

Untitled

The clear morning wakes
Flowing blood in heart;
The sunbeam shakes
My dreams apart.

And I meet the people
Of this English life
With so lacking and feeble
A bond of faith.

No, our bond is
The mutual work; is test
Of life's streamline;
The compact machine
Recording best.

Our eyes are clear
Watching the needle rise,
As 'there' becomes 'here',
And hedges sweep skies.

The precise definition
Of the swinging bend
Is the sorrow of speed,
The slower course we need,
To which our nerves are tuned
And our hearts attend.

But this morning we go
On the straight, through the city,
And you and I laugh so
Forgetting pity.

Forgetting shame, forgetting lust,
We forge new links
Of cold clean air
That chills the dust.

This is morning;
In the evening, slowing down
To another level,
An unpredicted world
And different, we own.

You would have thought
We had driven a car,
But rather we had caught
Something from a star.

And applying it to blood
As we set to morning work,
We held above the flood
The tight strung reins of speed;
And on this full-throated deed,
Our day's life, turning
To its end of morning,
This song is agreed.

The Thirties Marxist to the Bourgeois

Elementary desire
Repels a swift cruel decision.
But decision, stainless,
Will steal away the fire.
Desire awaits revision.

For the finer fires
Of vision have defended
Fearful ashy pyres,
Which else desire
Had ended, self confined.

The iron grey hand
Has grown upon the sinew:
Strained no more in sorrow
Is the sinew free
From morrow of regret,
And grateful can desire
What inhabits keener air,
What is yet gained higher.

March

Blowing across the plain comes March
Again tormenting us with cold,
As cruel winds with hollow touch
Show Winter's not yet gorged her fill.

But through the blast of Winters old
Who have held dour man to home,
Pierce sunlit arrows imminent
With a birth of Summer on the hills.

The valley's spiring songs of gold
Rise in the blast from feathered wells;
Then tall as poplars sway, till dispersed
Like ghosts in the hurrying winds that throng.

Man and tree burgeon in windflower song,
And hedge scents float green on rivers of light.

Psyche

They in the valley
Thought Psyche was a butterfly.
We who have climbed to the stone heights
Turn and think otherwise.

We see the butterfly
No more hastening among the flowers.
We hear the loud wind raised in our soul
And the stonechat's cry.

The bird's cry drops stern
On the hot stones of our dismay;
They could allow a butterfly,
But we must turn our hearts to the heights
Where the stone winds betray.

Untitled

If the age of thunder declares
Your night lying conceit to the world's ears,
Spend salt on wound
And wind your unfinished romantic story
Up to the master sail of glory.
Or take fugitive action, fleeing the crowds
In their teeth; let them chew hard upon shrouds.

When the parson is proper at the moment,
Sow from the blazing firmament
Your justice integral.
Write for the great no seasoned lies
Consulting precedent; order your spies
For a bond of darkness against dumb days;
Make even the shadows of spleen speak of praise.

For the earth in which all will lie
Along with the monsters curled and dry,
Lets tumbling seed
Flame fire of life to light our fall.
Sir, no man's enemy, lift us all
From morbid will and dead convention,
Be prodigal for our new contention.

The Analyst

Into a powder of moments
Of bitter and differing taste
Goes the high song analysed,
The remembered moments' waste.

To the thousand shot down birds
There goes in the bracken jungle
The disintegrating thorn
Who, finding death, will grumble.

But this tight celibacy
Of fact on fact close packed
Will render us no new-born
Fancy-bright pinioned act.

The bird with the birds will sunder
In stars to the light song trees,
And the black locust moreover
Will profit by death's increase.

But night comes over the desert,
A scale may drop from the eyes,
The metaphysician may slumber,
A bird in the darkness arise.

It mounts, soars high and hovers
Above his desert grains:
The Phoenix risen above him
Burning in splendour his pains.

Untitled

This stone and tree solitude
Of moor and silent sedge
Bears away lightly
With lark song rising
All unfenced passions.
Fragile scorns and honour,
Washed clear away by acid,
Cease to beckon. Breath
Folded in the earth
Sings in hard streams
Which chortle and cascade
Down in gritty cadence
To the green hammock dreams
Of ordered endless fields.
Who look on this, know derision
By the desert machinery,
Soil and bog condition
Determining Flora;
A ruthless right construction
Is unfolded here
That has the name raw life.
Feel it tell the gentleman
His flattery of blood
'Man upon earth'.
Hear in the tilted strata
The trilobite rejoice
At the head of creation.
This is lotus solitude,
Absorbing independence;
Here is reproof whereby
Man's laughing emulous trend
To form the world anew
Under the exquisite passion
Of his creative hand, desists.
And here can nature comfort too,
Brought to heather bosom,
Those who discourage fight
Of motion, the shelter folk
Who, rubbing eyes, dream
Of the bed, the rock and stream.
But here also she goads

By a larger sustenance, the wind,
Man to turn again yet
To conquer gravitation.

Therein the romantic view,
Apparently so smiling,
Is the earth's wrest and the wind's goad
Testing creative force.

The Limitations of Classroom Biology

As purveyors of knowledge we risk to inoculate
With dead abstractions; and to raise an anti-bard
Enclosing life's lovely cageless flow
To define a set standard.

For the imposed relation is only a wilful dream,
Dreamt out of facts and senses' information.
We plan channels for infected floods forgetting
The torrents not yet begun.

So without any warning our pupils are then deceived
By a monstrous wall of water bearing them down;
In erecting barriers we're soon believed
Where a deluge of doubt would else drown.

But no – Arrowsmith, Gibson, Horrocks, Jones –
The swelling list I'm told to misinform –
In class I'm not speaking of life at all
But only its retail form.

The storm has not arisen when you will know
Angry old heads of the frustrate demons of learning
Like a cloud on the hill and a sense of failure
Disowned but in you burning.

So in truth please reject from your knowledge for examinations
The simplistic theories that are deemed to edify,
Though such science is the fashion and growing
To which we have to comply.

Look first to the heart, teacher, learners all;
It is dark. Turn straight your searchlight probing in;
Then take what the wise can offer: A mirror
For wonder, without and within.

Surrealist Prose Poem (Written at Shrewsbury in 1937)
'Out'
For G.B. Griffiths

What is ordinary in our thoughts is not ordinary tomorrow, is bizarre, is strange as a dream. Why should there be a defence, when the water has seeped into all the ditches? Why serve for comment, when one serves as an example, a perfect pawn in a marxist hand-made game of chess?

'We are the morning' cries the clock to the farmyard, 'We are the morning' toll the bells to the town. 'We are as great nations, We surge' cry the boulders as they blunder down the stream. Envied by the ferment, who acts and is gone to another engagement; they, the heavy ones, proceed, nosing their way like blue-nosed fishes through the weeds to the corner where the current is known to change.

'We have been seen', several cry. In they dash, into the weeds, Widdershins, crawling and sucking, waking muckado, and squirting each other with little songs of praise – 'Detected' ticks the old clock: and they all scurry for the shadow of the bathroom door –

Purify our sins, oh Lord – And they emerged clean, and went into a far distant country – 'Which', as the orchard observed to the apple, 'was not half so far off as they had speculated.'

Coming, porter – oh Lord, no not you, you're always turning up-Go and hold the patients feet – 'Murmur', cried the child, 'I don't understand all this'. 'None of us do', barked an old tombstone and hid his head in green ivy, green ivy for disgrace.

And as the sun went down behind the row of pine trees, a cry went up among the chickens, that Old Elsie was out pouring seeds on the land again – So we scuttled out of our favourite grubbing patches, and all jostled round to the rally. The speakers were 'my thumb', 'my idea of my thumb' and the Very Reverend Dean of Garner.

We clothed her for the great event in various but rather boring garments, and the Lord of posts blew a little tootle on a tin trumpet from the torch tree on the left; and the company fell in.

This went on till an inner circle train came: and then, of course, it was each man for himself – I sat opposite a fat broker, and his knees shook. Above his head was an advertisement for dentifrice, 'Personal Salvation' it began –

My head sunk, the needle crept down, we should only be 18000 now and
the fog belt lay below. Turning in wide circles, we pressed our way with
the fuselage shaking like a leaf in the winds – Michael oh bother sweated
in the hand of God. And the crowds were silent and in winter plumage.
'Overhead one looks in Autumn' so the line runs but below us lay moun-
tains, alps and shoulders straining up from the churn of earth foam – We
paused, was that one disinfected? to light a cigarette. 'That's mate I think'.
And the match was quickly blown, Seven a side when the ground's as
hard as that, 'Out'.

First Published in 'The Salopian'

When bright sea flakes dance under the prow,
And belts are tight up at the bow.
When toiling high we crest the peak
And flooding sky nor rest nor speak.
When slow the owl hoots in the night
And paths retrace their steps to light.
I willed it not the worm would say,
I willed it not this world at play,
But shortly they will come this way.

When silent cables lace the deep
And youthful fists are clenched in sleep.
When night winds ruffle curlews' heads
And angels tumble from their beds.
When silvery rain the sweet grass slakes
And wide across heaven the dawn song breaks.
I willed it not the worm would say,
I willed it not this world at play,
But shortly they will come this way.

At Mitchell's Fold Stone Circle
First Published in 'The Salopian'

Almost three hundred years had past
Before he found their sprinkled ring of stone:
Then a six month's hunger drove him back at last,
But this time not alone.

Since they had chosen well the place,
All round the changing features looked at him;
The brutal slant-cut stones, the whin-grown grass
And the horizon's rim.

Upon the floor of sacrifice
He stood alive: life seemed a static thing
When he saw in the other's uncaring lips and eyes
The men who built the ring.

First Published in 'The Salopian'

He watched the worm stagnation
    Creeping beneath the skin:
But he had left the bedside
    Before the rot set in.

The light beyond the shadows
    Was what he went to prove:
Now raise him a graven head-stone
    And write: 'He died for love'.

He stopped the moving pencil
    Before the downward curve,
While I live on who admire him
    And haven't got the nerve.

Unititled

Yours is my gravity,
The cause you own,
Who with your graven beauty
Will have me in stone.
Cold with the stone to lie
While you depart
And ease your stargiven fancy
In another heart.

Untitled

O friend, that you should turn
    for a love that else was lost;
O grecian, that you choose
    to turn again and cleave
To a distant summer vow
    of an unforgotten past!
How can such things be?

The Forest

The minute sibilance of the goldcrest
Falls on the forest ear; and between
Straight pines, like strings to the wind's
Chord, falls to the leafy quiet
A whispering on the ivy carpet.
Through brake in the shadows of the sun
Grisly moving, the shy deer jerk
Then stop to pause: and in that pause,
As in the peace, between the straight
Tall spears of the sun's knowledge,
Between the earth shafts, is a certain
Watching – the forest eyes that come
Between the shadow and the trees,
Between the tree and tree; no one ever
Sees where they may be: but, always,
A short distance away are eyes;
And a strange bird's heavy fluttering
Dissolves away into watchful silence.

To a Boy (in imitation of the Greek Anthology)

I, boy, to best inspired by your fresh hand;
You shape and knead the lovely day of youth
And wisdom scorn.
And then you turn your slender glance
Keeping your lover to the road that leads through spring.

Untitled

Fiery traveller, the cold unfriendly wind
Is stilled in your eye. The groaning of the spheres
Encompasses your hidden further wish
And through suffering your fire of faith endures.
Endure well, lad; for all's not over yet.
Last out now well; Oh well last out a stay
Till summer calls from the cuckoo-burthened wood.
Call then lad too. I'll answer you on that day;
Led to your lips by an antique warbling flute.
Then if we perchance should meet again,
With woodland balm we'll kiss lad and rest mute;
Answering the wild flood that calls in every vein
As the heavy bee about his business moves
And the leaflets stir with the scent of summer loves.

Anguish
For Dennis Russell

Bound on a stubborn wheel of weeks and days,
I hate the malady that will not go,
Nor let the hoped-for hope as yet erase
The taunting solemn features that I know.
Since memory is cruel, remembers part
And will not add the rest, the immortal time
Of meeting; such eternity can't last;
And now for ever stops us being sublime.
For so I'm tortured thus withheld by fate
From beauty that is offered me each day –
The forerunner of every heavenly state.
His merry look I no more can obey
This morning, than I could when first he read
A signaller's code of fire and answered.

Two Sonnets for John Day

I

At peace, at ease, the tide of grief has swung
To its low ebb; the waters steal by slow;
Slow are the eddies of my sighs; but young,
Young is the way of those sleeping eyes I know.
The night has taken us both now separately,
Laying aside our ills and cares awhile,
Has left you serenely sleeping, and helpfully
Shown me where curled up asleep you smile.
This the assurance that I asked, this calm
Has followed after jealousy, alarm;
If no one else has proved to be more true
Then happier I sleep forgot by you.
Tomorrow let your enquiring way depart
To storm the cliff face of every new found heart.

II

From dark, cold dawn and pestilence you steered
My shrivelled dream of every human need
And quickened all my senses near to you
To flower again upon an open road.
I travelled with you through the hills; you spoke
But rarely as we climbed each gradient,
Dipped and then fell upon the massive plains
With the open roar of an endless time's assent.
We drove withdrawn from every lesser tie,
Attentive to the hedge, the wheeling sky;
Till evening drew us to the one sure hold
Where night with her resigning gesture bold
Would gaily close our eyes, ere we moved on,
Drifting our voyage and our oblivion.

Simple and Hard
For D.T.R. (mountaineer)

Simple to rise
From shoulder to peak;
And to peer with surmise
Where sharp screes fall
Away under feet
Into cavernous mists
Which echo your call.
Simple to lose
Your way and to fall
From crevice and schist
Into the mist,
Or from sandstone and shales
Into turbulent gales.
And simplest of all
Whatever befall
To follow your nose.

Hard it is only
To hear yourself speak,
To think of your safety
And not try that peak
Without compass or map
Or someone 'who knows'.
For if any mishap
Should mishappen, who knows? –
But for pegs and packs
And piton and axe,
You'd be eaten by crows
Or buried by snows,
And not be able
To go after
That rarest rock rose –
Or even (far worse)
Be rescued by Pros!

To D.M.G.

As the lightning from the dark mountain
Now flashes close, now dwindles in its order;
So your vision lingers through my heart,
Now blows strong, now idles on the water.

The waves bear in your message, morning's smile
Carried in on a lazy flood of foam,
That closer moves and closer, then hapless turns
Leaving my senses colder for a while.

For you are untamed substance, my delight,
And I receive you rarely when I will;
Though when I do there's order everywhere.
As sentinel my humour aids your flight.
And, all in all, how savage is my mood.
Does the wild wind blow so irrational and rude?

London at Night

Here is the wriggling worm intelligence
In the deep-at-heart spiritual rot.
Here are the two feet spanking the pavement
Gone on down to the crowded station
To wait on platforms where a brisk waking echo
Heralds the shining glare-glory train;
Here, with the pain's ascent, the whined
Complaint draws out, rocks, bumps, confides;
And the strap hangers cling in the empty corse
Like parasites in a lighted coelom.
Burn through the embryo darkness, night –
London, the gay advertisement;
The world prostitute on parlous walk,
Painted up to journey the streets as a magus,
Splashed black round scarlet, a sunlight trough –
In the neon nightglare the throbbing taxis
Hurry impeccably forward on thrust
By the glittering faces of the crowds.

By a Dark Loch on a Dark Morning

Farewell Loch Scridain;
Never perhaps again
Will I see the dark rain pour
In glistening cascades down the scaly slopes
Of your volcanic shore.

The barren hills abide;
But I cannot provide
That certain future which bears
One ever northward scattering geese again
In swiftly flying years.

My bed may never be
Set in such scenery;
Nor passive eye reflect
The even shades of memory folded back
To calmly recollect.

Silk waters scowling dark
Repeat no waking spark
Of morning light from me,
Who by your placid waters roaring run
To darker eternity.

Farewell Loch Scridain;
Never perhaps again
Beside your muttering shore
Will I throw hoody's shadow mirth or mark
Nor dangle eagle claw.

Untitled

Observe the birdman
Watching with glasses
The fluky amethystine bird
Of chance who never passes
Twice in the longrun day,
He is catching the sabbath morning.

Study the dance of the balletomanes
Who, seen from above,
In the city of grief and hunger
Make formal gestures
On a frozen stage.

Turn wheel with traffic stream
Around the vicinity without
The great halls where the concerts play
To our much admired audiences,
While the beggars pass by each day.

Then skim with a pigeon
Up to a ledge of St. Paul's.
Review religion's rituals.
When you hear the vestry whisper
And the loud Amen,
Stones will be turned in the wall
And blinking the people will crawl out
Into the summer sun.

The fine adjustment is their major care
Who would live free of interference;
They take their given pauses from the air
And synchronize experience.

Untitled

Can I ignore the blank leaderless passage
Within me whirling,
The convolute chaos? Unable
Am I to consider unable
Chaos in relation to chaos
The downsliding of my close-fingered class,
Within the heart subconscious.
No, ring wide the bell
The curtain is called
The curtain is down.
Gone is the pitcher
Shattered the well
Of dream, and life's lovely lease:
In 'death's dream kingdom'.

Untitled

Eight of them, eight of them answered the bell,
And death's smile stole from face to face;
Eight of them, eight of them knew it so well,
The attempted grimace.

In the hall the showering fell
Of a shadow of old ghosts
Fell on them there;
On the hall table, the showering fell
Ghostly fell on them there;
The shower bath shower fire free fire sparkle
Led from the crackle-dark crimson spurt
To the unvoiced oracle.
Wishing them well, Wishing them well,
Truly, truly, better to shut
                hurry to shut the gate
Before
Too late is the answer.

For A.J. Pearce
A boy in the Sixth Form at Shrewsbury School

O sleep soon comes upon us, Pearce,
Our nose is on the wheel –
Then the tiny playmate creeps to us
To ask us what we feel.

Though oft I eat the cardboard rue,
Woe which I once would eschew,
And sometimes sit upon the top
Of beanstalks made of glue,

I feel a Saviour's ecstasy,
A cabbage's broad aim;
I search a lunar heresy;
Examine a pail for shame.

Sin and subsidies subsided
In the nurseries vast empire,
And emphatically most were soon
Corrupted in desire.

For servants with obsequious might
Once stretched the cloth before us,
And laboured daily all the night
To do their utmost for us.

But the years clang over, sliding doors,
So Pearce, be no postponer;
Now the wild sea waits and waves for us,
That collar but names its owner.

For soon the sea with carrion claws
And soon the mariner laughing;
And soon the grandmamma haw-haws
Her paltry little coffin.

Fly sin resolved, fly hate unknown,
Fly power beyond recall,
As the caged bird when once uncaged
Will not look back at all.

O Pearce, young Pearce, the earth's still young
That you're let loose upon;
So dance while the dawn's courageous then
Dance on till the dusk is done.

Summer Holiday, Scotland 1937, with Basil Gough

I take a clue from you, my friend,
To deal with this time we cannot mend;
Inimical to vagueness and to self;
Hating both poverty and wealth;
Owning solitariness her charm;
Loathing and fearing romantic balm
With a fierce single hatred, directed chill
Against drowsy moisture that saps the will,
Making need a distance and distance a dream.
Now we tramp together by the highland stream
Ticking over. The heather smells good.
We've brought the glasses; we've packed the food,
For a long day's trudging – Why so poor fools?
We pore on the sunlight, the sun scorns our rules,
He probably doesn't think us of much worth
With all that human folly has brought to birth,
As we listen to echoes on wirelesses at eve
Of awful bombs we still needn't believe
As they're not yet too close; our season, we say,
Won't start for at least one more holiday.
So we scribble our postcards to favourite aunts,
Our feelings gone underground, fearing advance;
We hitch up our rucksacks, fondle a pet,
What we're afraid to consider we decide to forget.
Before Summer is over and the days are grown short,
Like horsefly, like mayfly, we'll frolic till caught.

Autumn 1937

Alone the oak holds leaves above our head;
Autumn is down at heel; we shuffle through;
Sludge that was once green glory now lies dead.
Decay seems all that the diary points forward to.
Our plans are short; waters dark in wall
Meet our eye. If we peer beyond weekly events
The cinemas on Saturday night seem all
Suddenly more attractive experiments.
The snail is asleep. Gone are the birds who sing.
Gone are the animals to warmth or sleep.
Draining our car radiators now we bring
A mechanical acquiescence so as to keep
True to the season's temper: A respectful mark
Of the native ancestor in us who fears the dark.

The Naval Review at Spithead, 1937

Oh look! Between the sullen straits they lie,
Stretched out line upon line of broken power,
Placid, to receive applause and nervous praise,
These shining lethal threats of steel and iron,
Expensive wolves, that are fun for admirals.
Oh, I approve. Who could do otherwise,
When all the navy's ships are so arranged,
By catalogue, and sailor's sweated pride.
These flags, these guns, the tossing sea so brave,
Blue with the white flecked foam, the crowd's glad din,
And town holiday, make this the perfect pageant;
The people believe they see the King's right arm,
History, or something like – The lucky poor,
To keep so out of date a fleet, for war.

POEMS WRITTEN IN WARTIME, 1939-1945

The Pleasures of Drink
First Published in *The Clayesmorian*

I pressed on the bell at a neutral hotel –
'A stormtrooper's knockout' I cried;
For this Nazi aggression
To Czech my depression
Was certainly one to be tried.

I added two doubles for troubles like Goebbels,
It's his fault the papers are boring –
Full of pictures of sick 'uns –
And I ordered three quick 'uns
To get rid of my vision of Goering.

Then Hungary once more, but not quite on the floor,
I decided to Haifa refresher,
And Benesh my jitters
In pink gin and bitters –
Could anything really be besher?

'Ale Munich' I cried, and thus ailing inside,
I began to Silese on the Polish,
And fell on my Hamm
With a Han'over slam,
Now there isn't much more to demolish.

Army Training Camp, Trowbridge, 1941

To the North, to the South, to the West and the East
The searchlights snap their empty claws;
And far away beyond the earth
The lonely missionaries travel,
Weary above the world they walk
Rubbing the wheel of empty space
To bring the unfortunate bitter unction.

Our troops encamped in the West Country town
Have had various ways devised for their employ;
There are organised ways of marking time
As atom on atom is duly piled.
The eager anticipating young who serve
To fight for the vital pattern of freedom
Have their angered and injured faces forced
Into the stupidity and waiting about
While the bombers menace over the earth.

Here are the errors crouched in the dark
Who whimper for our approbation.
They are past the sentries who are doing their job;
They are into our hearts; we are caught in their trap.
And no longer good are the longings of statesmen;
No longer good the ideals in the storehouse;
They have waited too long in the idle storehouse,
Abandoned projects through lack of funds.
The successful Caesars are rising up;
Who powerfully peer at the forming cloud
To divine some fully successful conclusion
Of so many movements of men and steel.

The trees are now discarding their goodness,
Throwing down leaves in disapproval
Like biscuits the damp has got into-gone rotten.
While petrol is thought out and everywhere felt for,
Desired as the smile that is sought among strangers.

Our ways, our wealth and superabundance
In a close-column jolts slowly forward,
With minor repercussions that are tiresome
For the individual with too keen a sorrow –
The noise kicked up from unhappiness,
Jolting of trucks on the line in the morning,
Sum total of all our discrepancy.

Number 4, A.A. Site
First Published in *The Clayesmorian*

I climbed up Hambledon Hill,
I met a Iwerne shepherd driving sheep;
Said Bill Hatchett, 'How's the war?'
I said, 'That'll keep.

Tell me how's the countryside,
Hills and dales that used to be,
High and low and far and wide –
Will they wait for me?

When the war has had its fill,
Will the hounds be on the scent,
Will the fox be on the hill,
Tell me is it meant?

Will the huntsman leap the ditch,
And Iwerne rabbits still be white;
Will again the dog and bitch
Salute the morning light?

Sun and water, sail and mast,
Riding boots and Turner's hack;
God knows when I saw them last –
Shall we get them back?

Nights when the butty lamp burns low,
Doubtingly my spirit broods,
Lest the remembered things should go,
Like starlings from Iwerne woods.

I love the Inn. I love the thatch.
I love the sunshine and the rain –
Red blinds and the door on the latch,
Will those times come again?'

'It'll finish, never fear,
Killing and much else beside.
Green lawns and English beer
And Summer skies'll bide.

Bide till the foe is beat,
The boys are back and folk again are free,
And me and you'll be here to see it.
Never fear.' Said he.

Grabberwochy

'Twas Danzig and the swastikoves
Did heil and hittle in the reich;
All nazi were the lindengroves
And the neuraths julestreich.

'Beware the Grabberwoch, my son!
The plans that spawn, the plots that hatch!
Beware the Judah purge, and shun
The fuhrious Bundersnatch!'

He took the aryan hordes in hand:
Long time the gestapo he taught
Then rested he by the Baltic sea
And stood awhile in thought.

And as a Polish oath they swore,
The Grabberwoch, with eyes aflame,
Came Goring down the corridor,
And goebelled as it came.

Ein Zwei! Ein Zwei! One in the eye
For Polska folk alas, alack!
He left them in dread, then as their head
He came meinkampfing back.

'And hast thou ta'en thy lebensraum?
Come to my arms my rhenish boy!
O grabjous day! Sing heil! heilley!'
He wortled in his joy.

'Twas Danzig and the swastikoves
Did heil and hittle in the reich;
All nazi were the lindengroves,
And the neuraths julestreich.

Wartime Leaves from a Naturalist's Notebook, 1941

Coming up wooden steps with the dark day
Still dark upon Trowbridge, stone and shut window;
Within, lights, stirrings, a multitude of equipment,
Rifles to be cleaned in a lighted attic,

And a period elapsed, a period of care.
Impartial the weak rain, drilling skies,
Skies with no sorrow, hills and drenched woods
With no dread of tomorrow, no fearful fancies.
For us the despair of uncompromising dawns,
On our faces a gleam
Of unnatural determination.

Seasons unfold to our world of choice,
Which choice so chosen spills down
Upon all we half-treasured;
As the walls of a coffer house rent apart,
Doors torn wide exposing our treasure,
A few occasional aspirations,
A number of the accessories of comfort,
A few books and ideas on a shelf.
Our decision taken, the lobster fixes his claws;
All contribute without their knowledge;
As hundreds of feathery medusae
Sinking to a lower level as if to press
Level fingers on a counter, creating a need
Or dashing away a previous distribution.

The creatures have all come to know their arrangements.
The dry blind pupae stirring in the dark;
The young delicate thallus, spot of green,
So important, hiding itself away;
The flattened nymph clinging to the boulder,
An age in its hungry eyes;
And the careful construction piece by piece of a caddis' world;
All move in a measurable, wondrous and positive dimension.

The living shoots will take up their new positions
As if accustomed to having their way,
Their various adjustments have come to be accepted.
With all such minute delicate testimony before our eyes,
For us the plans of reform are laid aside once more,
The financiers refusing to budge.
We build alone with shock assault of headlines,
Platforms, slogans, conduct for forty millions;
And, as we wait for the sudden moment of campaign,
We blindly obey all the schedules.

Charlton Hill, Shropshire, 1941

Through the summer heart descends
The Pipit's parachuting song;
Sleepy summer's hour extends
The pardon of her paragon.

Inviolable, shy to us,
The lark is summoned to the sky;
And the nodding grass inclines
To act the wind's inconstancy.

Foxglove spires and shady trees
Move on the background of the hills;
For peace and peace and peace are these
Upon the major world of ills.

To strive to brightness, steers the heart,
Shade and beauty to resolve,
While aircraft drone above, apart,
Intent as insects to evolve,

Beyond the parallels of hate.
They deal alone in deathly trial,
Assist the European fate
With our unnatural denial.

Yes, the shot in Wrekin wood
Is blind like theirs, as the crushed egg
Lies in the hot and sweaty hand,
Too late to signify regret.

Now natural the herb alone
Presents earth's argument as final;
Beauty blossoms near the bone,
Her early enduring duty, spinal.

Through the summer heart descends
The Pipit's parachuting song;
Now resolute, the earth attends,
And shields her safe where blossoms throng.

And the Beasts all Good
Some Wartime Observations of a Natural Historian

It is to climb inwards down hundreds of steps
To come to animals' world. At many grades we pause;
And we realize that our often all-too-human
Explanations of their lives are not enough;
We need impartial vision to unravel the truth.
We will consider, for example, the milk meek looks of deer;
They woo our attention to consider their lives,
The references in their frame of world.
How far, how much, of what kind is their illusion,
Whose eyes descry no colour in the tinted miles,
The purple heather and the grey sodden rock?
To them come important announcements by winds,
Little winds sharply cornering,
Who stream down corrie, who flutter the bents.
These, when the air's moisture every minute
Switches like lids across liquid eye,
Bear news of olfactory tidings.
The forefeet grow rigid, the neck stretched high,
Like spirits of an ancient world they loom,
With pricked ears, still, as warriors on outposts.
Then, to trot back over the shoulder
Out of sight with their information
Taken away from us; they quit the stage.

We will leave their world, though still as strangers,
And go through bracken across moist peat
Where the pale heather Tetralix and the squashy Sphagnum
Live with yellow spike beacons of the bog asphodel,
Where wind socks of cotton-grass, Eriophorum, are blowing for danger,
And where crawling on ground the Sundew spreads pretty fingers
Sticky beneath the noon, red and glistening
Alone in the silence of a usually neglected strath.
These quiet places have their own music
In the wandering hum of a bee visiting heather bells,
And in the hot wing beat of lonely butterflies,
Skippers, fritillaries, and the dark-eyed argus,
Who chase for ever beneath June sun,
Fluttering and veering with merry dashes;
They play round some hillock, or glide up to a thistle restaurant,
Clutching grass with light feet, when clouds appear.

Like them it is hard not to dally in the quiet places.
But the pale beady leaves of butterwort in bilious sweat
And the purple fragments of forgotten lava
Lying in the burn are a warning.
A dark wing floats in the sun stretched heaven,
A shadow to send pipits lisping and chasing;
A spider crawls out from the roots of the heather,
Trundles out on her web; millions of stomata
Are quietly breathing; and the hour is held in pause.

So let us move far on, to where the small waves
From the Hebrides and further beyond that
Lap round the dark Fucus, the glistening weed with a secret;
There the shore haunting Sandpiper whistles with urgent emotion
A challenge to each wave that comes.
A crowd of Oyster-catchers will fall to such piping
For half an hour maybe. It has often been noticed;
So why should I make a simile
To attempt to anchor such to your mind, dear reader?
More likely you would rather know why it is
That these birds in such desolate places
With the painted, deserted mountain and moorland
Stretching forever behind them,
With the silent vacancy of the ruffling sea
Like a blue empty cloth flung out before them,
Why, where no humans, no hostile disturbance
Comes to them, these birds should so fall to piping,
Whistling and echoing up the still afternoon.

Well there is a possible reason or so it would seem,
Though we are only beginning to get near to the idea;
That is, that when some birds gather together
And start hollering or dancing in a public frenzy
One thing leads on to another and little by little
There is built up a threshold of excitement,
Which apparently is necessary
For successful breeding and the nest making ritual.
And the louder the noise down on wind blown skerries,
The sooner will appear high up on the beach
The pointed eggs. I imagine you have heard how
Most of the flock, black and white, will be huddled
The red bills silent, each still on one rigid coral leg,
When perhaps only one or a pair are awake,

Who then sweep out to where the laced foam sinks
Between rocks, and rises with each incoming billow;
They'll circle screaming above the changing surge,
Piping like the damned, to make one more circuit
And then sail up, stall and settle,
Their red toes clutching the barnacled surface.
With a shake of their wings they'll continue to scream,
And the whole flock opening their probing mandibles
Will shout down the airway their scarlet screams;
You would think the whole company were being murdered,
But the piping falls on a vacant afternoon,
Where no step of danger has advanced to their shore.
Their excitement may lead them to leave,
With a sudden hush to swing off and sweep
Round the bay. In fantastic and graceful evolutions
Turning first white, then black, in a well timed squadron
To fleck out quite distant into the blue
And then to ghost in with silent rush of wings,
Clamour for landing space, and pipe again.
Such action is common before break up of flocks;
And even when pairs have assorted their territory,
They may meet with non-breeders and let out their calling;
A haunted alarm heard in neighbouring bays.
I would point to no easy explanation
Which pulls it all back to human terms.
If we follow such action and steep ourselves in it,
We move inch by inch nearer to another world.
And the first human thought that obtrudes here by giving
Some too easy conclusion leading back to ourselves,
Will frighten the animals out of their world
And we will see but sea-birds, wheeling and turning,
Background to our emotion, our holiday scene.

But to go through Environment, the new magic door,
Is the new transformation, where one can step
Free of our world. One can step into strange glass seas,
Hear the crackle of crystals, step between atoms.
You may now if you make yourself small enough
Look up to see Celandine towering above you
And tall straight spears of green forest grass.
For there are two knowledges of nature
And either is there for a choice:
You can draw in all trinkets and number and measure them,

The bleached bone rests on the black cotton wool,
Or the germ spores are counted by rough estimation,
Leading to a reduction in the incidence of fever;
And there is the agitated warehouse manager
Who wants all larvae destroyed at all cost;
And the patient expert selfing the grasses,
Dreaming of an appreciable rise in the graph.
All these to their point; but it's not these I speak of,
Though their work it is true will outlast their tired bodies.
But others can go through environment into a different world.
It's not wise to refer to them as lovers of nature,
Since in nature there is much that's unlovely
And a great deal goes on that should normally scare us.
The giant female spider descends on her husband,
The graceful winged tern will brood a tobacco-tin,
And the finest of deer will be crawling with vermin.
There are savage events under upturned stones
And in dark caves evil things flutter towards us.
But these are all nature's angles or corners.
What makes more men fearful of nature
Are the silent boulders encrusted with lichen,
The desolate areas of similar flora,
The long stretches of gravel and the brittle stars
Covering the lap of the ocean shelf.
It is this very inhuman element in nature
That makes some men shy away from her;
Shunning the crags, the precipices and the lonely places,
They slip out in saloon cars and streak through forests
To stop for lunch near a friendly stream.
The long ranks of larch woods in the main they neglect,
And to them the thought of the thousand split boulders,
The acres of grass tossing seed to the wind,
Or the warbler incessantly shivering his song,
Would cloud their horizon with need for home.

To enter the beasts' world leave sentiment behind you.
And don't plunge downstairs to grab some evidence
And then scuttle back to the well lighted lab.
You must sham stiller than nightjar on bough,
And possibly consent to forget your own eyes
Until carried on by the beasts' way of living;
You must unclasp the fingers clutching so hard
To your own species self, the theories you own,
And then perhaps for a moment comes vision.

Sea Elegy
For Peter Paine

Slowly tumultuous wave
Drop on his ocean grave;
Your white seething resolve
And ambitious fury dissolve.
Snarling foam line recede
From the pitched up desolate deed
Of destruction strewing your shore.
Eye wind whistle no more
In the teeth of the rusting groin,
Salt spiked with spray flowers blown.
To the burthen of the sea
Now echo my elegy.
Vainly I ask this accord
Through love's tremulous word,
Uttering an appeal
Neither wind nor sea can feel.
For below his flesh grey lid
Now scale worm and polyp slide;
And in the sealed water's moil
Where zoophyte slowly uncoil,
Fanning encrusted shell
Beneath the oblivious swell,
Corrosion ravens the world
Where his untried flag was furled.
Of the best that the sea has taken,
Its beauty now forsaken,
Of the gladness his friends would share
In his youthful promise fair,
Of all the fresh joys he knew
Which time's vivid moments grew,
But an uprooted shredded wrack
Will float and wander back,
Now cast up here as I grieve
Where the nagging waters heave
And strike with unpitying hand
On the gnarled and gravel strand.

Gulls over dipping wave
Indifferent to his grave
Loitering scan the waste

For any dead morsel to taste.
Quenched now to Winter's grey
Earth's lolling light will stay;
As the waves and days return
But to silt his funeral urn;
And dull grey sand to bury
What once was blithe and merry.

Loss

Give over winds nor grieve
His passing, for much fame
Will spread with famished Spring
Sparkling to shed his name;
Or morning siege will bring
Him live to every leaf.

Steep your fresh eyes with Spring,
Sip too the fluid dawn;
For his dead eyes do see
From hollow oaks outworn;
Will stir in pools now free
His spirit, pulse or spring.

Grip cleaner season's grasp,
Grapple to self each lean
Lithe shoot of grieving earth
That wears his worth in green;
For floats on the dewy air
Who gave to earth at last.

Sorrow no more for sure
The floods and thaws of Spring;
Bring, bury deep below
Many a lovely thing
That of his own will linger; go
Down for undying Spring.

To an Arab Boy in Aran

O sure-footed boy, whose breath is the wind
To nature pledged, you are guardian
Of youth for a world who youth laid by.
Foresworn to fight unceasingly
For livelihood;
Go to your business, go, go out
Away from us forgetting.
And on the cliffs, live hard
And die, folded at length
In the arms of Neptune, he your
Greatest love and your defender.

And then at length your memory may
Join the waves to stir and heal
In the unquiet heart
Of an old onlooker.

Desert Palm Trees and Wind

Lean out as hardened preachers to the wind,
Swaying your rigid doctrines above the air,
Above the oil, odour and dust of circumstance.
Put out your hands in supplication
Above the columns of your husky stems,
Your rugged birthright, hard as nails.
Compact the substance of your argument
And firmly armed with spikes against the world,
A leathery fibrous resistance
To all change, all weather, and all going forward.
Impervious your doctrine, for after all
You are there because you have grabbed water and striven
With each of your tall striving neighbours.
You cannot bow and smile;
You are the desert warriors
Who have fought the hot miserly sands.
Your mouths have been filled with the dust-storm;
And you have glared back balefully in the eye of the sun.
Siliceous, intransigent, you wave your plumes
Rigid above the Moslem world, your world.

You have known other doctrines but these have departed
As the first good downpour into the sand.
The sons of the Prophet have at last learnt their lesson,
Unbowing they have fashioned a life from their doctrine.
After this triumph, they have no more to say.
The birds call from your minarets
With a metallic chatter. Your gifts are few;
Fallen to the ground they soon grow dry and brittle,
As if you half regret your offering
To a generation that will not know of your hardship.
You are lean and niggardly old men of the desert.
You live high in your pride and with a fine contempt for all others
Who are not lean, niggardly and hidebound as you yourselves are.
You shake your manes in the evening sunlight.
You flourish your crown and coxcomb
Independent beneath the stars.

                                        Kut-Al-Imara

Music in Wartime

Music in wartime;
Pinched in between the wavelengths
The orchestra's beautiful libation
Is poured out on the ether.
And Beethoven's gift of phrase
From the grave adagios
Is like a comforting arm on the air,
But of no avail.
The armies clash in the ether;
Arms swinging in the dark
Land hopeless blows on truth.
War's tyranny grips all.
The music steals and rises
In my veins
Like the scent of dried grasses
From forgotten Summer pastures.
The phrases grow in my veins,
As the gentle voices of those
Who made this music for others
Pour out for others now their consolations

Which are scarcely listened to
And cannot properly be known.
The slick announcers puff out to the future
Their stale communiques.
But how long are the values forgotten
And the music unremembered?
How long will the valley of truth
Be no longer frequented
Where children sought with their questions
The long heritage?
The music steals over the ether
Forgotten, unheeded, back into the air;
As a traveller returned to his valley,
Out on his own into space, unwanted.
Out into the air the music
Flows away from the bows and the woodwind.
But it reaches us who are listening,
Pouring into our hearts through the weak spots;
Joining their truth and their sorrow
(Beethoven, Brahms, Mozart, Handel)
To our truths and to our sorrows.
There should be no music in wartime.

Kut-Al-Imara

CLAYESMORE HARVEST
1946-1966

Hellas 1947

This never forget:
That in Greece there is no dying.
Regrets may linger
In the hot spiny valleys
Where the pine trees fasten
Round dry rock fragments,
The Regrets may last
From strife of the past,
But there is no dying.
Never forget either if you visit
The hot dry hillsides,
Now tenanted by lizards
And a few soil-scratching peasants:
That Beauty is secret;
It is not a shell
Which careless fingers
May pull apart.
If you visit those islands,
Go alone,
As only one who is alone
Can hear and feel distinctly
Old things and past things –
Behind the breeze in the pines,
Behind the small scuttling movements
Of insect and rodent,
Behind the blazing flowers
And the incense of xerophitic shrubs,
Behind the still shadows
On the parched lions of Delos –
Old things and past things.
They lie around for us to tread on.
But do not forget
That there is no dying,
Never a death in Greece.
And the snatch of imagined music

Broken by waves on the marble shore,
The call of migrating curlews
And the names of the islands,
Mykonos, Delos, Thera, Zante,
Have been there continuously
With the surf continuously.

In Europe there are too many deaths
We are weighed down by deaths
And the rain and the wind
And the chill scattering of leaves
Make our own sad testimony
Of drift, dark drift and death.
There are countries of legends,
Climates and ranges of myth.
In the north we live in the shadows of mountains,
Returning at night and deeply sleeping.
But in Hellas,
Where the open eyed sun like a flower
Drinks the last drops from the dusty earth,
Where the people say 'Yes',
In Hellas there is gladness and brightness,
Gladness and foam white brightness.
The Gods were no fools
Choosing dry soils and gentle wave-rocked sleep.
For who slept in the arms of old ocean
Could never die.

And the Greeks
What shall we say of them?
They are noble and quarrelsome,
Greedy for corn and small town politics,
But they too could not die,
Once set foot on those islands;
For the Gods were there first
And have changed them.
It is a land of legend –
Legend greater than all history,
Deeply settled, and pervading
All the long eras of petty strife.
You may go there, if you like, and draw up statistics –
On the impact of Western commerce,
On the total export of raisins,

On the breakdown of civil transport,
And the spread of schools, sanitation,
On the depth of their bays, on their morals,
On the number of political dailies
Snatched and scanned in the smallest cafes
From Peiraeus to Ioannina,
And the usual mountain gangsters –
But this is not new
And this is not why people have lived there,
In a peninsula of trickling tracing streams
Linking their way through a limestone land
That juts into a scarf of amethyst sea
With a misty web of islands
Carelessly scattered;
They live there because
Their days are light
And their sleep is gentle,
Gentle with dreams,
And the music of legends
That have never died.

I have looked from a hillside on Ithaca
And listened
Hearing Easter hymns drift upwards;
And then turned westwards scanning the blue gulph
To Cephallonia, listening,
And hearing their voices still.
I have sought out sea beasts and purple nereids
On the sandy shores of Skyros.
And I have heard their voices
By the broken columns of Olympia,
The shelly limestone columns strewn among flowers.
This never forget:
That though regrets may linger
On aromatic hillsides,
And though the wind of history blows
Now as always on the plain of Thessaly,
The Gods are still there.
It is holy ground.
Go there, alone, and listen.

Mediterranean

Lie still: the hour is not for new design
Of unresolved voluntary powers,
While sleep may whisper low as you recline
On ocean's hem of salty-scented flowers.

Let the drowsy roar of the sea, the sun and the air
Drug you until, the painter leaving go
Which moored your waking craft to conscious care,
Out on the ebbing tide of sleep you flow.

Lie still: and let the sound of the broken surf
Lull you to charmed sleep with melody
Of rock and wave and sky and sea and earth,
Poured in your ear with strenuous minstrelsy.
Pillow your fancies far on the wandering deep;
Leave go, and sink into the arms of sleep.

Some Portraits of the Olive Trees
(Written at Banyuls, Southern France)

Grey guardians of the soil under whose leaves
The silver hours and shadows grow and pass,
You are the coinage and history of these hills
Who have handed down age over age by tilth
Your fruitfulness, like reason grey and wise;
Subduing the talk of fight, and easing the ways
Of those who struggling on these rocky hills
Have here carved out their arid livelihood.
On these red-terraced vineyard slopes you grow
Clinging to rock and soil in silent groves,
Where he who rests beneath your shade may learn
An inward spirit dwells, and rest at ease.
You grow, like those who work, clear limbed and strong,
Your features shining separate in the air
With silver greeting to the encircling sky.
At night though often hidden as the moon,
Your gleam sails out unveiled from swinging clouds
And secret leaves unfold their silver bloom.

. . .

And in bright Hellas where the Castalian spring
From Delphi falls from out her trickling gorge
To feed the groves below, where slanting wing
Of painted butterfly vies with the scented breeze,
And Hoopoe and Oriole call in glaucous glades,
Your serried ranks spread out their grey mantle
On haunted slopes beside the Middle sea.
Athene's gift to Athens long before
They raised the Parthenon to virgin honour,
You were her chaste rich benison for her own
And the staple of their civilisation.
O ancient trees, you harbour magic still;
Beneath your shade that glory is not past;
Ever the youngest of the ancient groves,
In you the misty legends breathe and last.
What are your leaves? The blades of Grecian oars,
Athene's silver spears through which the wind
In shrunken whisper goes telling of those
Who came in ships and gathered on the shore
And sped the stars across the board of sky
Night after night with talk of men and gods.
And you have heard, and seen their bodies laid
Beneath the earth and ceased their living tales
As camp fires guttered low upon the shores.
Only the names have lingered in the breeze
And whispered leaf to leaf with you repose.

. . .

Where we may seek the Olive, there is found
True ancient ease – as where mighty Taurus' ranges
Fling their last dark battlements down before
The rich grey rolling plain of Mosul corn;
There creaking wheels feed the young green wheatstalk
With precious garnered drops from mountain springs,
And there at the dry cliff face, in green gullies,
Haunt of the Wheatear and his scratchy song,
Poured out of silence on the vibrant air,
Cool streams arise and round them Olive groves
Have gathered to mark the site of long-known shrines
Where ancient peace for ever dwells; and the wise
Yezidi tribesmen with their simple lore,
Hallowing places where old Nature grows,
Rejuvenate and build white fluted cones
To consecrate the spirit of the fane.

There in the crowded shade beneath a bower
Of green Olives, the traveller may pause,
Kneel on cool stones and look into the clear
Pure icy fonts and drink refreshing draught;
Oft laying aside his rifle to recline
And sleep awhile where spirits still abide.

While in a hut nearby an old man dwells,
Bearded and wizened, owning but his robe;
He guards the shrine: to him the traveller brings
Khubz and oil and tea and swelling fruit,
A pilgrim gift to nature's own retreat.
Thus the Yezidis' ancient ministry
Where the peaceful Olive casts her grateful shade.

. . .

The shepherd boy beneath your shade reclined,
While guarding his herd of shaggy nibbling goats,
Will pour wild melody upon the hills;
From rock to rock it echoes loud and still;
And then he is silent, or speaking to his herd.
At other times he pulls forth a simple pipe
That he has fashioned in hot leisure hours
And spins the time upon the loom of day
High up and out of sight among the crags
With mountain warbling, ending on a drone
Like stealthy bees in heather in the noon.
This is the time when your shadows gather close
And the flocks draw in beneath what shades remain
To avoid the sun's eye searching from above,
Excess of blazing molten metal poured
From the travelling chariot to the zenith borne,
That burns the very stone till it would cry;
The birds are silent now from their sharp song
And insects cease to wander with the breeze;
Only the lizards creep or scuttle home
As black marauding pinions sail on high.
Then, gentle Olives, tried to the extreme,
You let not droop your silver standards down
In token of submission, as the weak herb
Is made by inner weariness to bow
Upon its cushioned green. Proud to the air
You raise your steady branches to ensnare
The mazy sunlight and to bring it home

To cease from angry glancing on the hills
Where like an unwanted guest it scorning scans
The unresponding features of the crags.
Rather you drink the sunlight and declare
Its errand to the roots who grope below,
The old blind water-carriers who provide
So you may raise your beauty in the air;
Your smooth grey stems are vessels of light upheld
To feed the gay and silver-lanced leaves
In the dry groves above sparse ancient lands.

Southern View

Judas tree flowering
Above river wall,
Peach blossom foaming,
And above all
The clear blue zenith
Lets sunlight fall.

The wistaria in tangles
In trellisses hide
Shades who would mingle,
As dogs that are tied
Waiting for evening
To wander wide.

Distant lie mountains
Resting in Spring,
Passive their features
Not menacing
With cruel iron spurs
Humans who cling

In small tiled villas
Under their lee.
In vineyards the tillers,
The sails out at sea;
All the hot landscape
Smiling and free.

Migrating Swallows

Here come the swallows hurrying in ones and twos,
Drawn like blue beads upon a string
Beside the plaintive Mediterranean surge.
Steadily North with glancing wing they go;
Heed not the churning spray nor barren roar
Of wave on arid rocky shore, but on
Following the coast line as a mapping pen,
They curve and skim beside the shining sea,
Bearing perfection North in fragile lives,
As sure as ploughman's furrow onward drawn.
Their steel-blue arcs soar the caressing waves
Who speak of tideless peace and quiet caves
Where the long legends uncoil and tritons glide
Mid wavering Nereids in the cobalt shade.
And the faint names of heroes and of gods
Are tossed in music on the sun-drenched shores,
Attis and Hylas, Glaucus and Amphion,
And Aphrodite, sea-born of the foam.
All of the drowned who slumbering drift beneath
Soothingly call on the travellers to abide
And lay aside their haste for ease; but they,
As if they slept within a field of force,
Follow the driving impulse of their wills
Unyielding, anchored alone in unalloyed
Shackle of home to harvest onward speed;
Like the returning soldiers from foreign wars
Move to the North and home in streaming horde;
Bare their red throats to hazard, chuckling fly
Across woven surf, nor heed the blind blue eye
Of Poseidon the tempter, the Mediterranean sigh
Which calls them to rest and forget their urgency.
The seas slip back with all their alluring calm
Distant as memories, now they forage on;
Challenging sweep by tower and bridge and stream;
Ancient as heralds their constant news to bring,
The joyous daring outriders of Spring.

Landing at Dover

Curled in like a chip of rock from the bouncing waves;
Onto the foreshore slid from the salt sea drawers,
Addressing, caressing the stone-heart beach; wild shores,
Where the loose swan wan went up from the hurricane's jaws;
While the wind like a knitting fanatic loosely raves;
And the ivory sea mews spin as spume in the rotting caves.

The tattered leather whips of the gale decide
A discarded eel flung again on the beaten shores.
And the sucking hungry surge in pain withdraws;
Shuddering up the wind-piled foreign floors
The sea-thigh billow strained in the harness tide,
To crash in its misery and splendour, while winds deride.

The swaying boulders roll under the salt green curls,
Toppling as loaves or casks in the undertow,
A loose loot scattered on the rocks below
Or back into the coffer where the lolling corpses go.
And gold from the elf wreck trickles mid ingot pearls
Where the tempest hushed in green gloom his racy standard furls.

So the tempest threw me, a chid speck of gravel chip,
From its scarring warring heaven-wounding spray,
Quiet, right up on the beach, removed from the affray
(Though the swaying giddy pendulum did stay);
And washed me into the hotel mouth to strip
And down into the green gulf of sleep to slide, a drowned ship.

Invitation

You may invite me,
I will not come;
You may delight me,
I have found some
New way of wasting
Precious hours hasting;
You will not come.

I may invite you,
You will find other
Ways to incite me;
Looks for another
I'll be exploring,
You can go soaring
After another;
I will not come.

All things deride us.
O Nature inside us
Have pity, have pardon,
'Tis thy will divides us.
I will invite you.
But you, will you come?

Spring Feeling

Ringing with song
The feathered field
Ladders of leaf green yield,
The sharpened spears
Aspiring pierce
The ringing Weald,
The sky-blue shield,
With song and thrust
From every field.

Man swallows hard
To feel the Spring
So humbly hurting sing,
And shifts his blood
To greet the flood
Of everything
So carolling
In curl and flick
Of bud and wing.

Four Poems for Michael Riddall
I. Lullaby For Michael

Little Michael sleeping high,
Breathing on your pillow lie,
Above the windswept pageantry
Of snow and ice and frost and flake.
Do not from your slumber wake.

Dreaming from your darkened tower,
Out of reach of waking power,
Let your sleep in snowy shower
Fall with softest flake till morn.
Do not wake before the dawn.

Sprites now gather in the trees
Tinkling with their icy leaves,
Lonely hearts without will freeze.
But let your dear head on pillow laid
Sleep innocent and undismayed.

I would never have you know,
Sleeping high above the snow,
Black wind's icy fang below.
You a sighing child shall rest
Warm and safe and unoppressed.

II. For a Confirmation

Receive, O Lord, this child into Thy hands,
Whom Thou through us have furthered on to place
One foot this day upon the starry stair
That from our impermanence leads on
Through hazards fine and dull to lasting rest.
From out our leaden wonders and our cloth
Of mortal erring darkness may he be
The bearer of Thy fingerprint to Thee.

Though he unknowing, fanciful and free,
Lightly imagine daily burden's woe
And skip towards Thy seasonal embrace,
Unfolded now in splendour to receive,
(He clothed in shyer shade of reverence),
O take him safely in to grow with Thee.

So that the flower who later will bear fruit
May from his sweetness never of his own
Seek willingly to err nor mar the web
Of Thy design within our wasting lives.
O he may sin, or die, or be a wound,
But never cast into a refuge of despair;
For Thou within him, he upon the stair
May always knock, nor ever fails reply.

If we could but eliminate routine
Of chatter, forceful thinking, nervous will
Of wearying emotion, and clearly see
Thy radiance, so familiar, yet unknown,
Now as of old fallen on bowing heads,
Breathing the purer air which us surrounds.
O if we could but grow such fruits by Thee,
The rotting thorn might fall on thankful ground.

To be as a child, but not the wandering child
Who deviates among delights of hours
From the straight paths of wonder which diverge
More variously throughout the starry bowers
And glades of innocence, O it were fine.
No other act of self than to approve;
To be in all the child, who magnetised,
Draws shyly near within his serious heart;

And cherishes the dream all men have held
Of following a world within Thy ways,
Till by distraction naturally it folds
Away, forgotten toy, more rarely used,
And grows alone. And each his festive path
Takes separate, astray from Thy true home.
We too, alas, most often absentee:
Lord bring us home this holy day to Thee.

This Thee and Thou and Lord and Thy true home
Are childish symbols which we have prepared
Before the mystery which right here is shown
Of one going boldly forth from what he knows,
In courageous darkness stumbling to the known;
These are the only words we know to choose;
They are rash words, where silence would alone
Prove our intent. May they themselves atone.

O may he joyfully go out today,
With symmetry of perfect blessing found.
And for the eternity this day in him
May these poor prayers stay freshly green at home;
My best, for him with Thee for ever sound.

III. Hic Iacet Mickey, Anima Obtusissima et Dolcis

Is it now, Mickey, only Sir between us two?
The you that I knew before this would obey as Mickey too.
You that are more to me than I to myself could be,
Why do you Sir me so? I am no longer free,
But bound as a servant to master to the moments spent with you.
Will it, Mickey, for ever now only be Sir between us two?

IV. I See him as a Spirit

I see him as a spirit
Shining in clear flesh;
Nor does any blemish
Spoil his sweet and fresh
Responsive self. O spirit,
Guard him from his merit.
May life not disinherit;
Nor greedy age discredit
With bitter touch his spirit;
Time, tarnish not nor perish
The spirits you enmesh.

Flight
For P.A. Down

The Ways determine what we think we own;
What time, route, comfort, climate, chance
Through all the attributes of circumstance;
In what green weather we are grown.

A lucky flight of gulls obscurely drift
Shadows across our table, as you lift
Your head, meaning to say in fact, alas
It's time, so soon must our parting come to pass.
Such bare paining flight, it seems, must lead
Direct to nothingness. No use to plead.

The Ways determine what we think we own.
The snows of circumstance will melt finally;
And we must follow down the unending way
Of that green weather where we were grown.

Looking and Growing

Child, you may own to no other flights than these
Short tumbling fancies of your guileless hours,
But there is seed yet steady within your brows
Mounting and spreading strong branches upwards,
Rooting within young flesh the Old King's tale.
Though through eyes like saucy mirrors one may see
But a summer wantonness, a clear delight
In the common sparkling moment's elusive joy;
Shrewd to the pinpoint your laughing aching eye
Where pen and line must falter, fail to define,
As your gaze falls forward framed in reflective vision,
And the long legend of wonder within you grows.

Morning Rode in on the Day

Morning rode in on the day
With his sparkling frosty wine,
His breath came white from his beard
And his eye it was blue and fine.

As he looked on the yellowing stone,
It glittered and blazed at his stare,
He chuckled and pulled at his flask;
Rooks clapped and rose into the air.

And the small birds, flicked and settled
Within a few yards of his steed,
When he leant over his saddle,
Scattered like handfulls of seed.

Perched in the boughs, reproving,
They showered him with downfall of song,
While gulls soaring over the rooftops
Keeled at him loud and long.

For the wine that he drank it was golden,
And they feared he would finish it all;
So the clamouring ducks in their boldness
Set up an intentional brawl.

Tying reins in a knot he dismounted,
Crystal the turf at his feet,
The earth at his footprint singing
A Mattins full and sweet.

He cast shadows sharp as proposals
From his fiery bright blue eye,
But a weary longing to linger
Therein could be seen to lie.

As he gazed at the hills of creation
Out across field and copse,
Bird songs, fifteen hundred,
Echoed in silver drops.

And when church bells from Sutton Waldron
Swung out full and clear,
He would leave his mount to wander
And then would disappear.

Down meadows by frozen runlets
He took his retreating way,
Soon lost to view in the hazy
Advent of the day.

But if you gaze in the sun's eye
And keep your gazing bright
You may still see him thundering onwards
Ever frosty and white.

For each time he rides to our doorfront
He pauses for a while,
And, before again travelling onward,
Leaves this day her comfort and smile.

Benedictus
For Julian Rathbone

The full summer radiant peers between
Tree, box, window; lights with sheen
The peacock's eye; lifting the leafed screen
On our friezed alfresco elbow lives.
For welfare eyes welcome the tossing glance
Of light and dapple shade on lazy green.

She stares into courtyards, rewards and shines;
Hallows the short mote dance in dusty shrines;
Glazing the live leaf, with tendril intertwines
Happiness to going forth in hillock dawn
Of this pied and perilous May, so pined to stay,
So pinned with daisies charmed and chance designs.

O alloy May, where light and breeze may sweep
From airy downland blossom and petal deep
In the leafspin laugh, twirl and reeling steep
To skidding cloudslope step; O ever hold
Your bright fenced eyelids trembling, skimmed to scan
The treasured trust, the glance you fain would keep.

As leaves stir lightly in the morning shade
The querulous thrushes echo from the glade
Their answer to our seeming thought dismayed.
The mist-high chorus swell from leaf top tree
Their sunrise Benedictus, greet the field
And folded sweetness in the dew-grieved blade
Where God-grown treads all treasure, unafraid.

Coronal

Today the lark sings the whole length of his acre;
With a tight-rope dancer's verve he swings on his trilling threads,
Straining of tension reels, accelerates round his corners;
The quiltwork counties embroidered with silver sowing.

Today the wave mounts relieved, breaks with a special splash,
Dashing back joyous from scrabbling barnacle slabs;
Foams with delight in the sunspray, seethes with excitement in crevices,
Hurls, burls and swells his shoulders, barging the strict cliffs with horseplay.

Today the boy goes flat-out downhill on his bicycle;
The humming tyres tight, crackles the light gravel before him;
Hair blown streaming, eye on the speed poured out ahead,
Not spilling a drop, skims down the slope reckless, today regardless.

For today is festival and morning has started grandly
With the sun already high and smiling, viewing the fresh preparations;
And the long ranks of flowers wait patiently their review,
Eyeing the busy movers with attentive starry dew-shot eyes.

The trees adorn and shake their shimmering summer dresses;
And a light breeze skips bothering, everywhere asking unnecessary questions
Just from excitement. While the vicar thoughtfully fills in the forms
For the entertainment-tax people above, who always make such demands.

For once in a while there is no price to pay on this May morning;
And the lark knows it and sings on unrationed for gladness.
The motorist unfolds his map and plans an extravagant detour
For the fun of it. Today petrol is on the house.

Aeroplanes circle in abandon, describing their speechless cloud patterns;
And gulls dance round the trawler masts in the packed echoing harbour.
Newspapers, crisp and unread, lie warmed on the hotel hall table;
For today man for a wonder has let go of his visions and worries.

Financiers smoke and agree; the projected merger is settled,
And the minister carefully looks with his pen where to sign the encourag-
     ing pact,
Disarming the secretaries and newsmen with his smile and the flower in
     his lapel;
While the thrush shouts from the gable three times over his triumph.

A fresh breeze blows from the headlands; the islands too are rejoicing.
The linnets gawkily chatter from the cliff furze and yellow spiking.
The bells peal out in the valleys; the ensign flaps from the church towers;
The air hangs on the morning; the morning's announcement in England.

No Simple Thing

It is a simple thing astride a hill
To cast ambition out, with all attained,
Relax upon the exertion of the will,
The rider you had willed yourself explained.
Also an easy life to stay below,
Among the rambling nibbling sheep recline,
Await the pushbike postman, who you know
Will bring one day the masterful Design.
But these are ends with which you may begin
When all is over and there is no excuse
Or turning back to set the course again
Which you had grown accustomed to refuse.
Hardest, away from self to stem your way,
Among amiable crowds to receive, to create each day.

The Ancient Families

Duck blazon their heraldry on the winter mere;
Gun-metal green, pure molten white and chestnut brown,
Each ancient family their proud colours wear;
Brought from the high North to drift on ruffled pools.
With slanting wing and regal splash they land
Upon grey-lidded waters in the stately parks
Of noble families who have long packed up and gone.
Deserted their stone breeding sites; the towered halls
And Grecian porticoes now dank with cushioned moss.
Proud lineage clings as ivy to the yellow stone,
Their names all but extinct with autumn's breath,
The genius of their place scarce haunting winter's throne.
The pageantry of broader days alone survives
In these proud squadrons floating on the mere;
Pied ducks returned each year to preen and sail,
As sable fleets assembled for a royal review,
Dipping their bright standards in the noonday sun
With strident flash of white and red and glinting green.

The people pass in Austin cars and stare
Or picnic with their wireless by the side.
Startled by the intruders duck take wing;
Rising in fright the last bright families go;
They fly with clamour South towards the moon;
And leave their land to crowded emptiness.

Nineteenth-Century Slow Movement

Beautiful and sad
The leaden music on
Among iron griefs and trees
Swings aimlessly.
A century turning on itself,
Assessing bitter wealth,
Pivots by slow degrees;
To death bright honour goes,
Success succeeded by oblivion.

The way lifts weeping head
On rhythmic tip-toe sways
Seeking a new way out,
As a doped serpent fearing
The imperfection that is guilty heir
To the swan hopes we bear.
O broken our aim without
Aim as by catch in throat
Caught in the natural comment of our days.

Iona, Winter 1948

The islands are but voices
Murmuring in the sea,
Mid grey the rock and wave
From Islay to Tiree.

The airs that blow about them
Are bred from out the deep,
And whispering the island names
They never sleep.

The voices of the islands
Whisper in the sedge
As sea thrift blows and rattles
On barren salty ledge.

Grey geese in clamour rising
Vanish in the mist,
And with the clamour dying
The quiet is increased.

O'er rock and sedge and grasses,
Mossed miles of boggy land,
A swathing mist of memories flows
Twixt eye and hand.

The piping oyster-catchers,
Trooped spirits in the field,
Have souls of long dead heroes
In magpie breasts concealed.

The starling flocks are spirits
That drift and throng and glide
Then huddle on the skerries
Forlorn at eventide.

As acid waters trickle
Between the peat and stone
The Norsemen whisper secrets
Bone to buried bone.

The plunder that they carried
Was early fruit and sour;
Long after they were buried
Stands the isle's Abbey tower.

A hush of centuries
Fell on the island name;
No litanies were sounded,
No chanting pilgrims came.

Only the waves spread their increase
Upon the glittering sand,
Always to swell and carry
Their burthen to the land.

But Columba's light through the centuries
Has shone off Mull:
The sacred pinpoint glimmer
No death force can annul.

North in the grey Atlantic
The polar fangs of Rhum
Catch a roseflush in the sunsets
That tells of snow to come.

The criss-cross moods of currents
Where cormorants plunge and swim
In the sinking eye of Winter
Grow remote and dim.

There is coldness on the island;
Never a man about.
And the machair is deserted
As the day goes out.

Sprinkled snow on sand dunes
Calms the Atlantic swell;
Birds sleep on grey waters
Where the snow flocks fell.

The nibbling sheep grow ghostly
Cropping salt sweet turf;
And the rocks seem powers of darkness
Menacing the earth.

In the dark tower of the Abbey
Peculiar shapes will gleam,
And the wind brings in sudden gusts
The distant roar of a stream.

Not a man the path will follow
Down to Sand-Eels Bay
Till the island spirits scatter
At the break of day.

The dead all night in hundreds
On the headlands sit,
While the Kirk lamp flickers
Which the early Christians lit.

The Origin of Tyrants

On him as on the greenleaf spring light falls;
The Tyrant's sunny nature smiles on all.
Through jagged teeth his whistling virtue breathes
Mild benison of one who at his ease
May loose his vigour through their meek desire
And sweep his many victims to their hour.
The hour when they must choose, but of his choice,
Submit their conduct to white scrutiny

Within their judgement exercised alone,
But at his bidding, who, aloof and bland,
Pronounces what they would he understand.
And, when they feel they know what they have lacked,
Asking their luck their needs in level tone,
Then he will wield his right and judge them there.
His tyranny their own created will;
His choice of ills their active deeds in flower;
His brisk and quivering rod seal of their power;
They of their heavens a thunder playground made
Handing to him his sceptre, are then afraid.

Moon and Flower

Across the cratered heavens
The web of stars forlorn
Emerged from stormy headlands
The brimming moon is borne.

As breath from misty hollows
Where tree trunks drip and stare,
Thirsty flowers pierce up to
The lonely nightward air.

Selene freshly minted
Gazes on rick and farm,
Mourning the lost kingdom
She wooed, but failed to charm.

Her million silver arrows
Would pierce Endymion's heart,
But she was cruelly treated.
Endymion sleeps apart.

When he is softly dreaming
She may kiss him with a gleam
But he will never answer
From the caverns of his dream.

So she sails on for ever
O'er valley, river, stone
And sleeping forest shedding
Her anguished light, alone.

O moon for ever crossing
The empty realm of night,
Forgotten in the morning
Is your fevered haunting light.

As the gathered snow is melted
From the open upland pasture,
Your coverlet is lifted
Ere waking birds will stir.

A flower alone is watchful
And catches within his cup
The silver wisps of moonlight
As with fragrance he looks up.

Within his bell of silver
He feels her sorrowing pleas
As over clouds she wanders
About the friendless skies.

A secret of his being,
Pure essence of his life,
Distils a drop of nectar,
As moonbeams like a knife
Now lucid and exploring
Touch the veins of his desire,
Fusing joy with anguish
In her waning icy fire.

So the poet in his striving
Makes an offering to the sky
Of a secret he has cherished
Since in childhood he would fly
With a stolen gift to kingdoms
Beyond our mortal range
Where he wanders as the moonlight
Kindred and yet strange.

So Beauty across the world
Sails on remote and shy,
And mostly her flowing warmth
Is locked and frozen dry.

Man with Beauty rarely
May commingle while on earth
Though daily he remember
His union lost at birth.

Back into Dark
I

I thought they smiled: but in their hearts were knives
Directed outwards. How silly I should dream
One could turn off by comfortable streams
And flowers; and make believe one had not heard
Once sounding thunder rocking low.

Poor fool, I hoped they had a place for faith:
When in their eyes were only festering knives
And screws of wanting, twisting in their needs.
They had not guessed what lay below the rocky pass:
And I had seen below.

Below the laughing eyes and frank demands,
The daily need of banter, greed and fun,
There lay the War again, again alive.
This evil rose deliberately, delighted to meet mine.
My hurt and angry eyes
Led back to darkness; and they lived puzzled in their light.

II

In this, relief:
The shuttered room, the pouring groaning music
Giving the wellkin a ringing rhythm,
Catching the order back in a glut of bitter stars –
In each hard gem a spat of shining chords
And a tossed spray of hard silver notes;
Coinage on dank pavements,
Silver coin, rolling on down dank pavements,
Where iron railings loom in a whirling fog.
This is a simpler way: back into darkness;
To leave the old rose-bud encrusted world
And go further on down solitary paths
Where music blows, swings creaking on the wind.
Cherish a secret! That was a confidence
Whoever told, he spoilt it:
Trying to tell to eyes what music means;
What wasted time is vision on deaf ears!
Keep the delight and go on back into the dark.

Fell the Trees of Hate

Fell the trees of Hate,
Clear the thicket of Suspicion;
Let die and wither
Whatsoever is bitter,
Rancorous and apostate;
Negative Ambition.

Until the twisting briars,
Pride and Indignation,
Are hacked down from their rankling,
There can be no just condition;
Out of their bitter ashes
No green creation.

Forests of Fears and Phobias
Soon sway up in the gale;
Green tongues writhing and flaming
Sprung from a drop of wormwood
Or gall of past Blaming:
There lies a cause of tears.

To the young tears come easily,
Raining of gentle relief,
But to older the physical weakness
Is mute to the strength of Despair,
To the negative Will willing;
No easy solution there.

The burrowing root of Sorrow
Sore at its own consuming
Worms into utter darkness,
Drinking only the scalding
Bitter drops of Despair,
Rooted in darkest Willing.

O fell the trees of Hate,
Clear the thicket of Suspicion;
Let them die and wither
Down to the roots again.
To whatsoever is bitter
Let Pity enter in.

Only by letting in Light
For green fronds appearing;
Only by new growth of Right
Will shimmering glade and clearing
With forward growth of Goodness
Charm with its slow returning.

If I Remember

If I remember your gentle ways
That have come certain, all days
To my always, all nights, all days,
I shall not let steal regret
Into this memory. Have met
Not then, not now, nor yet
Always we have met, all days, all nights, all days.

Shadows

Out of cloud and tree and sun
I will make a verse for one
Who like sunlight in a tree
A golden shadow cast on me.

When the dancing boughs evade
Wind's caresses, light and shade
Of filigree in patterns make
This life with living shadows ache.

Five Poems for Jeremy
I. May Night

Jeremy, under this sky I vow
To sacrifice all interest now
For you and every boy who cares
For better things from life, and dares
To stride into a head-wind, sure
In his faith to triumph and endure.
What little I can give I will
To help you on the way to fill
Your later days with treasure stored
While still at school. You have explored
Few of the paths of beauty's realm,
Where music's voice can overwhelm
And verse reflect like tranquil lake
The natural joys of days which make
The most of evening's gentle hush,
Forgetting the hurried duties' rush.
This is the world I know and care for;
To it I would guide you. Therefore
Please accept this clumsy proof
Of what I know at heart is truth.
For me the journey, understand,
Is pilgrimage back, into a land
Of lost content, I thought had slid
Over the horizon, forever hid.
But you have beckoned me this way
Through faith and innocence so gay,
Back to belief in lasting good,
The hedge gate to the Sacred Wood.

II. Two Eyes

Two eyes like any other face contains;
Two eyes set in neatly modelled features,
Attentive and watchful as a ferret.
Why should I care what message they convey?

How I wish they were really just eyes in a face,
Compounded of customary structural features,
With no inwardness, no traffic of signals
Whose desperate import drives me to sun or cloudbank.

Two eyes set in a not very special face,
Clean and definite unsmiling features,
An oval new frame. But within, an ocean
Of wonder mirrored in two drops of reflection.

Two eyes whose messages I can hardly wait to read
Each morning, worse than anxious headlines,
So often convey not-to-be-spoken thought,
Some look that would accuse, but silent rests, burning.

So often from two eyes I go back discouraged,
To assume the heavy cloak of a purposeless routine;
To set my features to look as though it were nothing,
To say that there had been no awaited news that morning.

But to be fair, there have been other days,
When two eyes have looked at me steadily, unblinking,
Shining from radiant laughing features,
Eyes that give and forgive, eyes that transform.

Eyes whose lips cannot but follow suit and smile:
And then no garden scene transformed by sun
Is comparable to the paean of praise
That in one lightened heart will sing.

Sufficing this, gladly to work I go,
Each step is carefree dancing, a royal rout,
Each act a lightheart joy, unfounded mirth.
O eyes, the leaden age endures. How long?

III. For J.

I was a granite wall against chafing waves
Of caprice and circumstance, hewn, hardened by ill-luck,
Until you sauntered smiling in, eager to explore,
With your sunny ways firing the sober stone.
There and then a tiny crack in the rock-face
Developed, grew to chasm, a mighty fault,
And up surged subterranean fires.
In the cleft I saw your haunted sunny eyes,
No longer smiling, but gazing clearly on
The truth and chaos you had formed.
The ruin spread; you feared what you had done,
The ramparts grew oppressive, and you ran
Out into the sun, your timeless moteless ways;

Your pure stream chose another course,
Leaving this broken hollowed structure
Hard put to repair the ravages of eyes
And lips, and the glittering corn, your hair.
O now you have wandered two rows of hills away
I will repair the damage of those days
As the industrious mason wasp builds up the broken cell;
Unfeelingly I'll apply to toil, nor rest,
And so, by constant labouring, learn to forget.
You do not need from others help, you are the needed,
The chance wanderer who taps the rockface
And finds it brittle; sent by the gods
You smile and demonstrate, though without intent,
How small a thing our fastness, how unsafe,
And with your deep arrow shafts
Touch the quick nerve of love.
The pain is now subdued, and the heart has learnt it lies
For ever exposed to outlandish sun or cruel breeze.
Accustomed now to shock, it must live on;
But O my earthquake one, into these peaceful ruins,
Do, and do not return.

IV. The End of May

High and lonely, locked in a tower,
I'll not escape your lively power.
Prisoners scattered throughout the land
Reject and rebel, but heed your command.
You raise a finger, we slam the door,
And drop the key through a hole in the floor;
By our own choice incarcerated,
At your instance, immolated.
Why should Beauty enslave the Beast
In freeing a spirit love has increased?
Brahmin spirits rise as plumes
Of towering smoke from carrion fumes.
The ashes of that fire taste bitter,
Dead the motive, dulled the glitter.
Solitary I go my way
And heavily to the tower today;
In the thraldom of my willing
Still the patterned fate fulfilling.
Something in me cries: Release.
But you smile: Objections cease.

Passively we take our cue,
And stand around and wait for you
To point us to our lonely cages
Where delight with anguish rages.
Doomed to struggle with our pride,
Through foaming seas of wrath to ride;
Visionaries with earth-blank eyes
Brought to life by Beauty's ties.
Strain we to escape from Beauty
And from selfhood into Duty,
Deep in sweet molasses floundering,
Our foothold on the future foundering,
O spare each vivisected soul
And let us drown in sweetness whole
Or else take wing again and fly
Beyond your hopeful lands and die.
True, you did not will it so,
This trail of corpses, that I know.
Oppressive may be Beauty's crown,
Flashing bright and striking down;
For with those arrows from your heart
O innocent, you had no part.
Such arrows always will be flying
While there's wonder bright and dying.

V. For J.

You have been gone for forty hours away
And I have played Mozart all the day.
Already the wound is calmer, less inflamed;
Though I think of you, the sadness is more remote.
I see you walking towards me, but not looking at me;
You have retired in time, like a photograph,
Or a figure in a scene I knew; but viewed
As the dead look on the living, with unreal eyes
That do not lead to feeling any more.
And soon that crest of trees, those scudding clouds,
That summer evening setting (Claude Lorraine)
Will likewise be a fading memory gone
With every other face and flower enjoyed.
Oh war may drift me from this port again
And the reality then will be sitting in desert tents
Far from green, from healing friendly smiles,
Sipping from glasses sweet and acrid tea,

Scheming for information, a rigid scene;
And I will return to my truck and not think of you
Except on lonely journeys through the sand,
With eye and purpose glued to destination,
A mirage you, the focus then as now,
A thought only of you in red rock desert.
And try as I will I shall not make you smile;
Then as now will be gone that direct flash,
Leaving my heart a smoking shattered dump
Bombed out again by grief's wild bursting blows,
Disfigured all, and you not there to care.
Oh can you care for one so lacking faith
Who doubts what is for one sole instant hid,
As a savage fears at an eclipse of the sun
Crouches and moans, and fears to lift his eyes,
Believing the sheltered sun is pain of blinding?
I'll not trouble you with hurts you've lightly caused,
Such unmeant acts you never knew could rack:
No blame to you, there's no blame can accrue.
For Beauty is fine, it purifies and kills
And bares the bone, nor feels the smart endured.
Beauty is free and unrestrained to go,
It may not pause to linger where it fires,
Knows not its consequence till it is gone,
Nor how a trail of ruin marks its run.
How arid and puffed this speculation is!
For you, true to your true self, but still alone,
(And I too alas) must journey further on.
O will there be some distant gleaming strand
Where we perchance unshadowed meet again
And recreate such happy summer airs
And instances; when tongue again may fashion
Lightness and grace to speech and summer deed,
When eyes may shine again as in that June?
Oh hope should never die: it can create
Images and affections that will flower,
Though pruned back ever by the unkind hand of rumour,
The horny hand of popular displeasure –
The people's wish to kill such love that blooms.
But we will emerge unscathed through the ring of flames
Where towers of music triumphant will resound.
And we will keep the faith that outshines fact.
Till then it must I fear be said, farewell.

An Alpine Lakeside Idyll
For Jeremy

The daylight bids you rise –
You turn and close your eyes.
High up a wreath of snow
Curls from an eave and drops;
Springtime is moving in,
Winter removes her props.
The crusted cornice topples,
Sliding away the snow;
Coverlets slip, uncover,
Down in the farms below.
Deep in the shadowed forest
A bud begins to leaf;
Deep in your shaded dream
Uncoils a lost belief.
The swallow follows the Summer,
Summer follows the Spring,
And you will think again
Of every well-loved thing.
Person, scene and cadence
In patient jigsaw fall;
And waking you will find
The truth that is best of all.
Music by the lakeside
In the morning drowsily
Will reflect the wakening idyll
As your dream melts into day.
With gossamer on the meadows,
The model farms will wake
And milk spurt warm in the pail
Beside the placid lake.
Emerged from isolation,
Your spirit will renew;
No longer dreaming of blisses,
You'll wake to find them true.
You will stretch beside the waters
Lying in cool banks of flowers
And let the busying insects
Ransack the honeyed hours.

Your spirit's convalescence
Will be drinking to the fill
Wonders born of wandering
Streams on the Alpine hill.
From cares you'll go free as water,
Your afternoons will be spread
Among the flowering grasses
Like butter on your bread.
The past no longer matters,
Your new setting is too pure;
Heart's ills go unregarded,
This is the Alpine cure.
So be willing now to recover,
Your first-born right prolong;
Let creation's never ending
Renewal be your song.
Survey the blue with patience,
With vision scour the sky,
Glean all your belief can wish for
With a bold and vigorous eye.
And by lakeside meadows in peace
May your country goods increase.

Ski Tour

Ecstasy of ice and snow,
Crunching footsteps on we go.
Jeremy, in this white scene,
Your image often comes between
The blinding purity of snow
And the route my heart would go.
Pounding on we trudge to gain
The shoulder height, then down again;
Hissing through the powdered snow,
I follow you wherever you go;
And stooping with a falcon arc
I chase your image till it's dark.

Untitled

I questioned from the first: How long can this last?
I never asked to need to love you so,
You whom I found so fair, you stopped . . . then passed,
But you caused my frozen happiness to flow;

And dancing days of keen delight ensued,
The sun shone on us from a placid sky;
The earth approved; the fresh grass under foot
Sprang lightly from our tread; the days sped by

In innocence and laughter; but then there grew
A grim predicted tower of wringing pain;
Fiercer each time I was absent long from you,
This fever like the ague rose again.

I feared the inevitable; for gone was all trace
Of pleasure in work, or interest, save in one
Who grew alarmed and fled and hid his face;
While I like a savage crouched at the eclipse of the sun.

Untitled

The parched earth soaks up the friendly rain;
It is gone.
So I thirst for your presence though
You're only this minute gone.

Why burning by the pool in the sun's rays
Does the bather go on
Striving for further fevered heat,
Sunburning on?

The moth goes to the candle
But not for fun.
The bather burning in the Summer
Is never done.
And I to be again reflected in your eyes
Live crazily on.

On His Own Demise

I do not wish to have a son,
To bear with me, an aged one.
Age is horrid, nothing less.
And no one else should share the mess.

Sons and daughters make an issue
Of the breakdown of the tissue;
Either wishing you'd go off,
Or worrying every time you cough.

I shall die alone and poor,
No other will regret it more.
But if friends should then recall
Former days when love was tall,

Let them carry that torch on,
Rejoicing for me when I'm gone –
And none need too much grieve the event:
When you've spent your cash, it's spent.

Holiday and Term

In holiday one thinks and acts but slowly,
Piling the treasure of experience, examining each glint
Of golden chance-born beauty, and reflecting
Like scarce moved water in weedy pool at turn of tide.
The glistening shoals of oar-weed, their polished shoulders rocking
Gently on the salt stream, twist twixt yea and nay.
So one reflects at ease, and like the barnacled clicking rock,
So sharp and firm to foot, one sees the sea slide out,
Watches the waters withdraw, or powerfully impressed
Glide in again and flood the listening creek.
The history of events is but the shielded whisper
Of air in her pearly staircase;
The import, but the underwater boom,
Peacefully reverberating, fathoms down.
Kneel on the edge and look into the flow,
The suck and eddy of Time's achievements,
The little vortices, beneath which ghost the prawns
In glassy stillness; uncharted, undismayed.
Time for appraisal, time for discerning,
Oh time for a delicious yawn.

Then term draws near, with things to do,
Details to manage; the decks are throbbing.
Uneasily we pace the rail
As the great ship prepares to get under way;
Walk to the bows and anxiously peer
Forward to what will need to be done.
No time now for reflection,
Time only for each necessary action.
The bric-a-brac of holiday experience
Drifts back and floats like harbour flotsam,
Chased perhaps and inspected by the importunate gull of memory,
Guzzled, and then left. We are now all too ready and alert.
Everyone moves on the decks, with a quiet adult purposiveness,
And with suppressed excitement, as before a sacrifice.
This is no time for stock-taking, the hour of adventure draws near.
The convalescents are flooding in, and banging their cases down on the decks;
Ready for crew-work or for first-class complaining;
Prepared to put up with whatever is approaching,
Thirteen weeks of unpredictable steaming.
Cast away, O cast away, sardonic man with the ropes,
Cast away from the shore of settled knowing,
Far out from the harbour and from peace we glide.

To

Why vainly chase the harnessed Spring?
Let clouds come by, suns reappear;
Let plants appear in their order too.
To Nature give her natural due.

Your haunted power, passion of movement,
Let swallows' wings requite with grace;
And lazy flights of insects loose
Your wilful grip of frenzied purpose.

Hurry is so strict a measurer;
Measures out with tots and nips and gills;
Unaffected his hungry worried eyes
As obscure maturings large devise.

Let these restless ripples settle
On the blown silk water's face;
And your smiling cheek be dimpled again
By laughter under green roof fane.

Drip-Drop
To a schoolboy poet in Autumn

Mourn rightly, child, the year's declining;
More's the pity Summer's spent.
Bury her gently, whilst divining
Fit lament.

Leaf and flower grew and flourished
That you might perceive her reign;
Now the Year's Dead Queen retires unnourished
To her roots again.

Spring and Autumn, days of ferment,
Irritate the poet's gland;
So let us at the year's interment
Lend a hand.

Shroud her passing with your Sonnets;
Elegaic poets, plead;
With the whistling Autumn Robin,
State your need.

Strew her grave with shining tribute,
Poems sharp and light as foam;
To each meeting each contribute
Honey to comb.

Never heavily progressing
'Neath the weight of learning's load,
But as dancers featly stressing
Steps of an Ode.

Don't confine her corpse to coffin,
Straitened in a rhyme-scheme tight,
Or you'll hear her Image coughing
Late at night.

Learn to master simple rhythms.
Child, your statement should be pure.
Do not swallow Sixth-formisms;
They obscure.

Just write simply like a Junior;
Sing your lyric slight and sweet.
Prouder poets seem the punier,
Moderns bleat.

I will write a thousand verses
To encourage and incite
You to listen to your Nurses
– Not tonight.

Oh Dear

The Great Ship prepares to move.
Or does she?

There is argument above decks
Between merciless stevedores;
Argument over the waters,
Flowing in beauty, as spread oil
Peacocks the dark harbour waters.
And the poets gesticulating,
Hat in hand from crowded hatchways,
Address those who are willing to hear,
(The waters, they peep out, my people),
Through the continual hum of customs, emotions,
Whimsies, Officials, employees and Port Authorities,
All who are waving the important vouchers,
And the traffickers in each emotional licence.
See, at another exit, a down plank,
The supervision of bakers by master-bakers;
The victuallers, cold-storage men,
All of them loading important treasures,
Stacking the trays and shifting the cases
Corner to corner beneath the leaning hulk,
Loading the tribute.

We must have been stationary about an hour,
Or was it hours,
Hours sad days
And days eternity
That we fetched up on the quay with our bags
Prepared for a journey?
There are some mad Doctors on board
Declaring good deeds,
While underwriters assuredly complacent
Write out unreservedly
The feverish prescriptions.

'There is no sickness on board.'
And no one is sorry to leave
Since the tourist pamphlets promise
A place in the sun
Of undying torment.

The Great Ship moves.
Or does she?

Here comes an important Person
With a fur collar, brushing aside
All the unknown anchorless souls.
With impatient shoestep and agile tread
He mounts the gangway
Bursting with instructions
And decisive initiatory orders.
Obviously he has the Plan (Maybe the Key).
Before settling down to supper
With clean silver and a white napkin
(Fancy, my dear, on a ship), 'Steward!
Wind up the waves, there's a good fellow,
And please vary the tempests.' 'Very good sir, very good.'
He must make a few trifling adjustments
To the heroic age's pulse,
Adjust old frontiers
Of metaphysics realm,
Fold napkin, and benignly
Beam up at the stars.
But who is he?
He, stripped of coat, plain he?
He is not the plan nor the peacedom,
He is the masquerading whirlwind
Of the overconfident ego.
Anyway he, like the rest, has now gone inside
And is soon lost within the belly of the ship.

I do wonder who *will* start the ship going.
Or are we in motion?
I heard a throbbing, a pulse
Amid smells of paint on bulwarks,
As I saw the stars drift on a chequerboard,
Drift on overhead.
Perhaps the waters are moving
And the Great Ship's stationary shudder
Is mistaken for motion.

The gulls, like my queries,
Seek and glide,
Keel with their cries;
Frozen motes in eternal draught
Perform aloft in a cold beam
Their icy galaxy of question and answer.
The waves leap higher,
Foam strikes with salt fanged tooth,
Snaps at the answer.
Cry higher, great gulls,
With your white tumbling hair
And yellow wise human faces.

The ocean below is shuddering,
Scratching at heaven.
The hand grip of terror on your shoulder
Snarls from behind you:
'O all the motion, the restless atoms,
They evil ones,
Cannot, no cannot, atone.'
When, O when, my heart, will we move?

The Great Ship sways and heaves, she begins to move steadily forward
Breasting the deep steeped wall of green.

Or does she?

Ballade (Chopin)

Faint music yearning
Soft through the glades
Kindles the memory,
Stirs among shades.

Happy the sunburst
Lit on laced leaves,
Slender boughs lifting
Their limbs it receives.

Then comes a sounding
Dark through the shaws,
A rustle of torments
Restless as straws.

The way without ending
Weaves between trees
From far away music
Returned on the breeze;

It steals through the shadows
From over the hill
With unearthly beauty
Into the still.

In hot painted clearings
Beneath the sun's glare
Still heedless the butterflies
Sail on the air.

The carpet of flowers
Smile in the sun,
Drinking the summer
Every one.

But deep in the woodland
The green forest sighs,
For a pain in its roots
Which no soothing denies.

Still now the music
Still are the glades;
Their beauty is merging
In deeper shades.

Trees in November Fog

Trees in November fog take on the moon
In argument with white bone dialogue.
Stored memory as a river flows along
While small dripping twigs that flourish in the fog
Expostulate and call to witness earth's
Warm scent, her summer praise of breeze and fly,
All mingled costume of the greenclad May
That arches on hills mid many flowers and song.
These come to mind as scraps of catchy tune
To catch and enmesh the critical cold moon;
They clutch at her raddled hand with childish warmth,
Ask smile from her high frontal frosted globe.
But her distant plea returns: Tis death alone;
That our breath may no more know, as shadows sweep

Across the creepered ivy on the stone
Like commentary to stifle beauty's leap,
Memory's shades that gather round the bier
Of Youth the fugitive whose pleasures fade.
Bare above cocks and owls and village chime
The furious comets streak and glow to inscribe
A lettered fire whose alphabet is closed,
That came to us once and, coming again, is gone.
The eternal playthings race without our doors,
Painting their codes across the peopled skies.
While serene above all worlds in icy flight,
Severe her cold reply and sentence known,
The Queen of the Eastern sky sails on alone.
The trees below in dreamy ballet throng,
Their decorous shadows poised on trim starred lawns;
They lift misty tresses sighing at her stare
And make a tender pleading utterance
In human tone beneath night's alien laws.
Dear trees, your beauty's utterance is heard
By me, a stranger too, who walks alone,
Who would distil the silence, hear the stone
Speaking, that in the beginning was a Word,
When the Word was all the positive that shone,
Whose shine was all the sheen of beauty's home,
In ageless beauty before the bone began.

Revenge

Winter, the cruel boy,
Touches with his light breath
Upon my wrist.

Rose flushed
His swift limbs flash and carve
Live air with scorn.

He is Ganymede
Of the tousled hair and mocking eyes;
His wild shafts of light
Are lost to the world;

So he flies
Kissing the late leaves' tracery
With rime.

Untitled

When I hear the wind in the trees
I hold my breath
And think of Agamemnon and his death
And of how wrapped in the purple shroud he stiffened,
And history stiffened with his breath.

Long after was the Mycenean gold
Laid out on museum benches cold,
To feel again man's breath.
But the stones keep their secret
And talk to themselves,
Heaping us with clues
And chuckling with the long wind
As of old, as of death, dust and ideals.

Trees and Gale

The gale's sea force sweeps inland now,
Sways in and crashes on breakwater trees;
Smacks crests of tall high-nested beach;
Booms in the bugling oak's huge bough.
Aloft, as woodland rigging sings,
Fretting the tossing chestnut spars,
The birds are blown like windswept spray
Away into sudden shrill wind cast;
While down the hills the dead leaves splay
And scurry round tall masted hulls
That creak and thunder, riding the bay
Of valley fields. The lashed rain dulls
The bobbing forest fleet from view.
Beneath grass coverlets lie skulls,
And Winter buds and bulbs plan new
Tempests of emerald heaving fleece.
Unmindful of these Winter dreams,
The ice-dammed hopes of torrent Spring,
Above the rocking deep, the wind
Yet raves among the whistling shrouds;
Rants wild mid riot of spent leaves
In gusty sorrow; storm-crossed gulls
Chide and are spilled across the plough;
And trees, each a wave-swept wind-soaked mast,
Drive on their keels before the blast.

British Schools Expedition to Iceland, 1951
Last Day at Base Camp, West Hoffsjokull

Here in the centre of Iceland for once I'm alone;
There's nothing but water trickling over stone;
No bird, no insect hum, no human voice;
Even the boisterous wind has ceased to rejoice
At our discomfort, sparing us grit in our eyes,
And the tents like ships in gales. We have no ties,
Save man to food and air, to warmth and sleep;
And the need to move the flesh and bone to keep
These hungry simple petitioners satisfied.
This is a natural setting for man's pride,
He and the elements and some surviving birds –
Rare relief from that other life where words
Encase him in – only lava and ice-sheet and sky,
The rapid swinging streams, and the cold to defy.
The rocks are so old and no one says their name;
The gravel shifts in rivers, stays the same.
There is no comment: Others have gone South
And sought the comfort at the harbour's mouth.
The clouds drift Northward: Silence alone tells
Of some who came and struggled on these Fells,
And sampled a tired triumph over death,
By living harder, cleaner, with each moist breath.
Today the sun absolves; the tussle's done.
We bang and pack the crates: It has been fun.

Three Clock Poems
I. Clock
For John Appleby

I took my clock to pieces,
I laid them in a row;
Please tell me now, you little pieces,
What will make you go?

The cogs began to argue,
Wasting time, I thought;
But all my intervention
Merely came to nought.

The dial smiled serenely,
The jewels all glared back;
The trouble, said the second hand,
Is minute hands are slack.

The mainspring had a theory,
That time drives the hands,
And all the little cogs
Should follow in their bands.

An older cog suggested
That a thing which he called God
Should wind them up and let them play,
Some thought this very odd.

Now the hair-spring had been silent
Waiting for his chance –
But then clutching tight his little wheel
He began to dance.

The pieces took their partners,
The open case guffawed,
They all jumped in and settled down
And half past foured.

They all spun round together
And next they hopped past five,
They leapt past six with little ticks,
Ticking I'm alive.

I stared into my clock's face,
I looked him in the eye:
D'you know I believe he winked at me.
Clocks are sly.

II. An Old Doddery Clock

An old doddery clock
Perched on the top of a rock
Leant over one day
To a man passing by
Who has never got over the shock.

For the question the clock had propounded
Among respectable clocks was a crime:
He had plucked the man's sleeve
And would you believe it
Asked him the time.

III. Clayesmore Clocks

I like clocks that are smiling,
I like clocks that are gay;
I like clocks like bobbies
Who will tell you which way.

For sometimes I'm going forward,
And sometimes I'm in reverse;
I haven't quite decided
Which I think is worse.

To want to be, the future,
To have been in the past;
But Clayesmore clocks say always
Now – both slow and fast.

Into the Kingdom of Poetry I head My Steed

Into the kingdom of Poetry I head my steed –
To a quiet country house, set back from the routes
Of idleness and commerce; here colours blend,
As Chemists pour solutions, green to blue,
Mingling their potions in the cream of day,
And wedding the silver particles to grey.
With jingling bridle and an easy gait,
I enter over cobbles in the yard
Which is empty but for the white presiding doves
Who strut and flutter beneath the stable chimes.
A little wind raises up an idle leaf,
Kittens it round the yard; then quiet resumes.
The Masters are all out upon the day,
Hunting the Image, living the chase anew
Amid the undying fields and the morning dew.
The glittering pastures stretch towards the hills.
And trees stand breathless by the summer corn.
But over fields from afar the roving horn
Echoes the hours in the patient steadfast hearts
Who wait for a joyful homecoming, late in the day.

Untitled

High up in the hills, O living Lord, You travel,
With the unravelled wind hand in hand You go
Over the grass to the dells on Hambledon,
Where You visit and cherish the least of flowers that blow.
Always at hand in the noisy crowded passage,
It is You who say 'No need to push at all'.
And when our eye falls on leaning chestnut branches
Whose blossoms drift in the sun, we hear Your call;
As when the eye of a friend returns our love:
Lord, You have willed it this way to be so.
In each perceiving grace in man and nature
We worship without needing first to know.
You have startled us, Lord, to love and then to reason;
May we accept this order and obey.
And as You turn the page of Summer's symphony,
May we Your children following You find calm;
Beneath tall skies grow tender, straight and free
And render our high spirits to Your almighty arm.

The Wren with his Sharp Beak Told Me

The wren with his sharp beak told me:
The cross is a dagger
To pierce once for all unreality.
In the original mountain where no man came
It was begot, the steel sword of God's word,
Christ's cross indeed.

And the handmaidens spreading the veil of dawning
Knew of it with sadness;
For baseless is the texture of our mortal sorrow.
Above us the sky, above us the clouds,
And we quest their soaring
Quietly, pacifically dreaming.
Down came the cross
As hammer on finger
And down fell man's dreams;
Down came the cross
And took charge of man's dreams, as Reality awoke –
Gripping our destiny to that moment

When Christ flamed forth
As an ordeal to the fumbling flock
And a threat to the nations.
It is a pointer for each generation
To each moment its message is final.

And the wren scuttled off in the bushes
Fussy, with prophecy, busy.
Thank you King Suleiman
Who spake by the birds of scrub and desert.

Untitled

Out in the dew of morning treads the boy,
Crossing the crystal grass towards his garden.
He touches the cheek of the peony-blushing rose
And sees the shining dewdrops trickle and slide
From that peerless shell which time will never harden;
For from time and care he asks as yet no pardon.

But fresh he comes to each day's promised joys,
To each new hill-top keen with hope he rides;
There is no end to what may lie in store
Beyond each valley or deep in the heart of flowers.
The world is scarce astir but still abides
Lost in its pillows drugged by lunar tides.

As that world dreams, the dreams of the boy aspire
In sparkling day to tread the new born turf.
Into the woods and away where paths descend
Beneath hanging glades he'll brush his way, and learn
As he smells the rich preparing of the earth,
In the gloom of woodlands, imagination's birth.

Then still while pensive morning holds her breath
And the birds go privately about the glade
Making mysterious calls that lead him on –
With reluctance to the breakfast table he turns,
Where he will have to awkwardly evade
The adult questions which would his world invade.

Vienna

Three Somerset Poems
I. Let us go up a Somerset Lane on an Early Spring Day

Let us go up a Somerset lane on an early Spring day
When a warm haze has early settled on land,
Pink stretch of plough and grey green pasture on every hand,
And a blue hazy outline on nearest horizons.
We come on a stack yard with finch flock creeping forward,
Who then will flutter and scatter to every hedgerow.
Chaffinches of both sex, some will be paired,
Leave the public now for longer each day,
To sing and establish a nesting domain.
The twitter and chinking of Yellowhammers
Abundant now in these lonely hedgerows
Sing of the heat through a hot west season
Posted on every tree in the lane.

Where sheep are folded in fencing, on ploughland
Gulls will be wheeling, common with green legs,
Not storm driven, now; they are regular visitors
Flying up long lines both morning and night
From lonely coast to lonelier ploughland;
They string out like workers from factory to suburb.
On a morning like this one expects a Wheatear
To be bobbing on fence post or scratching out song;
And the little dull birds who chirr in the deep lane,
Cirl Buntings, fly up to cover unnoticed
And, overlooked, rattle from near top of tree,
But never on top twig, announcing incessant
Through all of the morning a ringing song as Chaffinch or like.
Out of lane over ploughed upland now we will wander
And marvel at air saturated with larks.
There is emptiness here with scrap farm implements,
And the countryside slumbers but listens for migrants,
Those bold ones who paused in Provencal meadows
Under clear air feeding and hurrying on.
Soon they will flourish their mottoes from branches;
High, hid from sight, their small yellow forms
Will slip among catkins bringing their tidings,
A new birthday in this our land.

II. Quantocks

The stags on the hill,
The people in church;
Peace in the air;
No need to search.
No breath of a motor;
Just a quiet buzz of flies
Beneath fern taunting;
And the scent of the heather
Held by eye-blue skies.

III. Quiet Elbow, Firm Hollow

Quiet elbow, firm hollow;
In Somerset, rock is keeping
A time to itself, sleeping
To a music of its own.
Fire slaking dew is sparkling;
Where the way between fields,
Cut by animal hooves,
Folds arm over hill;
And hides in a sun-shy hollow
What is not of now, not new,
Nor is any time's morrow.

The Witchcock Hour

The witchcock hour before the dawn
Coming across with distant thunder
Crosses the land with sounds and omens
Over the heads of the sleeping sighs,
Coming across with a trample of glory
The thundering steeds and the dust flying.
Returns with portents of suspense
Back into silence waiting.

Over to you, Over to you
Sleepless one all sleep defying,
The sunbow scimitar sweeps on you
Out of the eagled eastern tapestry
And the forlorn web of stars.
The sucking milkproud night

With talons grips on the dead days
Squeezing out their dew of pain
With the solitary cock-crow witchcock wail,
The mephitic chiding death-beat wail,
Of the lonely cry where the railways run;
Enfield, Brentwood and the lonely junctions,
The puff of trains and the dawn coming.

And I turn as I lie on my woken bed
Like one returned from the dead
Communing with spectres.
Unable to speak, unable
To resolve one deed; and hearing
The dogs bark back
To the tears of the Great Regret.

The watchman stirs.
The watchman shuffles and coughs.
He stamps his feet and the night is full of noises,
Night noises that give strength to shudder.
Keep still. Do not surround.

And I turn again as the witchcock crows
And creep on our first-born wail,
Hemming in from the past
With my dark sorrow,
My crowd stream of sorrows,
Into pools of old despairs
Where hopes drain back;
And resolution fades
Upon the crowing of the cock.
Dhavana Dhyana Dhivana

Do you recall the times of feasting,
Unity, consanguinity and mirth,
The curriculum of ordered days and settled ways
(Over the hills the summer bowling)?

At this hour between birth and dawning
I see only
Beyond the crimson barrier range
A blacker land where the leaves blow
As the Angels know
To the breath of desolation,
The witchcock land, the spider's grim terrain,
Where the bats flit to and fro
And a nothingness finally achieved.

Oh firmament oh stars oh dazzling cliffs of splendour
Oh night
Keep still. Do not surround.
Do not as yet propound this plight.
As I weep at morning's shrine
Do not ask me further to define this task.
Speak still from the heart of silence.
For the witchcock hour is here
And I wait in a sweat of fear
That the universe might go backwards
Jolt. Jolt. Jolt.

For J.W.B. aet 15 on His Playing the Oboe Concerto of Cimarosa on 10 June 1955 (in a concert in the Burney Library, Clayesmore)

The riches of the air distilled this live long day
Are now at essence: and hushed to hear him play
The wind on this clear evening in June.
Young Bridgen, oboe, fifteen summers fled,
Gave tune clear shining wings to fly,
Scamper and pipe above the congenial mutter,
Dip and soar above crowd's contented roar;
Spraying with pert staccato old grey heads,
He scattered his pollen to the flying air;
Chortling and crowing, he rode his presto steed,
Chuckling, leaping, revelling, he did succeed.

Sucked into the vortex of his pure soul,
Beauty he poured in measured plaintive joy
From Beauty's curved lip; the silver reed
Gave voice to melancholy, shadow to evening stream.
Here was heart's longing laid on the evening air,
Beauty and love of beauty, archaic, pristine, fair.
No shepherd-boy's lament on far Idalian hills
Could outdream this surprise; those fountain eyes
Did fondle the air of nature, gave repose
Her birth and place of gifting; he nigh burst
To float and sound the sway of hallowed waters in our ears,
Cockling the ocean of our longing to a minute's span.
Prime among his peers, this poet boy began
For me a recollection, a troop of thoughts like deer startled

Out of the forest of past experience; from tangled thickets fled
Out on the dewy lawns those lost anticipations
With liquid eyes, then paused as they surmised
And sniffed a newness in the air, the freshness of creation.

And as the lad played on, drowsy like bees on summer slopes
We lingered to his note. To his lulling we rocked.
Us he led on the thread of tune, now slow and calm,
Now clearing a silver bow-wave of desire.
Precision tore through the calm fury of his young hair,
Fingers plied to unravel the delicate knots
With lightning skill, desperate to weave
His tightrope to the stars, his giddy transit.
While tensed below, the orchestra restrained his nerved hand,
Guiding with tiller the flood of his outpouring lay,
To pace with tempo taut the leap and chant
Of his enjoying. But he outran
Their limping aspirations, as the butterfly
Will soar and flutter past the questing flowers.
This was his day. He had laboured to prepare
This clarion announcement to a lidded world;
He led us one by one and all away:
And piping Hamelin like he tripped ahead
In quest of fleeting beauty to the shades
Of woodland haunts and insect humming glades,
Where flowers with dewy eyes were hushed and sighed
To his enchantment. The soft wind
Played and dawdled in the grassy wold,
So lightly lifted that forever slipping lock
Of golden hair; which proudly he tossed back
And like a cherub puffed the frolic wind.
A stream of silver nectar from his throat
Grew in its gold and honey, channelled and piped
And rolled about the floor as mercury among stiff chairs.
The soul of boyhood was at flowering;
His eyes looked far beyond the present hills;
So flushed his cheek, so deft his hand, so fair!
It were beauty creating beauty, held on the vain air.
We hushed: the airy flight prolonged and vied its trills
Then clipped, dipped to land to us, now overwhelmed
And hushed in true humility.

A fraction point of quiet, and then the torrents gay
Of hand-clap-hands: O this was Bridgen's day!

Five Poems for John Bridgen
I.

I cannot bear to measure
The gifts you gave away;
Such happiness in Austria
Such tears in Munich lay.

The tears were of rejoicing;
The happiness is spent;
Though memory may recover
O time will not relent.

The mountains bear your dreaming
Light as the curdled cloud
And Austrian air with music
Echoes your thought aloud.

Who once has gone to Salzburg
May never leave it whole,
It's true they need your money
But, ach, they get your soul.

Now back in England's pastures
Forego das Fremde Land;
New worlds abide your knowing
Fresh themes wait your command.

Go steep in a cask of Schubert,
Till your hair flows over your ears
Like water lilies floating,
Drown in delight and tears.

II. Caring

Today I have a sense of something fair,
Maybe it is the lime scent on the air.
I woke from clutching in the mothy dark
A mote of your true being, a heavenly spark.
The breath of summer morning seemed to lie
Upon my longing heart so heavily
Until your ease and breathing presence came
To set my living heart of joy on flame.
The grief of caring melted in such fire
Wherein your recognition did conspire.
Again we held the thread of summer's dance.
The manuscript of season opened as by chance

On a white page of beauty for our joy
Whereon you set your seal, delicious boy.
Your smiles well up so easily to the brim
And fount of relaxation. Nothing grim
Could long oppose such trusting questing eyes;
And love regales your cheek so young and wise
With generous regard. O how did death
Stalk through the night to steal away our breath
And dull our being with twelve absent hours?
What legends would confute, what downdrag powers
Interrupt our future by the trick of time,
Can we but to the vantage of this dawning climb?
As trailing hands will touch a wayside bloom
Our being here will smooth away past doom.
O love must grow each morning from a spark
That is caught and fostered from the jealous dark;
It cannot like cash be stored for future gain
And, if squandered, the darkness steals it back again.

III.

My life a turmoil was until I soared
Into the blazing shadow of your love.
How long together we can our flight sustain
Depends upon the pattern of the rays
Of mercy shining on us from above;
How long we can defy the pull of earth,
And from action circumstantial be thus freed.
Our orbits met, we rose above each hour;
The broken petals drift alas to earth,
As if reminders whence our action comes.
But never let our infidel recurring selves
Refuse the high adventure; nor deny
The pull of limitation, or its scope
Allow to grow and smother in its clasp
The tree of unforeseen delight, confused
By ivy spread which chokes the breath of dreams.
For we have built a causeway out on hope
By gift our love, and, subtly engineered,
This fragile bridge connects our lonely slopes.
Past deeds and past ambitions deep flow on,
Dark by the drugged scent of meadow sweet,
Fed by the dews of lasting discontent,
The untroubled waters move and eddy on;

For through pool and shallow must our natures flow.
But high above the drumming snipe describe
Their arcs of fancy in the summer sky.
Boundless the pang of evening should we refuse
Our equal chance to soar through summer's realm;
Perhaps to move into another clime,
Do we but dare not to return again
Back to the little gate of former selves.
We'll forge new paths of promise in the air,
Plumed and defiant cleave with shining faith
Through shadowy bonds of mundane cobweb need,
And break from the earthly nexus of despair.
We'll build new highroads in the sky of deeds;
Our song we'll proclaim with powerful growth of words,
To hover and smile aloft in candled green,
Green laughter in the swarm of Summer blue;
And construct a living maytime to ourselves,
Dear to eternity and mutual fresh delight.
As airborne soldier clambers to the hatch,
Straightens his harness and from safety dives
Clear of the noise of engines, silent drops
To spread his wing and float, so equal we
Must face each moment with determined eye
And freed of set-backs step into the blue
To sail with courage above the pull of time.
Thus through uncharted volumes we'll drift apace
And let ourselves dare all; nor losing much
That matters when the wheel of time rolls on;
So to the future we will point the way
With our unsurrendered resolve of liberty.

IV. Edmonsham Woods, Dorset, 1955

Let not one lucky leaf of Summer fall
Upon the silent carpet of the glade
Where you and I 'neath interlacing leaf
Did read together in the dappled shade
How Keats with sleep and poesy did toy,
And you breathed quietly, dear sylvan boy;
Let not one thoughtless leaf of Summer fade,
But I with weakest trestle struts of verse
Set down the joys of that most graceful shade
Of Summer glooms and glories, and rehearse
That wayward hour from off the time trod path

Of muddled busy day; where younger dreams
Stretched in the filtered sun, and joy held sway.
How you were pensive, how your gay young laugh
Curled in the echoes of unnumbered streams
That mazed their crystal way as thoughts in dreams
On pebbly floors of English counties green.
Let not one ripened leaf of Summer glide
To curved and crinkled ruin on the floor
Of that old woodland ere our thoughts again
Go forth with ancient fable as our guide
To seek Endymion's dream in silvery shower
Of music, fresher than cooling shafts of rain;
And to chase the clouds on Dorset downs, as kings
On those bright pavements shout challenge to wind and sky,
And with laughter and clamour to hail Apollo bright
As with quivering reins he drives to the golden night.
From fired and resonant hearts with affirmation
Then let us praise our heroes; banners raise
To Truth and Beauty; stale custom's pen defy –
Schubert and Springtime; Mahler and sadness; joy
To moth-hunting Brooke; to Tennyson laurel leaves.
Let glancing light of Britten hither fall
With serenades; may Housman perchance too steal nigh
The closer to view this boy of Bacchic eye
Draining the wine of Beauty to excess;
And to make his joy complete in time
May Auden add confirming praise of him.
Let wonder crowd his waking, the hours caress
His brow with thoughts of where the gold light weaves
In hollow tunnelled woodland. To him may all,
All of his hopes come true, and may the Muses bless
And crown this youth with unfailing tenderness.
Then if the stars are right he will proclaim
His thanks in right creation, word or note,
Come true from this young nightingale's sweet throat.
Let not this bud of Beauty unfold in vain;
This breath of Schubert for life or cash be slain;
May he mature sound from Nature's root,
For many the promising buds, but scarce the fruit.

V. For Ever

Come leave us, Summer, melancholy
Quit the scene of your distressed encounter
With the hours that should have ever flowed
Harnessed as brooks to memory in the green
Deluded image of our fleshly eye.
The flowers blow on for ever in our dream
Though Summer lifts her skirt, and stepping wide
And proud and free, turns
And enters the dark barn of Autumn
Where harboured gold lies piled
Beneath her shafting beam.
Still, O friend, still do I see
Your eye for ever resting on that scene
As our shadowed ghosts are playing on the green
Warm fragrant turf of a vanished time that's been.
The scented days float back, their ache now eased;
In the scabious' warm heart is always Summer's hour.
Still and drunk as a bee in lilac nectar delving,
Plunged in the restful grass our memories lie,
High on the Wiltshire downs
Beneath the chalk-hued skies;
There ancient burials sleep and bones rest underground
Forgetting their encounter. But let us rise,
Turn back again the pages of our joys and griefs
(The passage of bare hours, the pause of solitude)
For therein reflection can as in a mirror spy
The uncompromising image of eternity.
Raised by the spirit of a mellower faith
We'll not lament those hours for ever fled;
Though that Summer time is past, its flowers are not lost;
Theirs are the verdant fields of paradise, whose unencumbered airs
Wander for ever as freely as shepherds on their innocent affairs.

The Quest of Apollo
For J.W.B. who had been reading Keats's 'Endymion'

Where the moon has stolen by
Over silver meadows,
Where the beasts in pasture lie
Deep beside their shadows
Ruminating in the dew,
There goes fancy's retinue
Across the dew-drenched meadows.

Skipping far ahead through flowers
Over wold and hollow
Brushing pollen down in showers
Truant runs Apollo;
Tired of sun and sun's vexed shade,
Keeping to a vow he made,
Endymion to follow.

As the cattle stir and heave
Beneath the starry drifting,
Comfortably gaze and breathe,
Their heavy heads scarce lifting,
He scours the meadowland to find
The haunted youth whose noble mind
Was crazed by moonbeams shifting.

Light over meadows and long through shades
He treads and ranges, glancing
Down between waving grassy blades
In search of the youth entrancing.
The moonbeams chuckle, the moonbeams slide,
And silver the lonely cropped hillside;
Then away with Endymion prancing,
Across the waters, the rippling sea,
Stretching before them wide and free,
The silvery beams go dancing.

And ne'er can the sun with hot tight hand
Catch up with the shadows that over the land
Flee at their Lord's advancing.
When later the chase is left behind
And night her watch is keeping,

The child has forgotten the tale he had read,
The book has slipped from his hand and the bed;
And the cattle are quietly sleeping
In meadows where the herbs respire
And the moon shines with ghostly fire.

On the Ionian

All I hear is the wind in mast and shrouds
And the tireless whisper of the sea.
Behind unrolls, with Wedgewood curls and scrolls,
The stately, boundless plains of folded blue,
Where chop the unspoilt waves with subtle sighs
That little winds have made, their kisses furled
In the blue hair of the Hyacinthine sea.
Astern like gods we drift above the sea,
Indifferent to its terrors, remote
From its jaws of slavering foam;
There glides our path as track of amethystine snail,
A sleeve upon the labouring blue.
Below which toll in rusted bronze
The bells and armour of once ancient foes;
While oozy worms devour the shattered prows
Of their bleak ventures, and hypnotic eyes
Painted on bows once proud
Now peer into the sand dismayed.
To leeward lie Albania's eagle snows,
Their frozen talons clenched on the horizon's rim,
And a blue space between, like depth's reflection
In a considerate gaze,
Candid and truthful as of friend and friend.
Untroubled by the past, from present cares remote,
We sail upon the calm immoderate sea;
Spreading our daisied carpet
With smoke and mast aslant towards sleeping Greece.
The natty steamer tips its cheap-jack hat
Back like a traveller in 'lines' and cheap success,
To conquer Athens, flourish a kerchief, blow
All thought away save profit
And tourists' foolish gold.
But it is more than this we mean
Who scan and scour with hope the lifting main.

Happiness

The mistles have laid their fifing by
And the sun spreads his paws on to my window sill.
From the gramophone the Matthew Passion
Winds its choric floral way
With a Death and with a Life
And the burgeoning of the repeating seasons.

'Look for his memorial at Cape Harris in the Dardenelles,'
Said Matthew in The Talbot this morning.
'My brother, Reginald, he was in the Dorsets,
Same as has his name on the village cross –
I was at Lemnos then, it must have been nineteen fifteen,
And we were up at five thirty, and the sun scorched our legs raw
In the day in those lemon groves,
And their farming was forty years out of date, so it seemed.'

And today, now forty years further on it's spring.
The chiffchaffs have spread from the lake
And are slicing and chanting in the trees;
The jackdaws are clicking their tongues,
While the rooks, shaken matchboxes, caw and cry;
And the stockdoves contentedly pump and groan.
And tomorrow, leaving green April to bud in England,
I will be off to the flecking and thirsty Aegean.

TR-2
For Bobby Hill

With a broad swirl of pattering gravel spray,
The road took note of the hollow throat
Of a TR-2 under way.
With a surge of power our metal flower
Growled at the opening road;
And as my foot went down, any protest was drowned
In the roar of the visiting air.
Like a hungry hound we shuddered and shook
While the farmsides fluttered by
Like the laughing pages of a story book,

And the driver purred and sighed.
Till a chance in the form of a blind double bend
Led into the Victory slide.
The hedges flipped up and the trees kow-towed
And the sky came tumbling down,
But the wheel sailed round and we gripped the ground
And fled to the Postman's Corner.
Not caught that time by the hands of earth,
We danced on the crest of the morning.
The flowers waved hands, and the smiling lands
Basked in reflected glory.
Gravity attended to, gravity defied,
'Mind out, hold tight now for another slide,'
Says the muttering voice of our hero;
As he storms the gap in traffic, he's simply terrific,
Singeing the beard of tomorrow.
Man's life may be a poem ever greenly flowing
Between the safe banks of his ageing,
But his youth is a cordial and the chance of an ordeal,
So let's press on regardless and get weaving.
Oh the children weep as speedometers creep
In the crisp new air of the morning;
And the pampering winds cry out through cupped hands
Their livelong evergreen warning.
But with scarf and with frown I shout the gale down,
And I cry – 'You're too late, I've a fixture with fate,
And I'll not be the loser this morning.'

Swollen Eye

There was once a giant who pressed trees in a book,
He liked to show them to his friends at night.
And models of men he'd set down on a board,
Sprawling and carefully pinned; he labelled them
And wrote notes on such as when they first wore long
Grey flannel trousers. He was rather queer.
He liked to strip the railways up for fun
And watch the elaborate expresses fail to run
On time. Mid crowds and waving flags he'd duck
An embattled warship then dash on up to the hills

Where Government officials come rarely nigh.
And floating at sea he'd gaze at the sun going by.
He was a 'one'. The neighbours even said
His irresponsibility was quite
At variance with the birds he lived among.
But he sang with wonder o'er the shining spheres.
For his book was heaven, and daily he turned a page,
Leaned heavily over and scanned the immortal news.
It was but a carefree jest for him to stir
The pool of life and see which folk would dive
In zigzag terror chaotically spare
Clutching their money bags; but he approved
The poets soaring up to breathe some air.
These were his fancies. Yet each night put him to bed
Where he would snore as sound as you or me.
There was no Mrs. Swollen Eye; he was the last you see.
Since my childhood, when all this happened, he's mostly forgot.
For times are so much safer now he's not about.

Sonnet – June 1955
For J.W.B.

Fled, fled for ever is that golden June,
Our footsteps vanished from the woodland rides.
Your joyous laugh which mingled with the tune
Of singing birds is silent and abides
But in the cloisters of my mortal heart.
And you who saw and loved each passing flower
Have journeyed on in sleep and grown apart
From that sweet moment of love's temporal power.
I, lost in absence of our secret joy,
Must grip the rope of fraying time and pull
Me up from sad dispatch and sad employ
To stock a tower of wonder which will school
My fancies to enthrall your lips in rhyme,
And kiss hard back the urgent lips of time.

South Terrace, Clayesmore, 7 August 1955
For J.W.B.

Clouds drift serenely on;
Their ever whitening throng
Gathers as memories do
Within the leaden shade
Of graven cypress made,
As I dream on of you.

Above reflecting pool,
Mid water lilies cool
A grey stone cherub beckons,
Pointing to heaven the hours
Of seasons' wasting powers,
Ironically he reckons.

Wide spaced around, the trees,
In formal symmetries,
Re-echo a hushed charm,
Broken alone by martins'
Sharp chirrup of departing,
And then restored to calm.

Leaves, riding as I stare,
Sway to the silent air
In restless sea-blown fashion;
Bright trees in writhing green,
Bidden to tides unseen,
Shake in their emerald passion.

And I, alone, reflect
How Nature's dialect
In passing leaf and flower
Speaks of your quiet easing
Sigh in the breath of pleasing,
And my suspense of power.

Submission

I submit.
There is no more to it,
This tale of fruitless striving.
I cast my plan
Down. On my knees as man
I go, not journeying so
Through woes untold,
No way through, now,
No travelling, but
Arriving.

My Lord has said,
Lay first your head
Upon the first cold step of stone
And then atone,
For not alone
Should man devise Salvation
By progressing.

But pressing next
His heart to heaven's glass door,
Should ask his Lord
If one, so poor, might part from stressing
Into blessing.

Untitled

In the Northway valley stillness lies
Safe beyond the tides of man;
And the little road bides
And the little stream glides
Sparkling beneath the midday sun.

The blackbirds whistle from copse and hollow
Where the rabbits play no more;
On the steep green shoulder
Sheep graze by the boulder
And the buzzards mew and soar.

Felled are the alders by that stream
Where my memories have lain so long;
Though small is the range
Of outward change,
From my heart's brook has vanished its song.

Untitled

On this hard silent upland,
Rain-carved, stone-washed, sun-bleached,
The brusque leafless branches of Beech rattle lightly
Beside waving carpets of unrolled plough;
Grooved terra cotta, inlaid with shadow;
And a staunch tree of holly
Stands solitary in the cropped hedge –
A tidied, shorn and active upland scene.
While yonder the clouds roll on and dream
On Quantocks brow,
Whose classic hill line slants
To the pencilled blue shadows
That lie over Taunton dene.

The Currant Cat

Sadly the cat sits and purrs,
A paradox of furs.
And sleepy fumes attend
Her plump soliloquy.

Embers stir and readjust
Their fragile glowing cinder-crust;
An old and leatherproud armchair
Heaves a deep extended sigh;
A door bangs to, and round
The trinket-sprinkled mantelshelf
Puffs a cloud
Of
Sea green smoke.

Still the windows stream. . .
The currant cat swims in a dream. . .
Cream. . . .
Cream. . . .
Cream. . . .

Fingerday

Oh who when waking early
Has heard soft doves complain
While owls wide rings of sorrow
Echo again, again?

It is the time of transit,
Day treads on the carpet of night
And shades of fable and fancy
Gather and merge in fright.

Oh who when waking early
And hearing doves complain
Has not felt mankind's burden
Lifting itself again?

While the bright feet of the morning
Tread on the lintel of stars;
Birds in the dew rejoice again
And the first faint hum of cars
Pronounces that the roads are free
From the prowlers' hooded fears.
Dark faces set to the west again
On the caravan of tears.

But dew and the tears evaporate
In the manly warmth of day
As Apollo warms to stretch and guide
Our fingers on their way,
And the doves in their eased complaining
Croon on, for another day.

Poet as Maker

In a mortar of syntax and rhyme-scheme
He crushed the hard jewelled words,
Dulling their facets and innocence
To liberate a comparative meaning;
To distil a rational incense
In the tough senseless world of deeds.
But some words slip out of their orbits,
Not content to stand to attention in tiaras,
And wink and glitter as they slide away
And revert to their warm subliminal lives
Down the odd turnings, quirks and corners
Of our ignoble neural garden cities.

Par les Soirs Bleus d'Eté

The beauty of a Summer's dusk
Is shadow deepening into shade;
As the earth is etched on a darker blue
From which the hovering shadows fade.
Far over evening's tidal bay
A deeper confidence and peace
Folded beneath the foreign stars
Breathes in the silence of the trees.

The air is cool. The day is done.
Now lovers pluck a grassy stem;
Lovers who in the blue evening
Are lured by a more than mortal dream.
With hearts at peace these dreamers go,
Holding Poetry's magic scroll,
As silently by twilit paths
Through fields of gathering dark they stroll.

Untitled

What you are living and what you are thinking
Are not necessarily the self same tale.
For yesterday as we went together
Over the grey blackdown hills
In a mist I thought of solitude
And a blackbird stepping in a garden
With the weather slowly dropping down,
And I smiled at nature's divinity,
Knowing better than to walk through wet grass.
O soul, time's mover, o sense, heart's deceiver,
We are all of us ever, like Michael Robartes,
Trapped in our tower. This has been said
So often before. Many generations
Have assembled on the cardinal shore
Of a fleeing spirit's circumference
And discussed with joy the impending adventure –
But, like Coleridge nursing his woe as night neared,
Instead of striking new sparks from the dark,
They mostly took hold, like a clammy potato,
Of the cold dispassionate hand of Plato,
To pass into the mysteries.

Untitled

I lay and heard wind in the trees
Tossing its horns in the lower branches.
Scales were the leaves, black scales of heaven,
Studded with scales were the trees as a metal shield
Withstanding the thorns of darkness.

'What proof have you?' brayed the trumpeters,
In the golden velvet darkness.
'An echo' I cried, as the fish-scale stars
Slid at the tilt of the zenith.
An echo to the Poles went my answer,
To the uncrumbling absolute zeros,
Cold in the forest of fires and shoals of stars
Far above, luminescent and salty,
Far away spreading their skeins.

O Creator how stretched are your fingers!
Bewildered, the fringing reeds
Mutter and shake in the silence.

Untitled

In dim Brazilian light
Hot jaguars unite;
And dappled frogs perform
On banjos till the dawn.
While raucous parrot cries
Spread scarlet in the skies,
Piranas nibble chunks
Of what were human trunks.
Lugubrious as an owl
The mournful monkeys howl.
And down the great Amazon
The heaving currents run,
Wreathing as the dark
Swirls of the river mark
Where from branches smooth and wide
Dark anacondas slide.

Sea Island at Night

Where feeding sheep by moonlight crunch the turf
And stone walls loom, and hollow sighs expire
Upon the salty air; down by the cliff foot
Struggle and urge the silvered slavering tides
That lift the locks of seaweed in their surge
And boom afar within unsleeping caves,
Where nameless fish and oozy crabs abide
And jaws unfriendly lurk in ribboned gloom.
Sounds as each sea recedes the clicks and gulps
As winking bubbles break within the eyes
Of sharp spired winkles in the unfingered dark.
While out beyond the mouth of rocks and caves
The ocean wrestles and sleeps, pre-occupied
With the same deep problems; over and over as stones
The moiling waters rush, and waves in shoals
Quest in beneath a quickly freshening breeze,
Invading yet again once conquered bays;
And bringing their lament to sandy brinks
Of lonely shell-strewn beaches, where the song
Blown inland from the ocean never tires,
Telling of sadness from the echoing days
That knew not man nor his perplexities,
Ripples upon the swell of ocean's woe,
That, salty, rots the fabric of our earth.
List to the struggle borne in on the wind
Between the salt-flowered ocean and dour land,
Whereby the one would engulf the other quite,
And spread her restless peace above the capes
And scarps of our existence full submerged,
Like bottles sunk beneath the labouring tide
That swells and moans under a watery moon
And dangles tidings in our drowned ears.
Now on this short cropped turf the unseen sheep
In their familiar munching reassure
The safety of dry land and rocky pledge,
Here among thrift and granite to withstand
The countless murmurs of the sea, our foe.

Western Scotland

Nightwaking
For J.W.B.

The bread of moment crumbles.
Passions cease to flow.
What was a roaring cataract
Is hundreds deep below.

But through the icy caverns
Of an unremembered heart
Unheard there seeps the music
Of bitter springs apart.

And this in time of torment
Will well and flood the eyes
With memories of moments
That live on but don't arise.

Still in the heart's recesses
If we could truly mark
There dwells the flower of passion
That blossoms in the dark.

Like continents of childhood
That seem to have sailed away
The tragic flame of wonder
Burns quietly on for aye.

Now outward eyes but measure
And use not their regard;
Love that was tall now tip-toes
But rarely to the barred
Window of former loving
Where the air was light with joy
And peers through rain washed windows
With eyes love can't employ.

All death to flying moments
Creeps near to grip and tell:
'Little the satisfaction
That one has loved you well'.

Though life by love once kindled
Will outstare death's grimace
And bid him take his merchandise
To sell in other place.

The sadness will not leave us;
But lonely as saxifrage
Will linger on in crevices,
Forgotten stage by stage.

We never may recover
Nor hear the song again,
But the wound will bleed for ever
With the ichor of love's pain.

Earning is all in loving;
To save is storing grief
That sinks from hands of memory
For ever out of reach.

Soothed by the lulling music
Of metre's lullaby
We sleep and drown the music
That called to us from on high;
Sleep in our hearts' forgiving
And dreaming eye to eye.

April

The beauty is out of Spring again
And the leaden clouds are here
Tramping their way across sullen counties
Whose roads wind long and drear.

Seen by a roughly manged hillside:
A sudden rift in the cloud,
And a shaft of radiant orange sunlight
Pierces the drizzling shroud.

The people look up towards the hilltops,
Glance up from their heavy spades,
As glory over the allotments
Spreads and glows and fades.

Before Cockcrow

The web of silence spreads;
Night holds the summer in her stony hands.
The stars shine on hard in their stony brightness.
Pools of mist by distant railway tracks
Lie raw and melancholy in the moonlight.
A tethered goat chafes in his hut.
The early cockerel scratches.

Far off, the rumble of trains
And distant heavy traffic;
The congress of earthly cargoes hum.
First light is caught in an oil-silk puddle
By the looming shadow of a deserted signal,
A megalith of childhood.

The birds feet of dawning
Stir in labouring fields.
In the dewy web of morning silence
Naked bodies shift in bed,
Uneasily twine, their breathing heavy
Like the ancient dead.

Gaunt pylons watch,
Solitary and strict in inorganic fastness
Like metallic nurses of their creature man-child
Rocked in his dream of splintered splendour;
And a little wind plays in the grass of civilisation.

A cow shifts two plodded feet
In the mud of her earthfield.
As the mind like a fly crawls out to explore
Another broad table of day;
And the mood of dawning with cockcrow
Slides back to the timeless diamond stars.

Untitled

So up and out you sponsor
Of my pain's defined ascent,
Yours the privilege it is
To fight and not relent.

The Dead of Year

The world slides by; trees are drowned.
The rain drags drops to trickle down the pane:
The great siege of Winter is thus reduced
To tingling tight drops of despair, flowing,
Down cheeks flowing.

A starved and frightened crow flies out
Across the wreck and waste of waters.
Armies slide and plunge, and stick.
Thrush pulls at worm, reluctant thread of life.
In a sad stalk of grass, heeled into mud,
Lie years, passions, conquests.

Crude spiked railings loom
Where fog drips on raw, dank bark;
The trees' lank interlacing locks
Lie sullen in disgrace;
Caesar has spent the coffers
And sap is low in the well of their trunks.
A fox makes his skinny footway, trots out of winter wood
To sniff the carrion sky.
Steadily falling grief,
The rain, patters as he steals –
Methodic symbol of our deeds
And of our misdeeds.

And we lift our journals, settle in chairs;
See not the day, backward on moments lean,
The scarp twixt breaths,
The washed dead instant before becoming,
And long loth leave taking.
Swift ashes of ambition
And dumb acorn thoughts, not stirring.
Do we await a sign? No, for hope
Is not gossamered between gross browned leaves.
There is but richness, rotten richness;
There is but moil of mould, dead past caring.
And no point occurs.
Only relentless orbits.

Unleaving

Trees, lose not as yet your robes to winter's wrath.
Should careless storms rip off your summer's grace,
It were a loss too sudden to forbear
That so exposed you stand twixt bustling wind
And the stone hand of frore winter.
But destruction stalks the seasonal shores,
Tearing your tresses in his sore distress,
Cursing beneath his breath and at each gust
Scattering your level shade.
The scrambling headstrong wind
Then rushes in to tidy up,
Tipping improvident summer into a wry grave.
Oh wind desist and bide your biting tongue and blast.
Trees, my trees, part not so soon with these
Your tokens of summer's gift and shade
That later may with reverence be laid.
Such vain appeals I know are carried like the leaves upon the gale
And strewn aloft by laughing rollicking airs
To loss and mouldering in the season's grave.

Like Butterflies

Ambulances scream their way
Through the traffic of the day.
Sorrow is not so often heard,
But wings its way like a quiet bird
Into the foliage of the heart
As we drift on and sink apart.
Leaves to the ocean woodlands spent
Tumble to disfigurement;
Green thoughts in green shades
To a charred brown in stricken glades.
Hopes, like butterflies that hover,
Die and put an end to bother.

Untitled

What God does, that alone is right,
Herewith will I content me;
Though troubles ever in my sight
And pain and death are sent me;
My Father's care is ever near,
His strong right arm will shield me.
To Him I trusting yield me.

The Unfenced Mind

The sparrows' curtain flutters
Wallflower scent falls wry;
The putty on the window pane
Crumbles and grows dry.

Into a hand of moments
By chance's speckled ways
Touch points with index finger
To seal the lip of days.

The powder blue pronouncements
That puff the face of woe
Cause cherubs in the basement
To chuckle and sign and go.

The four ways of the compass
Were travelled round before;
Pointers swing in the gangway
And idle slams the door.

The goblin on the banister
Slides down the unlit stair
The powdered stars are scattered,
Blind dust in broken air.

Untitled

When they examined the hawser, encrusted with weed,
It led back very long to a friendship indeed.
True, he'd sailed far, while the anchor remained beneath,
But that had only strained, not snapped
His steel-cord of belief.

My Mind Woke up this Morning

My mind woke up this morning
From years of usual sleep;
Years when I could not sleep,
But only dreamed of burning
And, twisting thus and turning,
Drifted towards the deep.
The weir aware awaited,
The lasher sucked his teeth,
Straining his leash and foaming,
For most are sucked beneath;
Save, by an act, confiding,
One who treads a pace
In fantasy returning
By towpath from the place
Of ultimate derision,
And each pace drier learns
His foot upon the strata
To migrate though it turns
And spins bewilderment.

So move again by instinct,
Back by healing spiral;
With plenty to inform you
Of the way they went this morning,
The scent lies thick again.
And birds take up the challenge;
Suns again have meaning;
And enzymes are declaring
Hosannas in our bearing;
As we awake from sleep,
Dragged from the perilous steep
That drifted us so nearly
To pearly-toothed oblivion.
We waking rub our visions,
Feeling, seeing clearly –
Now joy has much to say,
Born on an endless traffic
To babble all the day,
For Spring this day returns.

18.4.64. Whitchurch, Hants.

Dawn Chorus

As the summer night lifts, birds mutter their prayers;
The querulous blackbird asks for a rainbow;
Throats re-echo fluffed and drilling,
Stirring the easy morning air.
Soon there is tutting, and reservations,
Strutting and bowing, the trickles spreading;
Trilling through copses, threads coalesce;
Silver as teaspoons their love they declare.
The argument mounts and the doves start pleading;
The ticker-tape gathers, woodpeckers typing;
Hectically reeling the larks are up, soaring.
Loud-mouth thrush is already boring,
Bearing down neighbours with proclamations,
Pinned to each tree-trunk, while barn-owl's snoring.
Over loved water meadows the mists are still hanging;
With the orchestra striving, the rooks are applauding,
Adding a comment or even a protest.
As the bowl of song rolls over summer morn spreading,
West country vales beneath blankets are stirring;
And the dew-shod foot of an early cowman,
Clipped and peeled like a cardboard puppet
Cut from the side of a cereal packet,
Shifts a quiet gate, and moves out to the meadows.

Envoi:
Now breakfast is over, the countryside tidied,
Here comes the cuckoo presenting his bill.

Untitled

When I look at the chewed pencil in my clumsy hand,
I see your acceptance, the golden principle shaped
To bind me, praise be, to the sympathy I need;
And will need, especially
When I look at the eager clumsy hand.

Untitled

Lie in the Spring and wait your cue.
Never let people decide for you.
The ore has waited long in the rock;
When Time wants you, Time will knock.

Untitled

Laughing and fooling may a barrier be
Between two sincerities,
When each by uttering converse praises
Says nothing he desires.
As poles drawn strong together once
May each repellent be
Shut in the fastness of their special powers.

Poet

A contemplative Argonaut,
Alert to watch and listen,
Casting into the brook for trout
With golden fins that glisten,
Who rise above the ripples and pout:
'The Lord indeed is risen'.

Untitled

At full extension sleep
Calls from the active process
Deeply outworn fingers
Of sense that often make much,
Sometimes reap and sometimes
But flounder on the deep.

Stonecrop

I crouched on a rock on the hillside,
Looking down like a Sphinx on the bay.
Stonecrop they called me, I think,
Those botanists.
Sedum Anglicum. Oh really?
Well, I suppose I have had my say.

Clerihew

Dr. Clemens Krauss
Was a friend of Richard Strauss.
Over a glass of beer
They wrote Der Rosenkavalier.

Wagner

The last of the unfettered magicians to break loose;
Like a lately active volcano, so close behind us.
Inhuman magic, with a coarse hand directing its flow;
Yet this is strong true wine, more true of man
Than ordered elegance would have us know.

Cuckoo

The cuckoo puts a spoon into our lips
And waggles it feeding us with hope.
He's a fly one, soon gone, when asked to perform,
To redeem his promise.
He stutters, falters, comes to a stop;
And then slopes off.

Untitled

There were some who said, and we may never hear that again:
'The great pianist brought them to their senses.'
Lies in the aviary, gone with the centuries wind.
Love the magician moves among his sheep
And shepherds guard the alembics of the mind.

Untitled

Perhaps where one is mad,
'Tis better to abide
Abed and endless laze
Than walk in mortal ways.

Perhaps where one is wise,
There's wavering whether to rise
Or wait on a dreamspun spirit,
Not wanting to spill a minute.

Bird Names

I hope to see in its abode
The Andalusian Hemipode;
But what I don't expect to find
Is what must be its state of mind
On finding that ornithologists
Have labelled it in lengthy lists:
The Andalusian Hemipode.

I knew a man who used to brag
About the habits of the shag.
He said that it is only found
Where Greenish Cormorants abound –
The simple statement of a wag.

Whenever my eye comes to rest
On a singular buff coloured breast
I think of the soul
Of the sweet Pratinole
Whose name is a name at its best.
Gloreola Pratinicola
Gloreola Pratinicola
A name after all at its best.

I hoped to see the See See Partridge,
I hope to see it still.
Although I know I haven't St. Francis
Of Assisi's ancient skill.

If a black-winged Stilt
Wore a highland kilt
And a Spoonbill came to tea
And Bonelli's Eagle
Was declared illegal
Where *would* the RSPB?

And of course these ancients –

They said as they followed the Auk
To his eyrie high up in the chalk
That the way that they went
Was an awkward ascent –
Such frightfully humorous talk!

When angered unduly, the Curlew
A look of defiance will hurl you
As much as to say
'If I had my way
I'd teach you, you impudent girl, you!'

And the great Original, Prime Mover –

There are those who live in hope to see
The Crimson Necked Phalaropee;
And there are also those who live in hope
To see the Red Necked Phalarope.

The Accent of Spring

The simple things of Spring are here;
Shy leaf and tender shoot appear;
Chaste catalogue of flower and song
Unfold each day from slumber long.

The brimstone hies on wavy flight,
The saffron herald of delight.
While tortoiseshells from lofts emerge
To flit and glide o'er path and verge.

In their dark eyes the myriad scene
Creates a pageant, whose varied sheen
Reflects from trembling velvet wings
The coloured radiance of things.

The larks applaud the rising sun;
Soaring and rippling to greet it they run,
And all the gamut of their blue
Zenith of desire pursue.

The chiffchaff's song will now commence,
Who then flits silent from tree to fence;
Slim voyager to these northern shores,
His song to all spring hope restores.

And as noble blackbirds strut on the lawn,
Sleek trespassers to scold and warn
Who dare to invade their private park:
Grey squirrels scrabble up the bark.

Lost in Snow

The snowflakes are falling outside.
Down, down, softly they condescend to pile
In a whirling moil of twilight twirl,
Feathers from the breast of a grey sky.
And my head, like a ball of wool sinks on to my chest;
Like an unwinding ball my thoughts unravel
And trail off lazily and travel
Into a tasteless, scentless future and past.

I present to the falling snow
An unfeeling sense, like the rosy breast of a bulfinch;
The soft cosy awareness of the bird's muffler,
Puffed out to ignore the ivory weather.
And the stuttered stamp of feet on the porch's steps
Are all drowned, drowned by the whirling pandemonium
Of silent madmen softly
Whispering down through branch and streetlamp
To alight and delight the freezing crystal snow way.
While away the squeaking crunch of padded footfalls
Are muffled and lost in the silent downfall,
Lost in the snow.

Entry Surgeon

Beautiful surgeon,
Where you cut, you should heal;
Though your blade is impartial,
Can you be as steel?

For the wound you have opened,
Not by choice on your part,
Cries out for the physic
Of a caring heart.

And Beauty like acid
Still burns as it spills;
In pity, Master Surgeon,
Be kind to these ills.

Untitled

Echoes the knock and bother
Of a distant Barnstaple train,
Rolling away through the vales;
By copse and quarry and stream,
Trundling through red and green.
Above Milverton dark houses raise
Their sandstone battlements,
Sombre at sun's abdication
From her glorious December throne.
Chartering country air
Smoke plumes rise and tilt;
Then under the Blackdown hills
Join Wellington's smoke and spread
With wrack and mist entangled
A legendary skein unguessed
Like forgotten bivouac fires.

Shoes

The life of the child is still house-slippered;
He tiptoes forth from home with caution.
While the youth sits, with his knees raised,
Tugging at the laces of good strong brogues,
Headstrong with hurry and swift ambition,
Ready to defy long roads and mountains
To prove his condition.
Then successful he, wearing a business suit;
With well shod stride he steps out, seeking to outpace
Destiny, his rival, or the cost of living.
What time man takes but little account of his shoes,
Unless they are dirty, insufficiently polished,
Or again worn out, and costing him money.
But the shoes and the life have a race with time,
Wearing out, now faster, now slower
Than his dreams and his hopes and his passion.
Oh at what sad cost does man his life so fashion,
When God may cobble all his schemes to nought.

On Revisiting King's College, Cambridge

The calm air sings among the divided traffic;
Spring and the May are constantly renewed;
Here at this well-head of God's English house
The stone balustrades smile like archaic statues
And the tall forest of stone is a perpetual celebration.

But the tides at the gates,
Oh the tides at the gates, bear down.

Within, the growing years inch forward to perfection,
Langorous as croci, whose short silent spears
Renew the Spring annunciation.
Our desires are reaped, transformed
To a jubilant exposition.
Notes run like rivers
Calm in the reedy boys throats,
Genes in their grooves perform
A marvel of exculpation;
The sainted air covers the tourist wave
Eroding, filtering the gates;
Reduces the throng to respectful behaviour.
Porters from Alice-in-Wonderland
Are the fabled beasts, allow access
To don or crazy march hare.
For here all is inscape, blessing,
The saucepan of rhetoric forever simmering,
And a flowering of art with the right decorum;
The straight-laced boddicing of College precinct
Sober as Sunday suits, enfolds the cherished patrons
Of incessant fermenting youth and freshness,
The acolytes of Spring.

So here let the fountains continue
To play their sweet theorems;
In the shrine resounds the blessed cadence.
Nowhere is Spring more sweetly served.

But the tides at the gates,
Oh the tides at the gates, bear down.

Mirrors

Time the faultless lyric breathes
Where a breeze its grace bequeathes;
Words to echoes answer long
Soliloquies of silver song.
Words and lyrics they are penned,
Though by the multitude condemned,
And speak through chance of poet's birth
Their sorry histories on earth.
Truth concealed in poet's guess
Glints with what they would express:
Patterns in the dancing leaves,
Purpose in the golden sheaves,
Truths in neatly fitting lines,
And terror in the makeshift signs;
Simple as a stone may be
That plummets down the silent sea.
Unresponsive storms may chase
From the haven of his face;
The scudding promises depart
From the fountains of his heart,
As bubbles breaking on the rim
Of perfection's chance in him.
Time suspends her motion now;
But in the trembling of a bough
Holds for a summer instant, while
The vision blossoms in a smile.
A glimpse is garnered, words perform
Their decorous duties as the storm
Is stilled into a dewdrop's quiver
Poised above the gleaming river.
But the hand that shakes the thorn
Now jerks the rein where time was born.
Perfection to the stream adjourns
While all without the bonfire burns,
And action into ash returns.

'Click' or after Hearing Britten's
'A Midsummer Night's Dream'

Now sweet delight create a gentle flow
Of moderate magic in the air we know.
No more are monsters met, no more afraid
We tread the leafy paths – they to denser shade
Have retreated and now in time's thick coverts are lost.
And still there hangs on woods a summer frost;
By moonlight slaked each thronging twig reveals
A clear identity, while music steals
Through banks and misty paths, threading the dark,
To vanish when cockcrow's curt denials bark.
When silence falls, bewitched, we strain to catch
The echo of a dropping garden latch.
Shut is the heavy book of summer's sighing;
But the web of summer's breath rings on undying,
As following in the tangled wood we stumble,
Hold melody by the hand in posture humble;
Lightfoot as children, charmed by Britten's wand,
We let it lead us, back to that unfading land,
His folded pageant from elysium retrieved,
The land in which once each one of us believed.

Poetaster

In carefully fashioned verses
The things that must be said
He left alone, and drifted:
His verse like him is dead.

And when the winds blow softly
About the flowering land,
They whisper of such promise
Gone beyond command.

The flowers grow up without him
And perish in their time.
But poets to fruition
Very seldom climb.

Normandy Morning

Orchards with warts of mistletoes,
Terra-cotta flowered poplars
Stand drilled by still lakes and ponds.
A land of rooks and furrows
With a spare sprinkling of larks,
Where bursts of pigeons fly up and
Are gone; while across brown fields
Swings a distant puff of starlings:
The earth awaits the sun.
Seeds in their millions smiling awake and stir
In the old drilled soil of France.
And we, journeying over,
Our holiday fancies rise and drift
As the engine's smoke-shadows
Start and fade and follow
Our train, scanning the verse called France.
It is a land which Virgil,
Appraising the dappled cart-horse,
Would delight in; and he alone,
Testing the country crumbling soil
Between dexterous hardened fingers,
Would choose to describe.
For us, our part, our harrowing,
Where lie so many human dead,
Soon crossed, soon passed, a prelude.

Impression

The paw of Africa thumps the yellow dust.
The fetid stench of breath
And a clout from the climate;
Though birds are bright as beads and green entangles,
The coffee rivers swirl, rock on
To an unmasked manifold sand-grained destiny.
Remarkable the mountains
How they boom back purple at you;
A torn calico skyline, a retching to heaven,
With thunder drubbing the distant carpet.
No skills here, the earth is symphony.

Death Wish

Tall as candlesticks,
Monocled and reserved,
Both icy and polite,
They watched the verse of rebels
Wash against the ruins;
The poisoned air from wartime
Corrodes the fretted stone;
And in the howling whine
Of jet and shell detect
Lament above the marshland,
Song of a shadowed future
Creeping over our maytime.
The blanket of denial
Is drawn across our culture;
The air left free for selling
Wares of a plastic kingdom,
Wiles of a sales-talk vulture.

From the Eagle-Haunted Summer

From the eagle-haunted summer
Shadows fly across the land;
Slant and glint of brassy thunder;
Hollow doom and golden sand
Sifting through prospector's fingers;
Mushroom cloud on purple strand
Spreads and stains the ghosted summer,
Conjured from a tiny hand.
To a mustard tree, enormous,
Bright with gas and poison dew,
Grows the cloud that will disarm us.
Strident trumpets herald new
Corrosive ways, so they inform us,
That will tarnish me and you.

Ageing

The sands of Africa drill in my ear.
And the great web of learning I'm afraid will not cheer.
In the grey marble rock pool antennae are flailing;
I can't wait to gossip, my biro is failing.
Drenched was the petal in spiked morning dew.
Driven to ruin the perilous few
Who rode over hump-backed bridges at dawn,
Chased by those cut-throats the rooks in the corn.

For Every Lucky Leaf

For ever lucky leaf
That downward as you fall
You cherish no belief
That you were meant at all.

When all your gold is sodden,
And sour your only breath,
You brood not with regretting
Nor hesitate ere death.

Past chlorophyll or caring
Of heedless summer days,
You drop to your disunion
Not knowing blame or praise.

Soon, Winter, cold, unfathomed,
Will grip life in its jaws;
When joy lies down to perish,
Life struggles within laws.

So, lightly, fragile token,
Fall to the bonfire's rake,
As in the smoke of autumn
Your exitus you take.

The Bronze Falcon (Die Frau ohne Schatten)

The Falcon calls. Out of Assyria
The Falcon calls, thrice calls.
From the steep barrier mountain
At our back the Falcon calls,
Soars as the Dove, uplifted,
And the sun's spears transfix him,
In loneliness and bronze he soars
Beyond our reach, beyond our stretch.
Before the mountain there lies a lake;
To the silken horizon only waters
Curl and reflect, echo and swell,
Curl and reflect. The Falcon's image sinks
Bronze in the reedy waters,
At sunset filigree luminous.
Beyond the waters turns the earth,
The rumble of commerce and oceans,
The unreachable earth of occasions
On its grinding necessitous pole
Where the sun sinks with a thousand horsemen
Trampling the carnage; and armies plunging
Down to destruction, as motes in the sun
Of a passing afternoon, burning plunge and go.
Away from kindness, from the wrists of kindness
And the brows of consideration.

Now the Falcon calls.
Powers of creation arise
Giddy as dust-devils,
Make new each moment
The sunset lakes, the ribbed violet mountain
And the tenantless desert,
Where floats the bronze Falcon
In violet shadow on the teeming waters
And the brass-tongued trees
Loll in a livid salty moon.
Here the Assyrian raised a stone finger
Beside the tumbling rock strewn torrent
And the gurgling peaty becks.
And in that finger
Was the inevitable slow cavalcade
Of all human endeavour,
Subject, alas, to the stone edict of a finger.

Hark, Armies of Moths, and a Cretan whisper,
The flaking off of giant crag
To tumble on his nose in the ruinous valley,
Scattering the Falcons
As an Emperor's gold-dust.

O trail beside the waters, hear my song,
There is no way to be that is not long;
And history is the powder on the face
Of history, to touch up Time's grimace.
O trail beside the waters, hear the song
Of Falcons who flew up from right and wrong;
Leaving the carcase, they rose up beyond
To threatening mountain ridges always higher;
Each beyond each rose up far beyond reach;
Proving the blood-drop true, and heart the liar.

Rebirth

The winds are torn and shrunken. Now left no mark.
The cows moan alleluyahs in the dark.
A shrivelled sprig of ivy taps the pane;
Flutter of dusty leaves and talk of rain.
The pensive stillness of the staircase winds
To where the tall No of a door reminds.

The pencil scrawls a line then stops: for look,
A clambering bee has crawled into a flower
And suddenly swung the bell of utterance
Down across the silent centuries.
Heavily and sweetly an angelus of light
Threads through the needle-carpet gloom like the sun:
The mood of resurrection is begun.

Spoil

Birds in the noonday
Sang from the treetops,
Reeled in contentment.
The sun as of old
Was lifting the green wrists
Of fresh tangled shrubs.

In the throat of the owl
Lay church bells and Christmas.
As snow billow tumbled
The ice on the pond's edge
Cracked in extremis:
The pause in a ballet
Of frozen ecstasy.

Now we have plundered,
Indulged and delighted,
Glossy with pamphlets;
The caves are all tenanted;
And the land lies ravaged.
Man is aware:
He is guarding his treasure;
Watching his dividend,
Getting and holding.

The scrape of a spade
Heard in reflection
Now holds more of truth
Than his armies of opinion.

What prospect for man
If he savage his mistress?
The hand of the snowman
Feels for his wrist.
The head of the Astrochimp
Closes on his.

Belone: Malta

The rock is too hot:
Dive in to the turquoise cavern;
Leave the shouting sun-brown boys
Hot in their sunburn,
And swim through shimmering curtains
Of ocean light, amethyst green
Under the shadow of boats
Blue keeled, red hulled;
Dodge the grey links of frayed rope
And explore the unsafe dimensions –
There, near the bottom,
A frilled flotilla glides off from us,
Rounds a rocky crevice to avoid us.
Here in the open spun emerald brine
Are the stranger Gar-pike, Belone,
Floating curious as needles;
They appraise our approaching
Then flash off to dissolve
In milk green shadows.
We stretch out a hand to grasp
Their silver denials
As they skip sideways and jerk to an oblivion
Of vistaed seascape.
Flat-earthers, we marvel at such salt solitudes
Ripening into unguessed vastness.
In such clear transports
We, fish and sunlight,
Inhabit separate jewelled courses
As remote stars ride their discrete ways.
Then from level shadows we emerge
Into the dry frolicsome sandwich day,
Where the brittle cars perch on the harbour wall
And among bizarre grey lobster baskets, the coloured boats
Dragged up out of reach, elude
Green fingers of the suppliant challenging sea.
And the brown boys rocket and plunge and shout,
The mackerel and sprats of this dry-palmed
Impoverished stone-aged kingdom.

To Construct Something on which to Rejoice

Declared affections close
Their eyelid on the morn;
Only those survive
In obscurest anguish born.

Disordered images flee
To the far corners of strife;
The luckless are overthrown
Rocketing back from life.

So little left for foothold
In the thunder of our days;
The walls of our possessions
Shield nought from death's keen gaze.

The castles of our belongings
Crumble at the touch
Of leering time's cold finger;
They don't amount to much.

No point can be in hurrying
From what's central to what's far;
Travel will bring no refuge,
Nor an abiding cure.

Now once again I circle
Solo around the earth,
In the orbit of aloneness
Seeking a new birth.

In the insecurity
Of the loving yearning heart
Lies the faintest hope of promise
As the seasons pull apart,

Like petals of the rose's longing
Stripped from the calendar year,
That through the heart's undergoing
Will fall the undrying tear.

Fall fresh tears at parting
From these burning eyes that gaze
Only towards the hilltop
For one lasting hope to praise.

The Broken Image, Katharos

His hair was an unmown meadow,
His lips a bubbling spring,
His footsteps spread like ripples,
He was by nature, King.

His song carved out of hillsides
Remote from later weirs;
He fingered frost on brambles
And froze the maidens' tears.

Giddy he struck the road rock
And knelt by folded doors
Where a quiet tangle opens
On a sweep of marble floors.

The ancient temple pavements
Depict a Grecian frieze:
A leaf unhitched, a memory,
Floats down the silent breeze.

It is the fountain's moment;
His hair is drenched in noontide;
The drops foam up and die.
The sun sets in his side.

A hero cannot vanish,
His parted lips must stay
To drink the heedless zephyrs
That wander down our day.

The Valley Rulers murmured.
Oh could perfection break?
High up an eagle circled,
An empire was at stake.

A crone below in Delphi
Fumbled in her cave.
The lightning flashed a warning.
Himself he may not save.

O, parched on stony hillside
His hair grew poppy corn,
While dust between the fingers
Crumbled and fell to thorn.

Powdered and white and broken,
He cracked and fell aside;
His symmetry had spoken
Its own resolve, and died.

His footsteps in the meadows
May now no more disturb
The teeth and roots and toiling
Of the everlasting herb.

Though hearts may glance in silver
Skeins of bubbling streams
That thread their way through meadows
Of the hinterland of dreams;

That cold and pure appraisal
Those lips may not now frame,
But the chatter in the pebbles
Will carry on the same.

No, stranger, pause and tarry,
Rest hand on this cool stone;
The sword is sheathed in the sunlight,
Azure and alone.

Fierce in her sable glances
The darkness bares her stars,
Her jewelled lances glitter,
The trumpets ring on Mars.

Shod in the dust of Nebulae
The chariots ride on high:
We raise our anxious faces,
And kneel, and pray and sigh.

Far out in space the Logos
Erupts in moted showers,
The timeless rain of atoms,
The dancing feast of hours.

Beyond our utmost orbits
The gates of Beauty clang;
Forgotten the face of the moment,
Unheard what poets sang.

No Communication in Eden

Solitary the snake slid forward
Into the accelerative world,
Exploring, tasting the hue-cornered meadow;
Wavered between lanced grass and the creeping buttercup;
By sun's occasional acts of kindness warmed,
Or by a shy boy's smile.
Led thus into coils of reminiscence,
He slides from tale to story
Expanding his grey mute scales
In the apparent warmth of a patient appreciation;
And Tolstoy spoke once to a lizard, who understood.
The tongue-tied snake can speak alone to a child,
Its secrecy clasped as an urn of offering;
Tongue darting and chrysostomic,
Nearer to the precipice of unknown vapours.
Then out slipped a quiet word, out of place,
A flaw in the logic of shining beauty;
Back steps the child, fresh faced,
By the wrong piece in the jigsaw baffled.
Back darts the snake as if bitten
By incomprehension, or a bitter summing up.
Snake then to snake, and child then to man
Break their alliance, paths crossing finally diverge.

Untitled

The rain has been falling on the tender earth
And in my heart at least the seeds give birth
To fairy flowers in silvered groves of leaves.
The rain has stopped. Now tender the night breathes
Of summer and all the oceans where the waves
Fall on a marble shore and cover graves
Of untried poets who must perforce be dumb
Until the Antique Trumpet bids them come
With laurel crown and humble lyre to place
Their simple offering in the hand of Grace,
Who trust and believe that as the healing rain
Falls on their husks of hope, such patient blooms
Will not expand and flower this time in vain.

LAST POEMS
1967-1968

Fishing for Legends
For Paul Valéry

The bare sea drifted in,
Over green wrecks
Spinning a sailor's yarn;
Spending spun thread
Over yard and mast and spar;
Spilling silt through,
Seeping over abandoned
Over encrusted hulks,
Long, long untenanted.
In splintered gangways spoke
The cold waves curling yarn,
The snarling foaming yawn,
The Jonah-swallowing gape of green.
Ocean of Legends, cruel receiver,
Swallow the baited line,
The fisherman's dripping line:
Fisher who hoped to hook
High leaping live, a story.

Cruel sea, surge over,
Turn bald shoulder
To fanciful story moulder:
Poet, perched he on pier,
Two eyes, two legs, and hope;
Who down gazes divining
In water eddies a deeper fancy,
A deeper drifting fancy.
Grey phantom shoals slide off,
Neglect the proffered shore;
Outflow with blazing flowers of tide,
Salt, reckless tide, outgoing glory;
Cohorts moving out,
Cohorts of hurrying riders,
Cry to the evening wind

Iconoclastic mocking;
Wave after wave,
With clenched indifference mounting
Above the fathomed fleeing shoals,
The nimble lives and legends,
Ride off from sorrow
Bitter and unrelenting.
O Watersway, why hastening?

The Untenanted House

Within, the creeping shadows
On yard bare floors; without,
A stealthy pitter-pat of rain
On dust-choked leaves, where staves of sunlight
Filter the air and motes eternal dance.
'Dust to dust' carefully whisper the spiders.
Crouching beneath its chestnut cloaks,
The house breathes personal messages,
Pressed by the weight of years
And languor of lost tongues;
Extends a skinny claw of time;
Toothless and shrunk and wrinkled,
Its skull of hollow history;
The haunt of pestering sparrows
That go about their business,
Restless as straws; they scarce disturb,
Confident in their acumen,
The mute abode of shadows,
As minutes in the years.
Livid-blotched and peeling the ochre walls
Are clasped by smothering ivy,
Which faithful climbs and clings
And taps upon the panes
And whispers in its ears.
Thrushes probe the once trim lawns.
While cedars lost in their glaucous frost
Drop trickling from needle drop,
Spread on the motionless grass.
And flowers raise imploring hands,
Greedily greeting the showers;
They are now struggling to perfection

With every humble weed,
With droves of crimson campion,
With hordes of blue speedwell
And glorious banks of dandelions
That crowd once cared for beds.
Long rusty grew the rake unused,
And leaves unswept on drive and path
Are strewn, grow brittle and curl
Like faded photo prints.
All is dejection and neglect.
The pigeons from their tilted cote
Fly to and forth, the day, as always, theirs.
Beside the lawn a cautious rabbit nibbles.
And foxes later prowl into the doorway,
Then lope out over sashes of dusty windows.

Retired into a shady corner to rest,
I close my aching eyelids on the world.
Long, long ago their last friends called
And said they must be out,
And, seeing the windows shut –
Maybe they are abroad:
Like the domed cubicles of fluttering martins
Fled to Africa,
Hollowly wait their return;
Or like a school whose children
From holidays are not back.

Death Heads

Foxes' heads rolling, severed, yowling;
Pink tongues like soapy hands overlapping
Basalt grey lips round white pillars curling;
Wet eyeballs rolling, at angles gaping,
Oiled globes tilting, swivelled by feelings;
Long drawn doling, keening, moaning;
In eyeball oceans, rip-tide roaring;
Piebald askewing, celluloid knowing,
Limited print world, final showing;
Mirrors of headlands, lost over wave tops,
Landmarks going, wet shine fading;
Memory dulling, last gasp stretching;
Foxes' heads staring.
Of kindness, bone survives.

Still Life: The Path

A plain sandy lane leads over the heath,
Sparkling with monsters. In the jewelled eye
Of the spangled turf grow reflections of ogres.
From far away to a lost content
Meanders a plain unpeopled lane.
Though insect breath inform of disasters,
Clangour of cuirass and helmet of chitin,
Imminent, crouching, such sheer clippers.
A trickle of sand gives the lie to the silence.
Echo, oh echo, echo, echo.
None saw the bird dip over the horizon,
Its secret huddled away in feathers.
A huge wing clouded a brown worm's passion,
Safety a worm thought, safety is better
In rules and burrows. But who can say
Whether the lane be of God or of man?
The bird was gone, on his own dispatch,
To inform fresh revolutionary landscapes.
There remains a plain unpeopled lane,
Wandering, bleeding, over the heath,
Over the groans of the ancient dead.
Still something here forever stares;
Something here still ripples in stone;
What in fact can still be left
That so indeed in silence stares?

Composite

Around the sated mirror
Marguerites abound.
Gold is the eye of Summer,
Quiet the air's sound.
Deep from their fretted skeins
Beckon the fruiting weed,
Sand in the hair of Summer
Slaking a sun-god's greed.
Roomy the meadow's elbow
Where streams gurgle through;
Patter the vole-foot shadows
By brooklime etched in blue,

Reflects the hue of heaven
In fields of plates of gold,
Whose blazons of rich image
Green tapestries enfold.
Light as butterflies landing
The air-twirled seeds descend
Through to the roots of grasses,
Gnawing with lust to mend
Torn calendar of seasons,
Rifling the meek soil's treasure.
All Summer now reclines
Outstretched on her bed of pleasure;
Toes to the distant murmur,
Finger tips to the noon;
Brushed by the lips of insects,
Quelled neath the breath of June:
The maiden meadows asking
A shower of gold from on high,
Content with a tickle of grass heads
Blown by the wind's hot sigh,
Relaxed and not expecting
The relief of Danae.

Age bends over the mirror,
Clouds cover the hands,
And rumours of mortals rumble
Through the sun-struck lands.
The finger of prudence fixes
Square in the eye of the dream
The date and the place and the provenance
Of a poet's instant theme.

Chaffinch Song

The chaffinch repeating his advertised mixture,
His same conclusion is tirelessly stated;
Like a youth at a fruit machine gormlessly pumping,
The same bell tinkles, the same coin rolls.
The street-corner newsboy, loud and unsmiling,
Repeatedly voicing to a world unrejoicing,
Though nothing is new in such love and such kingdoms;
The chaffinch and streetboy are calling their wares.

High August Noon, Cranborne Chase

The pathway through the clearing led
Down wild ungoverned ways
Where proud fritillaries would sail
On vaunted fulvous wing, bestow their praise
On modest clutching bramble
On sunny August days;
And greedy Peacocks flock and cling
Like business-men at bars
On coarse valerian's spread.
Steamy and hot this world where every foot
Must silent fall, while hoverflies
Refuse, decide, then raise their bid
Or whisk away to higher ledge
Of pulsing air. In this hot shimmering noon
Little is seen though life is close;
Adders through bracken squeeze and coil
In mailed threat. And harsh birds cry;
Magpie and jay ignite the taut
Observant fear in small bright eyes
Of fledgling and vole; while roe unseen
Move quietly out, from violence screened
By waving fern and hazel bower,
Treading the rides unheard.
Man is inside their biotope, and man is known.
Down from the leafy branch descends a thread,
On which unsavage world a defenceless larva
Clings, and with the wood's summer breathing
Ever so slightly swings.

Silence, Yorkshire Dales

Generally there is silence;
Water trickling away may be heard;
A sheep may mutter, a bird may splutter,
But generally only silence is heard.

Returned to the solitary house in the dales
For a long needed holiday from care,
I am enfolded here away
And I sink at first into recollection;
There is very little I need now to say.

Curlews inhabit the valley.
Their subdued occasional fluting
Floats into my slate back-yard;
But their pressure is secret, persisting
They accentuate silence.

An occasional car
Roars by up the stonewalled galley
And its echo is drowned in departing,
Restoring the mirror of silence.

I think if I now carefully listened
I could hear a drop fall from a bud
Or an insect cleaning its tarsi
Or an earthworm swallowing mud.

On the green upland the smell is different,
Fragrant and friendly; grass and sedge
Determine how near we come
On the wall-scarred moor
Where distant kestrels hover and soar
To the edge of pure silence.

In the mind's imaginary islands
The core of the moorland is always silence;
With the trickle of water repeating
Its benedicite of greeting;
But generally only silence is heard.

The silence gives a promise of healing,
Restoring inwardness.
And, forgetting self concern,
I feel little outward need
Nor any sense of lasting protest.
I am contented now
To wait awhile in suspense
Alone with this earth and sky
And to breathe with the ebb and flow
Of this listening upland silence.

The Stoat

Silent, selective, on steel cords treads the stoat;
Springy to snap and bound and dart.
Restive his eye, scent sniffing, with all his senses at alert.
He steps delicately through a world of odours
And hidden stained meaning;
Past a cathedral foxglove, then pauses,
Cranes up and stares; the world in focus:
The possible in the act of becoming;
He is all agin and aggression
And stinks like a fearsome nanny.
A threat among ferns, a sparkler
Who can rip out a belly as smartly
As you pull a mint bob from your pocket;
He is not a person to stroke, no dear sweet cub,
But a vice of nature.
The fangs of his canines are rooted in history,
His whiskers tickle the eye of the moment;
Like the market, he is woe to one slight slip
And packed doom to the let up, the lapse of attention.
If you are a vole, Jehovah is terrible –
For a mere split second uncogged from the mesh
And suddenly your sins are visited.
Then one fine day the current is cut,
And stiff his legs protrude and cool;
For the stoat too is mortal.
But fresh gods arise in the bramble shade
And lick lips, terribly eyeing the day;
Sneak out into the path, as avatars,
And scent the horizon, aching for prey.

Man's Loss: or Get Inside and Wait

His head was concrete gutters
And channels of emotion
Quickly drained away.
Fertility was fleeting;
Sorrow rose in the wells,
Swelled in the trough of his eyes,
But quickly sank and dried.
The mind's parched tension,
Temporarily eased,
Spouted from stone griffon
The ichor of consolation;
The jet of absolution
Into the deserts dried.
The scurrying feet of progress
Soon exclude the fountain.
The breaths of human purpose
Put fingers in those eyes
That wept for dappled clearings,
The quiet rural order,
The ordinary kindness
And sorrow for man who died.
Chilled by an autumn robin,
The unheard earth lay sobbing
In streams about our way;
A thin and listless music
Tinkled in icy cave
As winter rolled up her sleeves
And clad herbs in icy armour
That overlay the brook.
How could we tell the Parson
His favourite dog had died?
Creation swaying limping
Whistled through one wall-eye.
So now to the stone fountain
Our thoughts regroup, adjourn,
Trudge to the galleried mountain;
With trailing foot return,
Tongue frozen, heart cherishing
Long thoughts for one who died.
Long lasting as Hambledon,
Whose curve and sweep of line
Etched on the winter backcloth
An afterglow of time.

Quantock View

One Ionian winter
I looked across the bay,
The wide armed bay of Bridgewater,
To Wales not far away.
Primeval glowered Steepholm.
Rain in the fern smelt fresh.
The curse of docks just visible,
And winter on my breath.

Grey glistened the channel.
And Kilve's liassic shore
Had not of late felt footfall
Of wheezing dinosaur.

Could that be really Coleridge
Mouching along the lane,
Blithely threshing St. John's Wort
With his amber-headed cane?

Two threads of converse upwards
Rise from the leaf-struck combe,
As smoke from Holford's chimneys
Twirls upward curling plume;
No, it was just an illusion,
Wuggins and S.T.C.
Stepping out from Alfoxden
By the leaden Bristol sea.

They and the mottled saurians
Trudge this land no more.
We in our live day ponder
And look to yonder shore,
Separate for just a moment
From busy traffic's roar,
The hurrying salesmen, the profits,
And the mounting tip of war.

The Pity of the Moment

In the sigh of night
The naked soul uncloses
Fevers for the future
Plan to grip the world
In a loved enchantment.
And the blood announces,
Knocking on the threshold,
That in soft oblivion
Cares may all dissemble,
Leaving only yearning
For the one beside.

Breath upon your shoulder,
Cheek averted smooth,
Is the ages' sorrow
Is the praise of love.
Totally dependent
Lips disclose, declare
Through the wordless silence
Happiness laid bare.

Pilotless we wonder
In our cradled dream,
And the woken tongue deploys
Syllables in a stream.
Poetry from beauty
Bleeds from the inmost hurt;
The ichor in the tempest,
Tear grown in the eye;
Cast in a mould of words
For golden everlasting
The pity in impermanence:
The pity of the moment
Held in a human clasping.

To Bagborough in the Twenties

The church bells draw me through the dew,
Prayer book at ready; grass blades sparkling;
So much is new. The iron tongues gyrate,
Rebel and swell and beckon to a deep country faith.
And the sweep of the Quantock line
Rises to view as we leave, ready at last,
And click the gate.
Mother's glasses located, father steams at the wheel
As the family climb into the Austin,
And decorously we reel down the red lanes,
Shuttered in Somerset hedges,
Spattered through gleaming puddles,
To park by the font-spring wall
In the haven of Bagborough hill.
Walk up in our stiff Sunday Best,
With pennies prepared, through the park hillocked lawns
To the sandstone porch, where hats
Are discreetly abandoned.
And the sun streams in on the white and the gilt,
And the blue and the gold are refreshed
In the chanting and incense.
The upright families, with well cut suits,
The fox and staghunting gentry,
Bow in self-lost reverence;
As the robin trills at the window,
Sky framed in seasonal yew; and children fidget,
Following after motes in the sunbeam.
And Briscoe as ever fans the best message
With true-blessing hands;
We arise from our pews to trot separately
Or shuffle to the innocent renewal.

The grazing hinds on the hill
Pause, raise their heads,
Mark the blest alleluyahs,
Their nostrils wet and fresh
For the sign of a scare or a scent;
Not so noiselessly kicking dead leaves
With their feet, rough flanks steaming,
In the lee of harridan beech-hedge;
And, as Somerset rides moorwards to Devon,
Lower their muzzles to grazing, pace forwards,
By farmer or fly unsought for
A Sabbath sanctuary season.

Index of First Lines and Titles

Index of Names